P9-BIN-693

THE GUIDE TO LONG-PLAYING RECORDS

Orchestral Music

THE GUIDE TO LONG-PLAYING RECORDS

Orchestral Music

BY

Irving Kolodin

Vocal Music

BY

Philip L. Miller

Chamber and Solo Instrument Music

BY

Harold C. Schonberg

THE GUIDE TO LONG-PLAYING RECORDS

Orchestral Music

BY

Irving Kolodin

1955

ALFRED A KNOPF

NEW YORK

TO *Irma*

L. C. catalog card number: 55-5607

THIS IS A BORZOI BOOK,
PUBLISHED BY ALFRED A. KNOPF, INC.

FIRST EDITION

ERRATUM The "general preface" to which Mr. Kolodin refers in lines 5 and 6 of his "Prefatory Note" was decided against and omitted. It would have stated that because the huge number of long-playing phonograph records now on the market makes it impossible for any one critic to hear and evaluate all available recordings, we invited each of three well-known authorities to provide a list of recommended recordings (with explanatory comment) in a special musical field. Each of the three books will interest a particular group of music-lovers; together, the three books provide a comprehensive list of the best long-playing records. The companion volumes to *Orchestral Music* are *Vocal Music*, by Philip L. Miller, and *Chamber & Solo Instrument Music*, by Harold C. Schonberg. ALFRED A. KNOPF, INC.

PREFATORY NOTE

After six-years-plus of LP recordings, the pipeline from producer to consumer has been sufficiently supplied for a selection to be siphoned off which will neither accept all that has been produced nor reject most of it. The very good reasons for separate studies to be made of the several aspects of the total repertoire have been set forth in a general preface, and need not be capitulated here. Concentrating on the orchestral repertoire alone, I would say that its vastly extended playing-time dwarfs that of the total recorded literature as of 1941. In variety and inclusiveness, it challenges any individual's assimilation; and I do not doubt that here and there I have failed as a critical blotter.

As one who has concentrated on the orchestral literature in this volume after surveying the total recorded literature in several others, I would say, too, that one fact is immediately discernable to me, and must be shared with the reader as prerequisite to mutual understanding. It is my belief that the total of great performances now on records is substantially smaller than it was in 1941. The total of good ones is doubtless higher; the total of exceptionally fine-sounding ones is beyond question at an all-time high. But the repertoire represented by the magic digits 1941 (a time when the United States was not yet engaged in war and when our domestic catalogues were full of an unprecedented richness) was one that had been *accumulated* through a decade of intensive, discriminating effort in Europe and the United States. The six-years-plus since LP began have *created* a repertoire to fill a commercial need based on unprecedented consumer demand. The two are not synonymous and can never be compared—except to the artistic disadvantage of the current production.

Records unquestionably sound better today than ever before, a fact too often regarded as an automatic guarantee that they are better performances of the music as well. Questionable, highly questionable—and very often completely undemonstrable. Fortunately, the time-of-the-cuckoo duplication of the orchestral repertoire has also been blessed by the continuing good health of Arturo Toscanini, Sir Thomas Beecham, Bruno Walter, and, in lesser measure, Wilhelm Furtwängler; it has been a time for Ernest Ansermet to come to world-wide repute and for Clemens Krauss to make some imperishable recordings; for Fritz Reiner, Eugene Ormandy, Paul Paray, and George Szell to maintain established standards; for Dimitri Mitropoulos and Hermann Scherchen, Herbert von Karajan and Eduard van Beinum to manifest special sympathies, and for Guido Cantelli, Enrique Jorda, Ataúlfo Argenta, Ferenc Fricsay, and Antal Dorati (among others) to manifest hopeful promises of things to come.

But the old-time abundance in which England could show such fine workmen as Hamilton Harty, Henry Wood, Eugene Goossens, Constant Lambert, and Leslie Heward in addition to the enduring Beecham does not exist there now, any more than it does in France, where a long day of greatness has reached what seems interminable twilight since America has removed from their native functioning Monteux, Munch, and Paray. As for Germany, its promising men of the 1930's are scattered widely, with America providing residence for Steinberg, Klemperer, Schweiger, Rosenstock, Leinsdorf, and the older Krips.

The point would seem to be that the LP literature has not merely been created for a need rather than accumulated for a purpose: some of it has also been created for false reasons in the wrong places. All the able technicians sitting in conclave in Minneapolis cannot make the local orchestra and conductor a suitable voice for Berlioz's *Symphonie fantastique*, any more than the advantageous economic conditions of Vienna can make the local lips what Aaron Copland imagined his trumpeter should have for *Quiet City* or give the string-players the vibrato required for *Appalacian Spring*.

The marvelous flexibility of magnetic-tape recording has done wonders to perpetuate Toscanini broadcasts, even to reach back into the past and revitalize some seemingly inert. But it has also encouraged lax standards and a diminution of artistic integrity through its ability to track sound to its point of origin instead of making it of sufficient worth to transport it to where the equipment is based.

I do not know how many tape recorders there are in Stuttgart, for example; but at least one has obviously been running without cessation for five years, to judge by the amount of miscellaneous repertory (string music in particular) which has poured out of that city. Some of it is excellent, and much of it is worthy; but all the rest—amounting to much that seems at first glance to be in the tradition of the excellent, or at least of the worthy—is well-meaning, but musically useless. The wrong players are performing the wrong repertoire, with dismally audible results.

Needless to say, I have not been writing the preceding pages for diversionary or discursive purposes. These are the considerations, plus others to be mentioned below, which dictate the need for such a volume as the present one. No lay music-lover could be expected to know which of the Stuttgart recordings is excellent, worthy, or useless; but one paid to find out—such as myself—should produce the answer. The disorderly appearance in the "created" repertoire of performances made under vastly varied circumstances—tapes of concerts, reproductions of broadcasts, pilferings from experimental transcriptions never meant for public consumption in conquered areas now under Russian domination—makes the ancient and honorable accolade of "recording" a questionable endorsement indeed.

Omissions and inclusions in the text are mostly purposeful and critically ordained. Nothing good, I hope, has been omitted, and nothing very bad included, save where (by virtue of a famous name or celebrated affiliation) it carries a promise of quality far above the accomplishment. When, among sixteen "Unfinished" symphonies of Schubert, only eight are mentioned—two of them negatively, say—it may be assumed that the other eight were too expensive for the quality provided or too poor in mechanical resource for the economy afforded.

I may end by saying that I have praised nothing as the "last word in sound." A great concept—one by Richard Strauss, or Mengelberg, or Koussevitzky, or Weingartner—endures even when the means are obviously limited, just as a limited concept offends, no matter how persuasive the preservation.

Irving Kolodin

CODE OF RECORD LABELS

A440	*A440*
Ab	*Abbey*
Alc	*Alco*
All	*Allegro*
Am	*Audio Masterworks*
An	*Angel*
AS	*Anthologie Sonore*
AU	*Audiosphere*
B&B	*B&B*
Bar	*Bartok*
BG	*Bach Guild*
Bos	*Boston*
BS	*Bach Society*
C	*Columbia*
Cam	*Cambridge*
Cap	*Capitol*
CE	*Classic Editions*
Cet	*Cetra*
CH	*Concert Hall*
Cir	*Circle*
Cla	*Claremont*
CMD	*Camden*
Col	*Colosseum*
Con	*Contemporary*
Cook	*Cook*
D	*Decca*
Den	*Den*
Des	*Desto*
Dia	*Dial*
Eas	*Eastman*
Ele	*Elektra*
EMS	*EMS*
Ep	*Epic*
Es	*Esoteric*
Et	*Eterna*
Fes	*Festival*
For	*Forum*
GAR	*GAR*
Hds	*Handel Society*
HS	*Haydn Society*
L	*London*
Ly	*Lyrichord*
Lyb	*Lyrebird*
Mer	*Mercury*
MGM	*MGM*
ML	*Music Library*
Mon	*Montilla*
MT	*Magic Tone*
NE	*New Editions*
NR	*New Records*
Oc	*Oceanic*
OL	*Oiseau-Lyre*
Op	*Opus*
Ov	*Overtone*
Ox	*Oxford*
P	*Plymouth*
Pa	*Parade*
Per	*Period*
Ph	*Philharmonia*
Pol	*Polymusic*
Pro	*Program*
REB	*REB*
Rem	*Remington*
Ren	*Renaissance*
Roy	*Royale*
RS	*Rachmaninoff Society*
Sca	*Scala*
Sor	*Soria*
SPA	*SPA*
Str	*Stradivari*
U	*Urania*
V	*RCA Victor*
Van	*Vanguard*
Vox	*Vox*
W	*Westminster*
Wal	*Walden*
WCMF	*WCMF*

CODE OF NAMES OF ORCHESTRAS AND OTHER ENSEMBLES

ACG	*Amsterdam Concertgebouw*
ACMS	*Amsterdam Chamber Music Society*
AOR	*Augusteo Orchestra, Rome*
ASO	*Austrian Symphony Orchestra*
AUS	*Austrian State Symphony Orchestra*
BAM	*Bamberg Symphony*
BASO	*Bavarian Symphony Orchestra*
BAV	*Bavarian State Orchestra*
BAVR	*Bavarian Radio Orchestra*
BBC	*BBC Orchestra*
BCO	*Byrnes Chamber Orchestra*
BFO	*Brazilian Festival Orchestra*
BNO	*Boyd Neel Orchestra*
BPH	*Berlin Philharmonic Orchestra*
BPO	*Boston Pops Orchestra*
BSI	*Bolshoi Symphony Orchestra*
BSO	*Boston Symphony Orchestra*
BSOO	*Berlin State Opera Orchestra*
BTO	*Ballet Theatre Orchestra*
BUF	*Buffalo Philharmonic Orchestra*
CAO	*Concert Arts Orchestra, Los Angeles*
CBSO	*CBS Orchestra*
CCM	*Copenhagen Collegium Musicum*
CGO	*Covent Garden Orchestra*
CHAM	*chamber orchestra not otherwise identified*
CHO	*Chicago Symphony Orchestra*
CIN	*Cincinnati Symphony Orchestra*
CO	*Cleveland Orchestra*
COL	*Columbia Symphony Orchestra*
COP	*Copenhagen Royal Opera Orchestra*
CPH	*Czech Philharmonic, Prague*
CRO	*Cologne Radio Orchestra*
CZS	*Czech Symphony Orchestra*
DAL	*Dallas Symphony Orchestra*
DNO	*Danish National Orchestra*
DOO	*Dumbarton Oaks Orchestra*
DPH	*Dresden Philharmonic Orchestra*
DSO	*Detroit Symphony Orchestra*
DSTR	*Danish State Radio Symphony Orchestra*

EIAR *Italian Radio Orchestra*
EIDP *Ensemble Instrumental de Paris*
ERO *Eastman Rochester Orchestra*
FNS *French National Symphony Orchestra*
FRA *Frankfort Orchestra*
FRO *Frankenland Symphony Orchestra*
GFO *Glyndebourne Festival Orchestra*
GOH *German Opera House Orchestra, Prague*
GPH *German Philharmonic Orchestra, Prague*
GSE *Gothic String Ensemble*
GSO *German State Orchestra*
HAAR *Haarlem Symphony Orchestra*
HBP *Hollywood Bowl Pops Orchestra*
HBS *Hollywood Bowl Symphony Orchestra*
HEW *Hewitt Orchestra*
HIS *Stokowski and his Orchestra*
HO *Hallé Orchestra*
HOL *Haydn Orchestra of London*
HPHO *Hamburg Philharmonic Orchestra*
HPO *Hague Philharmonic Orchestra*
HRS *Hamburg Radio Symphony Orchestra*
HSO *Houston Symphony Orchestra*
ICO *Italian Chamber Orchestra*
IND *Indianapolis Symphony Orchestra*
INR *Orchestre de l'Institut National Radiodiffusion, Brussels*
JSO *Janssen Symphony Orchestra, Los Angeles*

LACS *Los Angeles Chamber Symphony*
LAM *Lamoureux Orchestra*
LAP *Los Angeles Philharmonic Orchestra*
LAU *Lausanne Symphony Orchestra*
LBE *London Baroque Ensemble*
LBS *Linz Bruckner Symphony Orchestra*
LCO *London Chamber Orchestra*
LEN *Leningrad Philharmonic Orchestra*
LGO *Leipzig Gewandhaus Orchestra*
LIV *Liverpool Philharmonic Orchestra*
LMP *London Mozart Players*
LOS *Little Orchestra Society*
LOUI *Louisville Orchestra*
LPO *London Philharmonic Orchestra*
LPP *London Promenade Philharmonic*
LRO *Leipzig Radio Orchestra*
LSO *London Symphony Orchestra*

LSSO	*La Scala String Orchestra*
MAD	*Madrid Symphony Orchestra*
MEX	*Mexican Symphony Orchestra*
MGO	*MGM Orchestra*
MGS	*MGM String Orchestra*
MIN	*Minneapolis Symphony Orchestra*
MOS	*Moscow Symphony Orchestra*
MPH	*Munich Philharmonic Orchestra*
MSO	*Munich State Opera Orchestra*
MTO	*Munich Tonkünstler Orchestra*
NBC	*NBC Symphony Orchestra*
NET	*Netherlands Philharmonic Orchestra*
NEW	*New Symphony Orchestra, London*
NFOM	*New Friends of Music Orchestra*
NGO	*National Gallery Orchestra, Washington*
NPH	*National Philharmonic Orchestra, U.S.S.R.*
NSO	*National Symphony Orchestra, Washington*
NSSP	*New Symphony Society, Paris*
NWDRO	*Nord West Deutsches Rundfunk Orchestra, Hamburg*
NYCO	*New York Concert Orchestra*
NYPH	*New York Philharmonic-Symphony Orchestra*
NYSO	*New York Stadium Orchestra*
NYWE	*New York Wind Ensemble*
OASC	*Orchestra of the Santa Cecilia Academy, Rome*
OBCO	*Orchestra of the Berlin Civic Opera*
OCC	*Orchestre des Concerts Colonne, Paris*
OLO	*Oiseau-Lyre Orchestra*
OMM	*Orchestra of the Maggio Musicale Fiorentino*
ONA	*Orchestre National, France*
OOC	*Orchestre de l'Opéra-Comique, Paris*
OPH	*Oslo Philharmonic Orchestra*
ORB	*Orchestra of Radio Berlin*
ORD	*Orchestre de la Radiodiffusion Française, Paris*
ORF	*Orchestra of Radio Frankfort*
ORS	*Orchestre Radio-Symphonique, Paris*
OSC	*Orchestre de la Société des Concerts du Conservatoire, Paris*
OSR	*Orchestre de la Suisse-Romande, Geneva*
OTCE	*Orchestre du Théâtre des Champs-Elysées, Paris*
OTLF	*Orchestra of the Fenice Theater, Venice*

OTN *Orchestra du Théâtre National de l'Opéra, Paris*
PAS *Pasdeloup Orchestra, Paris*
PCO *Paris Chamber Orchestra*
PERP *Perpignan Festival Orchestra*
PHI *Philharmonia Orchestra*
PHO *Philadelphia Orchestra*
PHP *Philadelphia Pops Orchestra*
PPO *Paris Philharmonic Orchestra*
PRA *Prades Festival Orchestra*
PRO *Pro Musica Symphony (Stuttgart, Reinhardt; Vienna, Swarowsky)*
PSL *Philharmonic Symphony Orchestra of London*
PSO *Pittsburgh Symphony Orchestra*
RCAO *RCA Orchestra*
RCAS *RCA String Orchestra*
RES *Residentie Orchestra, The Hague*
RHS *Rhineland Symphony Orchestra*
RIAS *Radio in American Sector, Berlin*
RIO *Radio Italiana Orchestra*
ROB *Robin Hood Dell Orchestra, Philadelphia*
ROO *Royal Opera House Orchestra, London*
ROP *Rochester Pops Orchestra*
RPH *Rochester Philharmonic Orchestra*
RPO *Royal Philharmonic Orchestra, London*
RSO *Rochester Symphony Orchestra*
RZO *Radio Zurich Orchestra*
SAL *Salzburg Mozarteum Orchestra*
SAX *Saxon State Orchestra*
SC *Società Corelli*
SCA *Scarlatti Orchestra, Naples*
SCH *Stuttgart Chamber Orchestra*
SCO *Saidenberg Chamber Orchestra, New York*
SFS *San Francisco Symphony Orchestra*
SOO *Symphony Orchestra of Olympia (Greece)*
SPO *Stuttgart Philharmonic Orchestra*
SRO *Stockholm Radio Orchestra*
SSO *Stockholm Symphony Orchestra*
STC *Santa Cecilia Orchestra, Rome*
STOC *Stockholm Concert Association Orchestra*
STS *St. Louis Symphony Orchestra*
SWO *Sadler's Wells Orchestra, London*
SYM *symphony orchestra not otherwise identified*
TCSO *Tri-Centenary String Orchestra (Corelli)*

TLO	*Louisville Orchestra*
TSO	*Ton-Studio Orchestra, Stuttgart*
USO	*Utrecht Symphony Orchestra*
USSR	*USSR Symphony Orchestra*
VAO	*Vienna Philharmonia Orchestra*
VDR	*Virtuosi di Roma*
VPH	*Vienna Philharmonic Orchestra*
VPHW	*Vienna Philharmonic Winds*
VSO	*Vienna State Opera Orchestra*
VSY	*Vienna Symphony Orchestra*
VTO	*Vienna Tonkünstler Orchestra*
WES	*Westminster (MGM) Symphony Orchestra*
WHO	*Woody Herman Orchestra*
WIES	*Wiesbaden Collegium*
WIN	*Winterthur Symphony Orchestra*
WKCH	*Wiener Kammerchor*
WSO	*Württemberg State Orchestra, Stuttgart*
WW	*World Wide (Philadelphia) Orchestra*
ZCM	*Collegium Musicum, Zurich*
ZRO	*Zurich Radio Orchestra*
ZS	*Zimbler Sinfonietta*
ZTO	*Zurich Tonhalle Orchestra*

THE

GUIDE

TO

LONG-PLAYING

RECORDS

Orchestral Music

ADAM, ADOLPHE *(1803-1856)*

Ballet Music

Giselle. *ROO, Lambert, 10" C ML 2117* (**Bliss*: *Miracle in the Gorbals*). *ROO, Irving, V LM 1092. OTN, Blareau, L LL 869.*

Lambert has the advantage, in plasticity and grace, over Irving, but more of the score is included in the Irving version. Also, it is better reproduced. The two-sided version of Blareau includes more than either (virtually the whole score), and the reproduction is excellent. However, it seems to embody some local tradition that is more balletic than musical, and it is rather boisterously delivered.

Overture

If I Were King. BAM, Leitner, 10" D DL 4046 (**Verdi*: *Overture to Sicilian Vespers*; *Boïeldieu*: *Caliph of Bagdad*).

Rather heavy wishful thinking, but vigorously reproduced.

ALBÉNIZ, ISAAC *(1860-1909)*

Iberia (*orchestrated by E. F. Arbos*). *OSC, Argenta, L LL 921* (**Turina*: *Danzas Fantásticas*). *OCC, Sebastian, U 7085.*

In saying the last word on these flavorsome pieces and Arbos's imaginative orchestration of them, Argenta reveals himself as a major artist in the interpretation of the music of his native land. Exceptionally firm, lifelike sound, which makes the ear tingle with pure aural pleasure. Sebastian's effort is creditable to him, but not in the class of Argenta's.

ALBINONI, TOMASO *(1674-1745)*

Concerto for Orchestra, in D minor, opus 5, No. 7. ICO, Jenkins, HS L 74 (**Geminiani*: *Concerto Grosso No. 2*; *Sammartini*: *Concerto No. 2 for Violin*).

A solidly musical work of the Vivaldi era, played with care, but not with all the cultivation required. Bright sound, a little wiry.

ALFVEN, HUGO (1872-   )

Midsommarvaka. *PHO, Ormandy, 10" C AL 35 (*Grieg: Peer Gynt Suite No. 1).*

The jolly tune that makes this work listenable can be heard as well in this single-side version as in the alternate 12" discs in which it is combined with much other material. Excellent sound.

AMIROV, FIKRET (1922-   )

*Azerbaijan Mugams. LRO, Abendroth, U RLP 7117 (*Arensky: Silhouettes; Liadov: Baba Yaga).*

Engaging local color, effectively delivered by Abendroth and well reproduced.

ARENSKY, ANTON (1861-1906)

*Silhouettes (2nd Suite). ORB, Lederer, U RLP 7117 (*See above).*

As suits a miscellany of orchestras and conductors, this reflects a miscellany of composers. The performance does not have the grace or charm desired. Fair reproduction.

*Variations on a Theme by Tchaikovsky. LOS, Scherman, C ML 4526 (*Rachmaninoff: The Miserly Knight). BCO, Byrns, Cap P 8158 (*Grieg: Holberg Suite).*

Neither of these is an outstanding performance, but the second side of the Scherman has more interest than the Byrns. Recorded quality in each instance is good, but no more.

ARNELL, RICHARD (1918-   )

*Punch and the Child (Suite). RPO, Beecham, C ML 4593 (*Lord Berners: Triumph of Neptune).*

A rather quixotic enthusiasm of Beecham, but one to which he applies his customary penetration. Good sound in both instances, with the repertory not likely to be duplicated.

AUBER, DANIEL (1782-1871)

Overtures

Fra Diavolo, Masaniello, The Crown Diamonds, The Bronze Horse. BPO, Fiedler, V LM 1049.

A simple solution to the Auber overture problem, with all the favorite works on a single disk, brightly played and vigorously reproduced.

AURIC, GEORGES (1899-)

*Les Matelots (Suite). HSO, Kurtz, 10" C ML 2112 (*Satie: Parade).*

A suitable effort by Kurtz, decently reproduced. The second side also fares well.

BACH, CARL PHILIPP EMANUEL (1714-1788)

Concertos

For Piano and Orchestra

*In A minor. Holletschek, VSY, Swoboda, W WL 5040 (*Sinfonias in C and D).*

The interests of this music are rather academic; the performance is of like spirit. Fairly good sound.

*In C minor. Roesgen-Champion, OSC, Goldschmidt, Per SPL 556 (*Haydn: Concerto in F).*

A small, rather weak-sounding orchestra and Goldschmidt's non-vital direction offset the merits of Roesgen-Champion's deft fingerwork. Fair recording.

*In D major. H. Schnabel, VPA, Adler, SPA 37 (*Trio for Flute, Violin, and Piano).*

Music of variety and expressiveness, played with excellent style by the team of Schnabel and Adler. Good sound.

For Orchestra

*In D (arranged by Maximilian Steinberg). MGS, Solomon, MGM E 3109 (*Haydn: Symphony No. 85). VSO, Prohaska, BG 516/17 (*Magnificat).*

Neither of these performances measures up to past standards phonographically. However, the Solomon version, on an individual disc (with a Haydn symphony), is a more accessible choice than the Prohaska. Both are well reproduced.

Symphony

*No. 1 in D, No. 3 in C. VSY, Guenther, BG 504 (*J. C. Bach: Sinfonia Concertante). VSY, Swoboda, W 5040 (*Concerto in A minor).*

Though these works date from a period (1780) when Haydn had long since given firm form to the symphony as we know it, they are much more amorphous works, sounding more akin to the concerto grosso. The Guenther performances are preferable in execution and sound.

BACH, JOHANN CHRISTIAN *(1735-1782)*

Concertos

For Cembalo and Orchestra

*In E flat, opus 7, No. 5. Leonhardt, VSY, Sacher, C ML 4869 (*Sinfonia Concertante in A; Sinfonias in E flat and D).*

This collection of J. C. Bach embraces several of his best-known works in performances of uniform excellence, brightly reproduced. Leonhardt is a keyboard artist of quality, and the clean-sounding instrument he uses is attractive to hear.

For Violoncello and Orchestra

*In C minor. Schuster, CHAM, Waxman, Cap P 8232 (*Schumann: Concerto for Cello).*

The notation that this is a transcription by Henri Casadesus raises the usual suspicions, moderated by the fact that it is basically an uninteresting piece, well played by Schuster, but recorded in a dismally dull studio.

Sinfonias

*In E flat major, opus 9, No. 2. LAM, Colombo, OL 50007 (*Sinfonia in D; Haydn: Concerto in D for Harpsichord).*

Not as interesting a work as the later D major (see below), but very well played. Note that the work is in E flat, rather than in E major as both the record jacket and label state. The annotation describes it as E flat, and that is the key in which it is played.

*In D, opus 18, No. 4. VSY, Sacher, C ML 4869 (*See Concerto for Cembalo). LAM, Colombo, OL 50007 (*See above).*

A vigorous work in the Haydn mold (or vice versa!), well instrumentated. Good performance in both instances, though the little Lamoureux ensemble has a distinctive tonal quality not matched by the Viennese group.

*In E flat, for Double Orchestra, opus 18, No. 1. VSY, Sacher, C ML 4869 (*See Concerto for Cembalo). CIN, Johnson, L LL 405 (*Schubert: Symphony No. 3).*

The size of the orchestra used by Johnson and its bass-heavy reproduction are not nearly so suitable for this music as is the lighter, more mobile group commanded by Sacher.

Sinfonias Concertante

*In A, for Violin and Cello. W. Schneiderhan, Hübner, VSY, Sacher, C ML 4869 (*See Concerto for Cembalo).*

An absorbing work, in the tradition of such duet-string works as the Bach D minor, the Mozart E flat *Sinfonia Concertante*, and, eventually, the Brahms in A minor. Beautiful string playing by Messrs. Schneiderhan (violin) and Hübner (cello).

*In E flat, for Two Violins. VSY, Guenther, BG 504 (*C. P. E. Bach: Symphonies Nos. 1 and 3).*

Rather stolid performance, well processed. However, more warmth and esprit in the playing would be welcome. The soloists are Franz Hegedus and Paul Riemann (violins), and Karl Mayerhofer (oboe).

BACH, JOHANN SEBASTIAN (1685–1750)

Concertos

For Orchestra

*Brandenburg, Complete Editions (Nos. 1–6). SCH, Münchinger, L LL 222, 10" L LS 226, L LL 144. PRA, Casals, C ML 4345/6/7 (*Excerpts from the Musical Offering). LBO, Haas, Wal 309. CHAM, Prohaska, BG 540/1/2. CHAM, Reiner, C ML 4281/2/3.*

Each of these has some notable artistic attributes, and they are all well recorded with the exception of the Casals, which varies in quality but is never better than acceptable. In addition to espousing some unconventional tempos, Casals dodges the difficulties of high trumpet part in No. 2 by utilizing a soprano saxophone played by Marcel Mulé. This liberty permits him an exaggerated speed which makes the music rather ridiculous. Haas, in his performance with the excellent Baroque Ensemble, inclines toward recorders, whose sound is woody and not to my taste. However, the reproduced sound is very clean, and the complete set includes the pocket scores. Prohaska indulges a similar taste in his version, also utilizing the *violino piccolo* and *viola da gamba* in suitable places. However, the performances are more interesting for scholarship than for expression. Münchinger and Reiner are both faithful to the traditions of these works, at least so far as instrumentation is concerned: the latter's tempos are almost always too fast and insistent. Thus, for my taste, Münchinger's fine-toned group, with such an excellent trumpeter as Paolo Longinotti in No. 2, produces the most consistently listenable music in the best reproduction. This applies not only to the total suavity and resonance, but to individual instruments and details of timbre.

Brandenburg, Nos. 3, 4, and 5. CHAM, DSTR, Wöldike, V LHMV 1048.

Clean, spacious sound is a particular attribute of these finely phrased performances. However, they lack the enlivening vigor and freshness of the Munchinger performances. (The reference to two performing ensembles respects the fact that No. 3 is played by the Chamber Orchestra of the Palace Chapel, Copenhagen.)

*Brandenburg, No. 5. PRA, Casals, C ML 4346 (*No. 4). CHAM, Reiner, C ML 4283 (*No. 6).*

The sound, in both instances, is the best in the two series noted, with interest heightened by the solo personnel utilized: Baker, flute, Marlowe, harpsichord, and Kolberg, violin (in the Reiner), Wummer, flute, Istomin, piano, and Szigeti, violin (in the Casals). In this sound pattern, the harpsichord has a more proper place than the piano.

For Harpsichord and Orchestra[1]

No. 1 in D minor, No. 4 in A, No. 5 in F minor. Viderø, CHAM, Friisholm, HS 92.

No. 3 in D, No. 4 in A. Rapf, CHAM, BG 509.

No. 4 in A major, No. 5 in F minor, No. 7 in G minor. Elsner, PRO, Reinhardt, Vox PL 7260.

The common ground of concerto No. 4 does not show any startling advantage for any of the performers involved. Actually my preferred way of hearing these patterns is in the version for oboe d'amore made by Tovey, recorded by Goossens on C ML 4782. Viderø's thoroughness is well reproduced, likewise Elsner's somewhat, but not markedly, more imaginative playing. As Rapf's No. 3 is the same as the E major violin concerto, and Elsner's G minor the same as the A minor for the same instrument, the musical pleasures of both will be found under happier auspices elsewhere.

*In D. Gerlin, CHAM, AS 31 (*Concerto for Two Harpsichords in C; Vivaldi: Concerto for Violin in D, opus 3, No. 9).*

The pairing here is not as pointless as it might appear, for the Bach "work" is his version of the Vivaldi which precedes it on the disc. Gerlin illuminates this intelligent procedure with his own vigorous artistry, though some of the finale is jumbled. Good sound throughout.

For Two Harpsichords and Orchestra

*In C major. Gerlin, Charbonnier, CHAM, AS 31 (*See above). Viderø, Sørensen, CHAM, Friisholm, HS L 93 (*Concerto in C minor).*

The disparity of sound between these versions is so great that

[1] Editor's Note: Inasmuch as the average purchaser is likely to search out a work in terms of the performing instrument or instruments, the arrangement herein follows such categories, though it is well known that Bach used identical or similar texts for different combinations of instruments. As an instance, the first entry under Harpsichord and Orchestra is the same music as the D minor concerto played by Foss on the piano and Szigeti on the violin.

useful comparison is virtually impossible. The French players use harpsichords of deep, stringy sound, the Danish prefer lighter, more bell-like instruments. I agree with the French, though the HS issue is more recent and cleaner in sound. This is, of course, the work also performed on two pianos (q.v.).

*In C minor. Viderø, Sørensen, CHAM, Friisholm, HS L 93 (*See above).*

Friisholm has a steady hand on the tiller, riding the waves of sound from the harpsichords resourcefully. However, this music sounds better in D minor, and from two violins. Very fine reproduction.

For Three Harpsichords and Orchestra

*In C. Fuhrmann, Seidelhofer, Heiller, CHAM, Heiller, HS LP 1024 (*Vivaldi-Bach: Concerto for Four Harpsichords).*

Careful, well-disciplined performance, but not as animated as these patterns can be made to sound. Good recording.

For Four Harpsichords and Orchestra (After Vivaldi)

*In A minor. Heiller, Seidelhofer, Fuhrmann, Rapf, CHAM, Heiller, HS LP 1024 (*See above).*

This might be a continuation of the foregoing, so closely does it duplicate those characteristics.

For Oboe d'Amore and Orchestra

*In A. Goossens, CHAM, Süsskind, C ML 4782 (*Marcello: Concerto in C minor; Handel: Concerto Grosso, opus 3, No. 10; etc.).*

Unlike musicologists who advance hypotheses without bothering to validate them, Tovey, in his arrangement of the A major concerto (No. 4 in the sequence under harpsichord), leaves little doubt about his theory that it was written for a wind instrument, probably the oboe d'amore. It is a live and warming experience as conveyed here by Goossens, in what is probably the best recording in a singularly fine disc.

For Piano and Orchestra

*No. 1 in D minor. Foss, ZS, D DL 9601 (*No. 5).*

The lightness and flexibility of this interpretation may not suit everyone's concept of proper Bach style, but it makes a spirited play of sound with Bach's patterns and a convincing thing of his structures. Particularly clean, resonant recording.

*No. 5 in F minor. Foss, ZS, D DL 9601 (*No. 1). Haskil, PRA, Casals, C ML 4353 (*Concerto for Violin in A minor; Trio Sonata; etc.).*

Nothing in the heavy treatment by Casals, which often blankets the sound of Haskil's well-phrased performance, alters my preference for the Decca product. Microphonically, the orchestra has all the better of the arrangement in the Casals, with a rather confining resonant frame.

For Two Pianos and Orchestra

*No. 2 in C. A. Schnabel, K. U. Schnabel, LSO, Boult, V LCT 1140 (*Mozart: Concerto in E flat for Two Pianos, K. 365).*

Musically, this is the same sound, slightly dull performance of 78-rpm days. However, the tonal values are better, with more resonance and less of the percussive effect previously deplored.

For Three Pianos and Orchestra

*In D minor. R., G., and J. Casadesus, NYPH, Mitropoulos, C LM 2196 (*Bach: French Suite No. 6).*

All-round sensitive work by the related soloists, and well-correlated orchestral playing under the direction of Mitropoulos. Nice, open, resonant sound.

*In C. Fischer, Smith, Matthews, PHI, Fischer, V LHMV 1004 (*Mozart: Concerto for Piano, No. 25 in C, K. 503).*

Those who are wise enough to prefer Fischer's performance of the Mozart C major, K. 503, will find this on the other side (if they can tear themselves away long enough from Mozart). Fluent, clean performance, but with the rigidity that must set in when three pianos are required to mesh. Uncommonly fine C major sound for minutes at a time.

For Piano, Violin, Flute, and Orchestra

*In A minor. Horszowski, Schneider, Wummer, PRA, Casals, C ML 4352 (*Concerto in D minor for Violin).*

The fine flute-playing of Wummer, especially in the slow movement, is the singular attraction of this disc. Clear sound.

For Violin and Orchestra

No. 1 in A minor and No. 2 in E. Barylli, VSO, Scherchen, W WL 5318. Heifetz, LAP, Wallenstein, V LM 1818.

Even Barylli would not claim to be a Heifetz, but in this repertory, his sound performance plus the vital leadership of Scherchen produces more that is Bachian than is produced in the over-silky, too finely spun presentation of Heifetz. The orchestral background does not have the energy of Scherchen's; the Vienna recording also surpasses the American in clarity and vibrance.

*No. 1 in A minor. Stern, PRA, Casals, C ML 4353 (*Concerto for Piano in F minor; Trio Sonata; etc.).*

One of the best in the series of Prades recordings, with Stern a more subdued, and hence more expressive, artist than in many of his own recordings, the rapport with Casals a pervasive thing. Acceptable sound, though the bass is all but inaudible.

*No. 2 in E. Goldberg, PHI, Süsskind, 10" D DL 7507. Francescatti, COL, Szell, C ML 4648 (*Prokofiev: Concerto No. 2 in G minor).*

Neither of these is precisely what I would like to recommend in this literature, for Goldberg's finesse is sometimes on the verge of delicacy, Francescatti's vigor definitely rough at points. I incline to the understatement of Goldberg rather than to the overstatement of Francescatti. Both are well reproduced, but the values in the Goldberg are more suitable to the work.

*In D minor. Szigeti, PRA, Casals, C ML 4352 (*Concerto in A minor for Violin, Flute, and Piano). Szigeti, NFOM, Stiedry, C ML 4286 (*Sonata No. 5 in C).*

The recent Szigeti is only to a small extent an improvement on the older one, for recording science did not have its happiest epoch in Prades, and the Szigeti tone is more alive on the old, though that was a relatively feeble recording. The Prades Orchestra is bigger.

*In G Minor. Szigeti, COL, Szell, C ML 4891 (*Tartini: Concerto in D minor, Sonata in G, etc.).*

Pleasure in the eloquent phrasing of Szigeti, especially in the slow movement, is offset by the harsh sound of his instrument in this version of the F minor concerto for clavier. The recent recording is very revealing of the shortcomings in the violinist's tone. Excellent direction by Szell.

For Two Violins and Orchestra

*In D minor. Stern, Schneider, PRA, Casals, C ML 4351 (*Concerto for Violin and Oboe). Menuhin, Enesco, CHAM, Monteux, V LCT 1120 (*Sonata in E for Violin and Harpsichord). Krebbers, Olof, HPO, Van Otterloo, Ep LC 3036 (*Beethoven: Two Romances).*

None of these offers musical values to compare with such a standard as that established by Szigeti and Flesch (C Set X90), for the Stern-Schneider is not well enough reproduced to represent this period of recording, while the Krebbers-Olof, which is, does not come within breathing distance of a live performance. The Menuhin-Enesco has its moments, but it too is a poor specimen of recording. I omit the Busch-Magnes, now unavailable, and the Heifetz-Heifetz, which should be.

For Violin, Oboe, and Orchestra

*In C minor, or D minor. Stern, Tabuteau, PRA, Casals, C ML 4351 (*Concerto for Two Violins). Compinsky, Schoenberg, SYM, Van Den Burg, Alc 1210 (*Rosza: Duo Sonata).*

Whether played in C minor or D minor, this is an alternate version of the C minor concerto for two claviers. Stern and Tabuteau nominally prefer the original key, but the sound comes out in B minor for mechanical reasons mysterious to me. However, there is little more to hear in their total than in the well-played, but not too successfully recorded, Alco product.

Concerto (Arrangement)

*In the Italian Style. BPH, Schmidt-Isserstedt, Cap LP 8128 (*Excerpts from the Musical Offering).*

No arranger or editor is credited with the transcription, which is on the whole tasteful and well done. Vigorous performance, good recording.

Suites

Collection of Four. CHO, Reiner, V LM 6012 [2]. VSO, Prohaska, BG 530/1. HEW, HS L 90/1.

None of these delivers the music with the straightforward emphasis and welcome clarity of the now unavailable version by the Busch Players. The best orchestral playing and cleanest sound are contained in the Reiner offering, which, however, varies from stimulating to perplexing in its musical properties. A prevailing tendency to slow tempos in the B minor suite possesses Reiner here, though his previous issue with the Pittsburgh Symphony (see below) is gratifyingly normal. No. 3 is beautifully played, and very well reproduced, the others acceptably. Neither of the other issues offers much that is aurally competitive, for the Prohaska is rather forbidding on the side of scholarship, the Hewitt disaffecting in its lack of ear-appeal. By far its most attractive element is the brightly clear sound of Jean-Pierre Rampal's flute in the B minor. (Julius Baker is his opposite in the Reiner, Karl Reznicek in the Prohaska.)

*No. 2 in B minor. SCO, Pepin, Münchinger, L LL 848 (*Suite No. 3). HIS, Baker, Stokowski, V LM 1176 (*Wir glauben all'; Jesu, Joy of Man's Desiring; etc.). PRA, Wummer, Casals, C ML 4348 (*Suite No. 1). PSO, Caratelli, Reiner, C ML 4156 (*Mozart: Symphony No. 35).*

The best totality of qualities, including excellent balance between soloist and ripieno, is offered by Münchinger and his fine ensemble. Pepin may be not quite the flutist Baker is, but Münchinger doesn't try to find the "soul" in this music as Stokowski does—and, in not trying, succeeds. The Casals orchestral treatment is a little heavy for the stream of sound produced by Wummer, and the reproduction is dull in timbre. The lightfooted string-playing in the Pittsburgh version and Caratelli's finely phrased playing of the solo part are, unfortunately, undervalued in the recording.

Miscellaneous

Musical Offering (Complete, Roger Vuataz edition). CHAM, Scherchen, W WL 5070.

*Ricercares a 3 and 6, Trio Sonata. CHAM, Casals, C ML 4347 (*Brandenburg Concerto No. 6).*

*Three Canons, Ricercare a 6. WIES, Weyns, Cap LP 8128 (*Concerto in the Italian Style).*

Completeness would certainly seem a prerequisite in music of this cumulative complexity, and Scherchen provides it in a performance of more life and detail than either of the excerpted ones. As between the versions utilized, I am partial to the Vuataz, which provides diversity of tone color in the use of flute (Cammillo Wanausek), oboe (Friedrich Wachter), English horn (Josef Noblinger), bassoon (Franz Killinger), and cembalo (Kurt Rapf), in addition to string quartet, whereas the Prades performance is restricted to flute (John Wummer), piano (Leopold Mannes), and seven strings. Finally, the Scherchen is a much better recording than either of the others.

Arrangements

*Adagios and Fugues (from Six Three-Voice Fugues), arranged by Mozart. JSO, Janssen, C ML 4406 (*Handel-Schönberg: Concerto for String Quartet and Orchestra).*

Some excellent music in this collection, mating Bach fugues (from *The Well-Tempered Clavichord*) with original Mozart adagios. Janssen's tempos are discerning; the sound is good.

Arrangements (Stokowski)

Chaconne, Passacaglia, and Fugue in C minor; Siciliano (from Sonata for Violin and Clavier in C minor); Mein Jesu was für Seelenweh. HIS, Stokowski, V LM 1133.

Come, Sweet Death; Jesu, Joy of Man's Desiring; Sheep May Safely Graze; Fugue in G minor ("Little"); Chorale from Easter Cantata. The same, V LM 1176.

Beyond stating that these two discs incorporate some of the finest sound RCA has offered to its public, I have no judgment to pass on the propriety of Stokowski's editorial inclinations or the taste with which they are translated into sound. I might say, however, that both now seem worse than when they were new.

Arrangements (Ormandy)

*Passacaglia, Toccata, and Fugue in D minor; Jesu, Joy of Man's Desiring. PHO, Ormandy, C ML 4797 (*Handel: Water Music, Concerto for Orchestra, in D; Corelli-Pinelli: Suite for Strings).*

Of their genre, these performances are relatively restrained, with the rich sound of the orchestra superbly reproduced.

Arrangements (Walton)

*The Wise Virgins. VSO, Litschauer, Van VRS 440 (*Scarlatti-Tommasini: Good Humored Ladies).*

The admirable choice of repertory and Litschauer's affectionate direction are offset by some misguided hi-fi accentuations in "*Ach, wie flüchtig.*" Wiry string sound, compensation or no.

BALAKIREV, MILI ALEXEIVICH (1837-1910)

*Tamar. LSO, Fistoulari, MGM 3076 (*Rimsky-Korsakov: Ivan the Terrible suite).*

Vigorous playing brilliant reproduction of a symphonic poem highly influential in the development of Russian music. The Rimsky suite is also well performed.

BANTOCK, GRANVILLE (1868-1946)

Fifine at the Fair. RPO, Beecham, V LHMV 1026.

A work of more quality than the composer's present repute would suggest, ardently expounded by Beecham, and warmly reproduced.

BARBER, SAMUEL (1910-)

Ballet Music

*Medea. NEW, Barber, 10" L LS 33 (*Symphony No. 2).*

Able performances under the composer's direction, well reproduced in the London manner.

Concerto

For Violoncello and Orchestra. Nelsova, NEW, Barber, 10" L LS 332.

Nelsova is an excellent interpreter for this work (which should be better known), and the recording is just.

Works for Orchestra

*Adagio for Strings. ERO, Hanson, Mor 40002 (*Essay, School for Scandal Overture; Gould: Latin-America Symphonette).*

A compendium of the shorter Barber repertory, persuasively performed by Hanson, and very well reproduced. The Gould work is also well played.

Symphony No. 1. SSO, Lehmann, CE 1011.

Far-fetched Swedish sympathy, adequately reproduced. Also included are Barber's "Dover Beach," with baritone, and songs.

*Symphony No. 2. NEW, Barber, 10" L LS 334 (*Medea).*

See entry above, under Ballet Music: *Medea.*

Work for Orchestra and Voice

*Knoxville, Summer of 1915. DOO, Steber, Strickland, C ML 2174 (*Four Excursions).*

Barber's success in effecting combinations of his own works in this sequence of discs is something any composer might envy. Here the apt singing of Steber is coupled with Rudolf Firkusny's artistry in the piano pieces.

BARTÓK, BÉLA (1881-1945)

Ballet Music

The Miraculous Mandarin (Suite). NEW, Serly, Bar 304.

As a kind of inverse justice for the neglect he suffered at the end of his life, Bartók is the first contemporary to have a record label in his name, and devoted largely to his works. Persistent traits are high-quality workmanship and the active participation of such musicians as Serly and Primrose, who worked with the composer during his lifetime. The recording, for the most part, is done in London's Kingsway Hall.

Concertos

No. 2, No. 3 for Piano and Orchestra. Farnadi, VSO, Scherchen, W WL 5249.

The advantages in this pairing are both musical and auditory, though I still regard Sandor's No. 3 as the choice in that composition. Scherchen's penetration of the coloristic detail in the score is an aid to the appreciation of No. 2. Extra good sound.

*No. 2 for Piano and Orchestra, Foldes, LAM, Bigot, Vox PL 8220 (*Rhapsody No. 1).*

Not the roundest sound, but a good interpretative effort. Preferable in the coupling noted.

*No. 3 for Piano and Orchestra, Sandor, PHO, Ormandy, C ML 4239 (*Miaskovsky: Symphony No. 21). Katchen, OSR, Ansermet, L LL 945 (*Prokofiev: Concerto No. 3).*

My preference here is firmly with Sandor and the fine sound of the Philadelphia Orchestra. However, if the prospect of the Miaskovsky does not appeal, Katchen's performance is the best of the others, and wonderfully reproduced.

For Viola and Orchestra. Primrose, NEW, Serly, Bar 309.

No question here of authority, for the work was written for Primrose and completed by Serly from sketches left by the composer. Very good sound.

For Violin and Orchestra. Menuhin, PHI, Furtwängler, V LHMV 3. Varga, BPH, Fricsay, D DL 9545. Rostal, LSO, Sargent, L LL 302.

A Menuhin in top form and a Furtwängler with a superior command of this demanding score are more beneficial to Bartók than anything provided by Varga or Rostal. Moreover, the sound is superior to either competitor's.

Works for Orchestra

Concerto for Orchestra. MIN, Dorati, Mer MG 50033. PHI, Karajan, An 35003.

Dorati's particular contribution to the unfolding appreciation of this work is a physical drive that makes certain aspects of it more dynamic than ever. Karajan does not match this distinction, nor is his generally excellent performance as well reproduced. If this seems to add to a distinction without a difference, the performances are that close in quality.

*Dance Suite. NEW, Autori, Bar 304 (*Two Portraits).*

An advantageous combination of elements, very well reproduced.

Deux Images. NEW, Serly, 10" Bar 305.

Excellent performance, clearly reproduced.

Divertimento for String Orchestra. *RIAS, Fricsay, D DL 9748* (**Two Portraits*). *MIN, Dorati, V LM 1750* (**Kodály: Háry Janós*).

Fricsay's sense of the appropriate style for this work is keen; the reproduction of his excellent orchestra is more sonorous than Victor's management of the Minneapolis problem. Also, the additional matter here is its best form on records.

Mikrokosmos Suite. NEW, Serly, Bar 303 (**Two Portraits*).

Rather fragmentary Bartok (arrangements of piano pieces), reasonably performed. Startling reproduction.

Suite, No. 1 (*opus 3*). *SAL, Fekete, Col 1010.*

Fair performance, sub-par reproduction.

Works for Orchestra and Solo Instrument

Portraits, Nos. 1 and 2. RIAS, Fricsay, D DL 9748 (**Divertimento for String Orchestra*). *NEW, Autori, Bar 304* (**Dance Suite*).

Although these pieces are customarily regarded as works for a "name" soloist and orchestra, the preferable version of Fricsay (preferable largely because of the combination with the *Divertimento*) leaves the soloist's identity unrevealed. In totality the Autori-conducted effort, with Jean Pougnet as the able soloist, is as faithfully Bartókian, and, if the *Dance Suite* is cherished, it is as good a buy. Both are excellent in sound, the Decca not quite so sharp or detailed as the other, Kingsway Hall, enterprise.

Portrait, No. 1. PHI, Szigeti, Lambert, 10" C ML 2213 (**Contrasts; Rhapsody No. 1*).

Inasmuch as this disc offers the composer as collaborator with Benny Goodman and Szigeti in works of his own, the Bartók enthusiast would not readily be without it. This performance with Lambert is a more recent recording than either of the disc-mates, and very beautifully done.

Rhapsody for Piano and Orchestra, Opus 1. Foldes, LAM, Désormière, Vox PL 8220 (**Concerto No. 2*).

See entry under *Concerto No. 2.*

Rhapsodies for Violin and Orchestra (*Two*). *Vardi, NEW, Serly, 10" Bar 306.*

Though Vardi is better known as a violist than as a violinist, he manages these works very well, and with admirable understanding.

Miscellaneous

Music for Strings, Percussion, and Celesta. CHO, Kubelik, Mer 50026 (*Schoenberg: *Five Pieces*). *PHI, Karajan, C ML 4456.*

Whether in combination with Schoenberg's *Five Pieces*, as noted above, or with Bloch's *Concerto Grosso* (Mer 50001), the Kubelik performance is substantially better reproduced than the Karajan, a considerable factor in such a work as this. The latter's forceful personality makes much of the opportunities in the score, but the sound is particularly confined and unresonant.

BEETHOVEN, LUDWIG VAN (1770-1827)

Ballet Music

Creatures of Prometheus. LSO, Van Beinum, L LL 577. WIN, Goehr, CH 1063 [2].

Either is rewarding, according to the listener's preference for the overture and excerpts (Van Beinum) or the total music written by Beethoven (Goehr). For those otherwise undecided, the Van Beinum is a customary concert selection and includes the best music in the score.

Choral Work

Missa Solemnis. NBC, Shaw Chorale, Toscanini, vocal soloists, V LM 6013 [2].

A product of 1953, in Toscanini's 86th year, this will long stand as a monument to his art and skill, penetration and insight. Superb orchestral performance (save for the violin tone in the "*Benedictus*") and a virtuoso choral effort offset the deficiencies of the solo quartet, in which Jerome Hines, bass, and Nan Merriman, mezzo, are suitable to the occasion, Lois Marshall, soprano, is powerful but edgy, and Eugene Conley, tenor, is rather out of his element. Powerful recording of the orchestra and chorus, but a distinct unbalance in reproduction of the quartet. They can be heard on a wide-open, wide-range machine, but who has a concert auditorium in which to accommodate that effect?

Concertos

For Piano and Orchestra

Complete Edition. Kempff, BPH, Van Kempen, D DX 125 [3].

It is an undoubted economy to have the five great works on three LP's, with no extraneous matter, excellent sound (Deutsche Grammophon in origin), and consistent work all the way through by soloist and conductor. However, there are a few qualifying factors. No work is complete on a single side, and the sequence requires a change from one to the next: No. 1 is the only one that begins a record, the others all follow portions of the preceding one; and Kempff, while a meticulous, thoroughly informed Beethoven player, is not a notably enlivening one. As noted in the following commentary, Kempff is at his best in Nos. 2 and 4, though even in the latter Gieseking is much more the poet required by the music.

No. 1 in C. Badura-Skoda, VSO, Scherchen, W 5209. Kempff, BPH, D DX 125 [3]. *Gieseking, PHI, C ML 4307. Serkin, PHO, Ormandy, C ML 4914. Dorfmann, NBC, Toscanini, V LM 1039.*

For the best balance of all elements, the pairing of Badura-Skoda and Scherchen offers the preferable value. Both Kempff and Gieseking dominate their conductorial partners (Gieseking's, though anonymous, is generally believed to be Karajan). It is also a suave, tonally equitable recording. The Serkin-Ormandy enjoys the full bloom of Academy of Music sound, but this is a "big" conception that strikes me as out of place in this work. The interests of the Dorfmann-Toscanini are diminished by the dry sound of a wartime effort tonally inferior by current standards.

No. 2 in B flat. Backhaus, VPH, Krauss, 10" L LL 421. Kempff, BPH, Van Kempen, D DX 125 [3]. *Badura-Skoda, VSO, Scherchen, W WL 5302.*

Both veterans are in splendid form here, but the broader range of pianistic colors available to Backhaus adds a dimension to his playing. Should either Schnabel version (preferably with Dobrowen) become available, it would be worth owning. The Badura-Skoda-Scherchen treatment here is not as suitable as in No. 1

No. 3 in C minor. Moïséivitch, PHI, Sargent, V LBC 1012. Backhaus, VPH, Böhm, L LL 289. Rubinstein, NBC, Toscanini, V LCT 1009.

In point and dexterity of articulation, Moïséivitch has long had a lien as a specialist in this work, which honor should not be denied him because the Bluebird series is sub-standard in price. Excellent value. For a bigger style, Backhaus satisfies all wants.

The Rubinstein-Toscanini collaboration is preserved, dimly, dryly, from a studio 8H broadcast. Power, yes; grateful sound, no,

No. 4 in G. Gieseking, PHI, Karajan, C ML 4535. Kempff, BPH, Van Kempen, D DX 125 [3]. *Backhaus, VPH, Krauss, L LL 417. Schnabel, PHI, Dobrowen, V LCT 1131. Rubinstein, RPO, Beecham, V LCT 1032. Curzon, VPH, Knappertsbusch, L LL 1045.*

Gieseking is the rippling master of this score, well companioned by Karajan, who may be expected to duplicate his collaboration at some future time on the Angel label. However, though this sound is not the equal either of the Kempff Decca (Deutsche Grammophon in origin) or the Backhaus London, it is quite respectable. Time has robbed the others of some of their previous attractiveness, but Beecham's delivery of the orchestral score is outstanding among all of these, and Schnabel's subtleties are worth knowing, if the sometimes wavery sound of the reproduction is not. If fine sound alone is demanded, the Curzon provides that in abundance, though I find his treatment of this score a little prosaic.

No. 5 in E flat ("Emperor"). Backhaus, VPH, Krauss, L LL 879. Schnabel, CHO, Stock, V LCT 1015. Horowitz, RCAO, Reiner, V LM 1718.

Alphabetically, as well as in every other way, Backhaus stands at the head of contemporary interpreters of the "Emperor." One of the great recordings of the LP era, musically virtuous, tonally sumptuous. Were time elements reversed, one might say as much of Schnabel, but this is not even the last version of the work he made (a more robust HMV product with PHI, Galliera). However, it conveys his largeness of thought and expression in a score for which he had profound affinity. One can hardly imagine the piano part struck off with more brilliance and clarity than it is by Horowitz, and Reiner draws sparks from the orchestra, too. But too often the pianist fails to accentuate the needed note in a rapid sequence, and the design suffers thereby. Brilliant sound. Budget-buyers are commended to the Matthews-PHI-Süsskind version on C RL 3037.

For Piano, Violin, Cello, and Orchestra

In C ("Triple"). Hendl, Corrigliano, Rose, NYPH, Walter, 10" C ML 2059.

The only contemporary version worth considering (the tempting one with David Oistrakh as violinist is poorly recorded, not too well played), this is in many ways an appropriate successor to the one conducted by Felix Weingartner. Columbia has, in its devoir to Weingartner, included that in its LP reissues (10" C ML 2218), but the Walter-conducted performance is in every way superior.

For Violin and Orchestra

In D. Francescatti, PHO, Ormandy, C ML 4371. Haendel, PHI, Kubelik, V LBC 1003. Heifetz, NBC, Toscanini, V LCT 1010. Hubermann, VPH, Szell, C ML 4769. Szigeti, NYPH, Walter, C ML 4012.

The above order is purposefully alphabetical, for none of the discs is wholly recommendable. The most exciting performance, to be sure, is the Heifetz-Toscanini, but the sound is poorish. Francescatti's style is not my choice in this work, and Szigeti's, whose is, suffers from pre-LP recording. The Hubermann (dating from 1932) is an interesting oddity. For the reasonable price asked, the Haendel-Kubelik is the best value of the lot. If none of the violinists attracts for intrinsic reasons, the purchaser should bide his time.

Incidental Music

Egmont. Laszlo, Liewehr, VSO, Scherchen, W 5281.

Laszlo is a capable singer, Liewehr an effective reader of the text; Scherchen exercises his usual orchestral powers in the sequence that includes, of course, the overture. Suitable sound.

Overtures

*Consecration of the House. NBC, Toscanini, 10" V LM 6 (*Schumann: Manfred Overture). LPO, Van Beinum, 10" L LD 9022 (*Leonore No. 3).*

Each of these performances exists in other combinations which may appeal to the listener more. (They are cited here in the combination which involves as little other material as possible.) The Toscanini has its typical power, the Van Beinum warmth and fine musical detail. Sound values are distinctly in favor of the London product.

Coriolan. PHO, Ormandy, 10" C AL 15 (Egmont). LPO, Van Beinum. 10" L LD 9021 (Egmont).

The identity of pairings makes a simple choice between these possible. In terms of total value, Ormandy and his orchestra give us more of Beethoven than Van Beinum and the LPO. However, this remains something less than the whole account of these works, and a later judgment might be different.

*Egmont. NBC, Toscanini, V 1834 (*Berlioz: Roman Carnival; Hérold: Zampa; Sibelius: Finlandia; etc.).*

In absolute terms, this is the great playing of the *Egmont* on records as of now, but I can hardly recommend it with enthusiasm, for the listener, unless he is agile on his feet, will immediately be plunged into a sequence of Brahms "Hungarian Dances," with the other items as indicated. (The best of them are available in preferable groupings.) Therefore the discussion under *Coriolan* stands as the wisest words I can provide.

*Fidelio. VSO, Scherchen, W 5177 (*Leonore Nos. 1, 2, 3). LPO, Van Beinum, 10" L LD 9024 (*Prometheus).*

The Scherchen collation of matter written and rewritten for various productions of *Fidelio* is a musical item of the first order in illuminating the processes of a great musical mind. The performances are outstanding in directness and energy; the recording is of prime quality. For those who are undisposed to the total sequence, the Van Beinum effort is a worthy one, as is the overside *Prometheus*.

Leonore Nos. 1, 2, 3. VSO, Scherchen, W 5177. See *Fidelio* above.

*Leonore No. 1. BBC, Toscanini, V LCT 1041 (*Prometheus; Symphony No. 5).*

The quality of the interpretative effort here is typical, but the fidelity of sound is limited. It is, in a sense, vintage Toscanini (c. 1940), but the dry wine of 8H (Symphony No. 5) is not for many palates.

*Leonore No. 2. LSO, Weingartner, C ML 4647 (*Consecration of the House; Egmont; Fidelio; Prometheus).*

A less forceful version of this work than the Scherchen noted above, mentioned here because it is the only other now available on LP, and might tempt some. In this group, the *Egmont* and *Prometheus* overtures are of superior style, though the sound is far from today's best in purity and balance.

*Leonore No. 3. NBC, Toscanini, 10" V LRM 7023 (*Wagner: Faust). See also Scherchen, under Fidelio.*

I nominate this as the outstanding *single*-side version of the *Leonore* No. 3 rather than the *same* version on LM 1043, in consideration of the couplings. LRM 7023 is a 10" disc which offers, on side two, as fine a playing of Wagner's *Faust-Ouverture* as one is likely to hear; LM 1043 is a 12" disc which is paired with the second suite from Ravel's *Daphnis et Chloë*. This is excellent, but hardly the last word on the subject. It should be mentioned, for Van Beinum enthusiasts, that his well-regarded versions of the *Coriolan, Egmont, Fidelio,* and *Consecration of the House* overtures are also available, in an omnibus edition with the *Leonore* No. 3 on L LL 357. In sum: the Scherchen totality on W 5177 and the Toscanini virtuosity on LRM 7023 will give everyone as much of Beethoven's thoughts on his *Leonore* problem as they can readily absorb.

*Prometheus. LPO, Van Beinum, 10" L LD 9024 (*Fidelio). See also Leonore No. 1, Leonore No. 2.*

The pairing with the *Fidelio* gives Van Beinum's *Prometheus* special attractiveness as a coupling of two of the less frequently played overtures of Beethoven. Those who are considering quantity as well as quality might consult the entries under the headings noted above.

Romances

*For Violin and Orchestra, Nos. 1 and 2. Heifetz, LSO, Sargent, V LM 9014 (*Mozart: Concerto No. 5 in A).*

This is not the greatest Heifetz, nor is it the greatest Beethoven. However, in consideration of the second-side Mozart (with Beecham) and the comparative values in other current versions, it is the most desirable disc in sum.

Symphonies

Complete Edition. NBC, Toscanini, RCA Memorial Edition (see individual entries).

*No. 1 in C. BBC, Toscanini, V LCT 1023 (*Brahms: Haydn Variations). NBC, Toscanini, V Set 6009 (*Beethoven: Symphony No. 9). ACG, Mengelberg, Cap P 8097 (*Beethoven: Symphony No. 8). VPH, Weingartner, C ML 4501.*

The Toscanini of 72 vs. the Toscanini of 86, with the BBC as marvelously responsive as the NBC. Musically, the earlier version is preferable, though many will acquire the brighter-sounding latter as part of the epochal No. 9. Mengelberg's Nos. 1 and 8 are part of interpretative history, as is Weingartner's No. 1. Gravely limited sound in both.

*No. 2 in D. NBC, Toscanini, V LM 1723 (*Beethoven: Symphony No. 4). NYPH, Walter, C ML 4596 (*Beethoven: Symphony No. 4). SFS, Monteux, V LM 1024. LSO, Weingartner, C ML 4502.*

Both pairings represent a better investment for the purchaser than the single-symphony discs, and the Toscanini disc is a cleaner, clearer statement. Of itself, the Monteux performance is notable for solidity, and Weingartner's verve is infectious even if his reproduced sound now is weak.

No. 3 in E flat ("Eroica"). NBC, Toscanini, V LM 1042. RPH, Leinsdorf, C RL 3069. ACG, Mengelberg, Cap P 8002. VPH, Weingartner, C ML 4503. BPH, Van Kempen, Ep LC 3016.

Allowing for a lack of the best sound, Toscanini's is the inclusive "*Eroica*" of our time, blending vigor with control. Leinsdorf's energetic, well-reproduced performance is an excellent value in a lower price bracket. Mengelberg's is erratic but largely drawn, the Weingartner substantial if slightly phlegmatic. For powerful sound and a very solid if not markedly personal treatment of this score, Van Kempen's is recommended.

*No. 4 in B flat. SFS, Monteux, V LM 1714 (*Schumann: Symphony No. 4). Co, Szell, C ML 4008 (See Symphony No. 2).*

For a pairing of Beethoven, the recommendation under Symphony No. 2 remains. I would, however, regard the Monteux as the best of all the performances of the Fourth (and of the Schumann) now available. The Szell is capable, but spread over two sides. For a best economy buy, consult the Harty-Hallé version, C RL 3034.

*No. 5 in C minor. NBC, Toscanini, V LM 1757 (*Symphony No. 8). ACG, Kleiber, L LL 912. LPO, Weingartner, C ML 4505.*

For fullest sound and a particularly powerful first movement, the Kleiber is the choice. However, the Toscanini of present mention is a decided improvement on the long-suffered Studio 8H version, though made from a radio broadcast; and its cumulative force is beyond match by other interpreters now on record. The Weingartner is an interesting relic. For economy, the Barbirolli-Hallé version on V LBC 1018 is first choice (it is coupled with the Mozart "Jupiter").

No. 6 in F ("Pastoral"). NBC, Toscanini, V LM 1755. BBC, Toscanini, V LCT 1042. PSO, Steibenrg, Cap S 8159. ACG, Kleiber, L LL 916. PHO, Walter, C ML 4010.

The circumstances of the two Toscanini recordings of Symphony

No. 1 are reversed here: for the later NBC retains all the freshness and spirit of the BBC, adding to it a considerable measure of realism. Steinberg's is lyrical and well reproduced, Kleiber's full of fine musical detail and particularly well reproduced. The Walter is mentioned for those who relish a concept much similar to Weingartner's, but reproduced with contemporary techniques.

No. 7 in A. NBC, Toscanini, V LM 1756. VSO, Scherchen, W 5089. BPO, Van Kempen. Ep LC 3026.

As in the well-remembered N. Y. Philharmonic-Symphony version (still available on V LCT 1013), the Toscanini concept of this work survives both repetition and challenge. Fortunately, it is powerfully reproduced, especially in the driving energy of the finale. Scherchen's is a fine example of his classic style, favorably reproduced, while the Van Kempen, thoroughly traditional in treatment, is also given imposing resonance in the Philips (European originators of this label) manner.

*No. 8 in F. NBC, Toscanini, V LM 1757 (*Symphony No. 5). RPO, Beecham, C ML 4681 (*Mendelssohn: Symphony No. 4). AUS, Busch, Rem 199-149 (*Haydn: Symphony No. 101).*

Those who accept my recommendation of a Beethoven No. 5 will automatically acquire this sterling performance of No. 8. However, those who want somewhat more lightness in this music will find it in the Beecham version, solidly reproduced and advantageously coupled. The Busch (the late Fritz) concept is durable, the recording acceptable for the price.

*No. 9 in D minor ("Choral"). NBC, Toscanini, V LM 6009 [2]. VPH, Kleiber, L LL 632/3. VSO, Scherchen, W 208 [2]. VPH, Karajan, El 51 (*Symphony No. 8). VPH, Weingartner, SL 165 (*Symphony No. 8).*

None of these is perfection, for such a Ninth Symphony is a rarity in the concert hall, and hence even less common when the problems of recording are introduced. It may be said, however, that the lacks of the Toscanini are not in conception, which towers above any other known to me. After a somewhat unsettled first movement, the power and fervor of the music are eloquently matched in the playing of the orchestra and the singing of the chorus. The solo quartet is not wholly first class, and the balance is sometimes poor. But it is a historic likeness of an unsurpassable experience. Kleiber's suffers from Vienna-echo, as do those of Karajan (a good value at the price, especially for the solo quartet) and Weingartner. The latter is one of the latest in his recorded sequence, wholly homogeneous in musical character, and possessing perhaps the best solo quartet of the versions noted. Scherchen's is to me ponderous rather than powerful, but the best in sound.

BERG, ALBAN (1885-1935)

*Concerto for Violin and Orchestra. Gertler, PHI, Kletzki, An 35091 (*Bartók: Sonata for Solo Violin). Krasner, CO, Rodzinski, C ML 4857 (*Schoenberg: Concerto for Violin).*

If there seemed a reasonable certainty in recording lore, it was that Krasner's pioneering effort would not soon be surpassed. However, Gertler, a Hungarian virtuoso long resident in Brussels, has a remarkable flair for Berg's melodic idiom, a warmer sound than Krasner, and—most important—decidedly high fidelity reproduction. Kletzki does his work splendidly, leaving no alternative—save for those who prefer the second-side Schoenberg to the excellent Bartók work strongly played by Gertler.

Concerto for Violin, Piano, and 13 Wind Instruments. PCO, Leibowitz, Dia 9.

Skillful execution, acceptably reproduced.

Der Wein. Boerner, JSO, Janssen, 10" Cap L 8150.

Both singer and conductor are in command of the problems in this work, and the reproduction is reasonably good.

BERLIOZ, HECTOR (1803-1869)

Overtures (Collection)

Beatrice and Benedict; Benvenuto Cellini; Les Francs-Juges; Le Corsaire. PHI, Kletzki, C RL 3071.

The classification in Columbia's economy-priced "Encore" series belies everything about this odd and valuable disk except that it is a "buy." Kletzki's direction of each individual work is hardly exceeded by any in the more expensive categories below (Munch's *Benvenuto Cellini* would be the exception). The orchestra fairly sparkles through Berlioz's challenges, and the recording, if not of widest range, is big, broad, and resonant.

Overtures

Beatrice and Benedict. *NYSO, Smallens, 10" D DL 4034 (*Dvořák: Carnaval Overture).*

Not nearly all this work is entitled to in performance or reproduction.

*Benvenuto Cellini; Roman Carnival. LAM, Van Otterloo, Ep LC 3054 (*Trojan March from Les Troyens; Three Excerpts from Damnation of Faust; Four Excerpts from Roméo).*

The engineers are really the persons responsible for mention here of this disc, for Van Otterloo's direction, though solidly traditional, shows little special flair for the material, and the playing is not outstanding. However, if it is loud, precise Berlioz you want, here it is.

*Benvenuto Cellini. OSC, Munch, 10" L LD 9019 (*Le Corsaire).*

Both in performance and reproduction, the Munch *Benvenuto Cellini* is superior to others separately available, and the coupling with the *Corsaire* adds to the attractions of the disc.

*Le Corsaire. OSC, Munch, 10" L LD 9019 (*Benvenuto Cellini).*

See entry under *Benvenuto Cellini.*

*Les Francs-Juges. ORB, Celibidache, U 7024 (*Franck: Psyché).*

Vigorous performance; powerful, but not too well-balanced, reproduction.

*Roman Carnival. NBC, Toscanini, V LM 1834 (*Beethoven: Egmont; Hérold: Zampa; Sibelius: Finlandia; etc.). PHP, Hilsberg, 10" C AL 34 (*Suppé: Light Cavalry).*

For those to whom this grab-bag of Toscanini "favorites" (a new commercial euphemism for a potpourri) does not appeal, the very well played Hilsberg (almost wholly Philadelphia Orchestra personnel) can be readily if not warmly recommended. The Toscanini is certainly more dynamic and powerfully reproduced, but it is the third item on a side prefaced by the Beethoven *Egmont* overture and a sequence of Brahms "Hungarian Dances."

Opera Excerpts (Orchestral)

*La Damnation de Faust. ACG, Van Beinum, 10" L LS 620 (*Handel: Royal Fireworks Music).*

Serviceable rather than brilliant performances of the customary excerpts.

*Les Troyens. LAM, Martinon, 10" MGM E 127. OSC, Munch, L LL 3 (*Romeo and Juliet excerpts).*

Martinon is quite as good a Berliozian as Munch here, and the brightness of the MGM recording compares favorably with the rounder sonority of London. In addition to the "Royal Hunt and Storm," the Martinon disc includes the Overture and Ballet Music.

Symphonies

Symphonic Fantastique. PHO, Ormandy, C ML 4467. LSO, Scherchen, W 5268. BPH, Van Otterloo, Ep LC 3005. SFO, Monteux, V LM 1131. CO, Rodzinski, C RL 3059.

No one of these is so superior to the others in all respects as to constitute a clear favorite. Considering all elements involved, the brilliant playing of the Philadelphia Orchestra under Ormandy's knowing direction, and its keen reproduction, speak more favorably for Berlioz than any of the others. Scherchen's rather opinionated statement of the music (by which I mean that when questions of doubt intrude, his inclination is to a textual interpretation rather at variance with most others) is strongly but not convincingly reproduced, while without the Epic sound the Van Otterloo conception would have little interest. Monteux has the most refined conception of the score among these maestros, but the likeness of it here is incomplete. For an economy version, the Rodzinski-Cleveland may be commended.

Work for Orchestra and Viola

Harold in Italy (*Symphony*). *RPO, Primrose, Beecham, C ML 4542. SYM, Riddle, Scherchen, W WL 5288.*

As Primrose was the preferred voice for this music when his effort was joined with Koussevitzky's, so he is, even more, in the company of Beecham. Good ample sound, if not the ultimate in fidelity. The Riddle-Scherchen performance is much similar to the latter's *Fantastique* noted above. Certainly it is outstanding in sound values.

Work for Orchestra and Voices

Funeral March for the Last Scene of Hamlet. OSC, Sebastian, U RLP

7061 (**Excerpts from Damnation of Faust; Franck: Redemption, Prelude to Part II*).

Sebastian omits the chorus from his version, which is not a serious blemish, as its part in the results is small. Good performance by the orchestra, and excellent sound. The playing of the *Damnation of Faust* excerpts is rather routine.

Lelio. PSO, Leibowitz, Vox PL *8250.*

The not-too-successful concluding section for the "*Fantastique*," not too successfully ventured by Leibowitz. A curio, but no more.

Nuits d' Été. Danco, CIN, Johnson, L LL 407.

In the absence of any other version, it is certainly fortunate that we have this one. However, Danco does not convince me in these songs (as Teyte does in her singing of Berlioz), and the orchestral direction of Johnson, though capable, is hardly definitive. Fairly good sound.

Romeo and Juliet (*Complete*). *BSO, Munch, Chorus, etc., V LM 6011* [2]. (*Excerpts*). *NBC, Toscanini, V LM 1019* (**Tchaikovsky: Romeo and Juliet*).

Munch omits nothing from his version of the score as Berlioz wrote it, though what Toscanini offers is much more intense, probing, and satisfactory (Part II, including *Roméo seul: Tristesse, Concert et Bal, Grand Fête chez Capulet,* and *Scène d'Amour*) as a musical experience. However, the march of improved sound is to the benefit of the Boston venture. Despite all, I'd be inclined to settle for what the Toscanini offers, as being insuperable of its kind, and to wait for another issue of the complete work.

Symphonie Funèbre et Triomphale. CSO, Straub, Chorus, Ly 40.

A rather odd and impressive work (with some decidedly "Wagnerian" brass effects before Wagner thought of them) played with fervor, though not with compelling orchestral power. The reproduction is more an approximation than a likeness.

BERNERS, LORD (1883-1950)

Triumph of Neptune. PHO, Beecham, C ML 4593 (**Arnell: Punch and the Child*).

A rousing tribute by Beecham to his countryman, and well performed by the Philadelphians. However, the drolleries of the score don't seem to register as well from the record as in the hall.

BERNSTEIN, LEONARD (1918-   )

Age of Anxiety. NYPH, Foss, Bernstein, C ML 4325.

A happy collaboration, with the composer in charge and a trusted friend at the piano. Good recording.

Fancy Free. BTO, Levine, 10" Cap L 8197. BTO, Bernstein, 10" D DL 6023.

Bernstein's version of his music has its own kind of drive and articulation, but Levine's has almost as much and is substantially better reproduced.

BIZET, GEORGES (1838-1875)

*L'Arlésienne (both suites). HIS, Stokowski, V LM 1706 (*Symphony in C). PHI, Hallé, Sargent, C RL 3051.*

Some of Stokowski's effects are a little highly colored for this rather pastel music, but the fine quality of the orchestral playing and its excellent reproduction are hard to resist. Of recordings devoted to the suites exclusively, the Sargent is the best value.

*L'Arlésienne (Suite No. 1). LPO, Van Beinum, L LL 79 (*Carmen suite). Hallé, Barbirolli, V LBC 1047 (*Schubert: Symphony No. 8).*

Van Beinum's work is worthy of admiration, but the second side (conducted by Collins) does not qualify in competition with others. A better buy is the reasonably priced, well-recorded Barbirolli.

*Carmen (Suite). COL, Beecham, C ML 4287 (*Tchaikovsky: Capriccio Italien). NBC, Toscanini, 10" V LRM 7013 (*Thomas: Mignon overture).*

No one can choose, as right, one treatment or the other of two espoused by two such competent minds as those of Beecham and Toscanini. The Beecham inclines to the French point of view, the Toscanini to a more general one. I find the former more to my taste, especially as coupled with the Tchaikovsky showpiece. It is also a brighter, more vibrant recording.

*The Fair Maid of Perth (Suite). RPO, Beecham, 10" C ML 2133 (*Delius: Over the Hills and Far Away).*

A fair view of the fair maid, admirably reproduced. The overside is not likely to be better played in any near future.

*Jeux d'Enfants. OSC, Lindenberg, L LL 871 (*Bizet: Fair Maid of Perth; Chabrier: Suite Pastorale). CGO, Braithwaite, MGM E 3000 (*Chabrier: Suite Pastorale).*

My inclination to the Braithwaite treatment of the *Jeux d'Enfants* is somewhat affected by the inclusion, on the Lindenberg disc, of the *Fair Maid of Perth* music, a performance not in the Beecham class. (The Chabrier fares about the same in each instance.) Tonally, the results are in the same category of quality, with the familiar difference that the MGM is brighter, more specific in detail, the London more resonant.

*Symphony in C. HIS, Stokowski, V LM 1706 (*L'Arlésienne, Suites 1 and 2).*

The gloss that Stokowski applies to his performance of this music makes for a brilliant surface indeed, though there have been more penetrating versions available at other times. For the while, its execution and reproduction are superior to those of any other.

BLISS, ARTHUR (1891-)

Ballet Music

*Checkmate. ROO, Irving, C ML 4362 (*Meyerbeer: Les Patineurs).*

*Miracle in the Gorbals. ROO, Lambert, 10" C ML 2117 (*Adam: Giselle).*

As the attributions indicate, both recordings derive from the repertory of the Sadler's Wells Ballet, and are authoritative. Good if not outstanding sound.

Concerto

For Piano and Orchestra. Mewton-Wood, USO, Goehr, CH 1167.

Good orchestral performance by the Dutch ensemble, and suitable virtuosity from the pianist. Better than average sound.

BLOCH, ERNEST (1880-)

*Concerto for Violin and Orchestra. Szigeti, OSC, Munch, C ML 4679 (*Baal Shem).*

The classic pre-war recording, with Szigeti in thorough command. The recording is less ample than we now regard as desirable.

*Concerto Grosso. CHO, Schick, Kubelik, Mer 50001 (*Bartók: Music* *for Strings, Percussion, and Celesta). PSO, Franklin, Steinberg, Cap S 8212 (*Schuman: Symphony).*

The two performances of the Bloch are about of equal quality, though the Steinberg—an actual performance "take"—has a little more vitality in the playing. However, the second-side pairing with the excellent playing of the Bartók makes the Mercury disk that much more desirable.

Israel (Symphony). VSO, Litschauer, Van 423.

Well-integrated performance, fine reproduction.

*Schelomo. Rose, NYPH, Mitropoulos, C ML 4425 (*Saint-Saëns: Concerto for Cello). Nelsova, LPO, Bloch, 10" L LS 138.*

A reissue of the superb Feuermann performance (Victor) would put this matter beyond discussion, but until that happens, Rose has more of the breadth and strength of that style to offer than does Nelsova. However, she plays well, and her version has the participation of the composer to commend it—also excellent sound.

BOCCHERINI, LUIGI (1743-1805)

*Concerto for Cello and Orchestra, in B flat. Casals, LSO, Ronald, V LCT 1028 (*Bruch: Kol Nidrei). Janigro, VSO, Prohaska, W 5126 (*Haydn: Concerto in D).*

Casals's playing of this work is as close to insuperable as interpretative art can come, and what sound there is doesn't offend. However, those who prefer equal balance in all respects are referred to the Janigro, a performance very much in the Casals manner and beautifully reproduced.

*Concerto for Flute and Strings. Renzi, GSE, Con 50 (*Marcello: Concerto for Oboe).*

A delightful work, well played. Fair recording.

*Scuola di Ballo (arranged by Jean Françaix). LPO, Dorati, C RL 3043 (*Field: Suite).*

Not the newest recording, of course, but still a decent likeness of the delightful Boccherini material considerately treated by Dorati. The second side is well conducted by Sir Malcolm Sargent.

*Symphony in A. VSY, Swoboda, W 5002 (*Haydn: Octet for Wind Instruments).*

A rather elusive work for Swoboda, and among the less notable reproductions in the Westminster catalogue, being one of the first.

Symphony in F, opus 35, No. 4. *ICO, Jenkins, HS 79 (*Rosetti: Concerto for Horn).*

Well-meaning, not too skillful work by Jenkins. Good reproduction.

BOÏELDIEU, FRANÇOIS (1775-1834)

Caliph of Bagdad: Overture. *LPO, Martinon, 10" L LD 9036 (*Dame Blanche overture).*

Highly adroit direction by Martinon, and a very proper kind of recorded sound.

BORODIN, ALEXANDER (1834-1887)

In the Steppes of Central Asia. *OSC, Ansermet, 10" L LD 9086 (*Mussorgsky: Night on Bare Mountain). NYPH, Mitropoulos, C ML 4815 (*Ippolitov-Ivanov: Caucasian Sketches). HIS, Stokowski, 10" V LRM 7056 (*Prince Igor, Polovtsian Dances).*

Either by itself or in the coupling with the Mussorgsky material, Ansermet's version offers a superior blend of interpretation and reproduction. The Mitropoulos is mentioned for some excellent woodwind-playing, the Stokowski for its advantageous combination with Borodin's "Polovtsian Dances."

Prince Igor (Suite). *PHI, Süsskind, MGM 3008.*

A decidedly worthwhile disc, which includes the Overture, "Polovtsian March," etc., in addition to the familiar dances. Excellent reproduction.

Prince Igor: Polovtsian Dances. *HIS, Stokowski, V LM 1054 (*Falla: El Amor Brujo). The same, 10" LRM 7056 (*In the Steppes of Central Asia). LPO, Van Beinum, L LL 203 (*Falla: El Amor Brujo).*

The 10" disc, though economical, omits the choral portions that contribute so much to the interest of the fuller treatment on the 12" disc. The latter is beautifully molded by Stokowski, and the spacious 34th Street studio gives fine perspective to the reproduction. Van Beinum's offers little beyond competent execution and good recording. No chorus.

Symphony No. 1. *BAV, Graunke, U 7066 (*Dohnányi: Symphonic Minutes).*

Energetic direction, powerful reproduction.

*Symphony No. 2 in B minor. PHI, Malko, V LCB 1024 (*Tchaikovsky: Suite No. 3, Theme and Variations). MIN, Dorati, Mer 50004 (*Stravinsky: L'Oiseau de Feu).*

In its price category, the Malko version is a better investment than the Dorati in its. However, if biting sound is wanted, Mercury has it.

BOWLES, PAUL (1911-)

Concerto for Two Pianos, Winds, and Percussion. Gold, Fizdale, SCO, *10" C ML 2128 (*Milhaud: Carnaval).*

Lively performance by a pianistic pair thoroughly attuned to the composer's idiom. Saidenberg directs his ensemble vigorously, and the recording is good.

BOYCE, WILLIAM (1710-1779)

Symphonies (Eight). ZS, D DX 105 [2]. *LBE, Haas, W 5073, W 5159.*

The Zimbler Sinfonietta (made up of members of the Boston Symphony Orchestra) plays these works with ingratiating style and fine sound. Recording is excellent. Haas and his players are no less skillful, but the distribution of symphonies 1, 4, 6, and 8 on 5073, the others on 5159, does not make compelling logic.

BRAHMS, JOHANNES (1833-1897)

Concertos

For Piano and Orchestra

No. 1 in D minor. Rubinstein, CHO, Reiner, V LM 1831. Backhaus, VPH, Böhm, L LL 911. Serkin, CO, Szell, C ML 4829.

As a combination of superlative pianistic resource, first-class orchestral execution, and broad, beautifully sonorous sound, the Rubinstein-Reiner gives a maximum of value to this chewy score.

The Backhaus is in every way admirable, though it does not rise to such heights of dramatic or lyric expression as the Rubinstein, and its tonal values, well realized as they are, nevertheless must defer to the intensity and power of RCA's accomplishment. The Serkin-Szell does not get at the musical essence of the score nearly so well as either of the others.

No. 2 in B flat. Backhaus, VPO, Schuricht, L LL 628. Serkin, PHO, Ormandy, C ML 4014. Horowitz, NBC, Toscanini, V LCT 1025.

The Backhaus and Serkin are the performances of current interest, for the Horowitz-Toscanini, despite its notable elements of virtuosity and power, is a faded page of earlier phonographic history and an interesting document as such. As between the others, I find the Backhaus effort more lyric in the dramatic passages, more dramatic in the lyric passages than the Serkin. In warmth and vigor, the Vienna orchestra is more suitable to the material than the Philadelphia.

For Violin and Orchestra

In D. Milstein, PSO, Steinberg, Cap P 8271. Martzy, PHI, Kletzki, An 35137. Szigeti, PHO, Ormandy, C ML 4015. Heifetz, BSO, Koussevitzky, V LCT 1043. Renardy, ACG, Munch, L LL 1. Stern, RPO, Beecham, C ML 4530. Olevsky, NSO, Mitchell, W WL 5273.

None of these fulfills all reasonable, present expectations for a work of this character. Of the newest versions, Milstein's has the most fluency, combined with proper recording and a sympathetic collaborator in Steinberg. Martzy (a Hungarian virtuosa now about thirty) has the most personal sentiment to convey, backed by a stunning treatment of the orchestral part under the direction of Kletzki. Szigeti's broad concept has not as much mechanical advantage as the foregoing, nor the silky sound of Renardy (a little wanting in dramatic emphasis). Stern's is finely fingered, but with too much microphone emphasis on the violin. Much of Olevsky's effort is creditable to his taste, and he produces a beautiful, if rather small, sound from his instrument. However, Mitchell's tempos throughout are much too leisurely, the total sound being somewhat muffled. My preference may not be a representative one, but, lacking a new Heifetz—the present one just does not have enough orchestra—I have been listening with most enjoyment to the effort of Martzy.

For Violin, Cello, and Orchestra

In A minor. Heifetz, Feuermann, PHO, Ormandy, V LCT 1016. Milstein, Piatigorsky, ROB, Reiner, V LM 1191. Fournier, Janigro, VSO, Scherchen, W 5117.

Despite its lack of tonal magnetism, the Heifetz-Feuermann standard is not nearly enough matched by one of the others to demand revision of a long-standing preference. If tonal fidelity is the determining factor, the Milstein-Piatigorsky partnership works more harmoniously than the Fournier-Janigro and with more orchestral justice under Reiner than under Scherchen.

Overtures

*Academic Festival. ACG, Van Beinum, 10" L LD 9038 (*Tragic).*

This disc solves the problem of the Brahms overtures, for all practical purposes. It is soundly directed and powerfully reproduced, and excludes extraneous matter.

Tragic. See above.

Symphonies

Set of Four; Two Overtures; Variations on a Theme by Haydn; etc. NYPH, Walter, C SL 200 [4].

For those who are devoted to the musical concepts of Walter, it may be said that these are as representative of those concepts as one could wish, in sound rarely surpassed by Columbia (save in *Symphony No. 4*, which dates from somewhat earlier). For those not so devoted, I would describe the performances as the essence of "comfortable" Brahms, with no striving for ultimates of power, pace, expression, or execution. As such, I find them a little lax and without the full impact of the composer, especially in the big moments of Nos. 1 and 4, and in the more mercurial aspects of the *Variations*. Should No. 3 become separately available, it might take precedence in that area; likewise, the two overtures. (The *etc.* above embraces a selection of *Hungarian Dances*.) Perhaps it should be stressed again that these are uncommonly fine-sounding discs, in the manner of several Mozart symphonies (*q.v.*) lately to Walter's credit.

No. 1 in C minor. NBC, Toscanini, V LM 1702. CHO, Kubelik, Mer 50007. ROB, Leinsdorf, V LBC 1004.

Whether for drama or for musical essence, the Toscanini is presently without close competition. It has substantial tonal virtue, also, though those who cherish Brahms in terms of high fidelity will probably find the Kubelik more to their taste. At the economy price asked, the Leinsdorf is excellent value, and well reproduced.

No. 2 in D. NBC, Toscanini, V LM 1731. VPH, Schuricht, L LL 867. PHO, Ormandy, C ML 4827. SFS, Monteux, V LM 1173.

The Toscanini is not the richest-sounding among these—that honor, in terms of traditional Brahms, would go to the Vienna Philharmonic-Schuricht, or if it is the sound of a great orchestra sumptuously reproduced which is wanted, to Ormandy and the Philadelphia ensemble—but it pursues the musical line of the work with the most persistence to the most satisfying totality. Of the versions that point for the surge of the finale as the excuse for underplaying the earlier movements, the Furtwängler (L LL 28) is the better-sounding. I have an affection, still, for the Monteux treatment, but the sound no longer suffices.

No. 3 in F. BSO, Koussevitzky, V LM 1025. ACG, Szell, L LL 487. NBC, Toscanini, V LM 1836.

Despite the revolution of LP and the creation of half a dozen new versions of this work in the last half-decade, the Koussevitzky retains its pre-eminence for broad sympathetic style and virtually impeccable orchestral execution. Moreover, the dubbing, though a bit different in focus from current recording techniques, shows the orchestral tone in its very best Koussevitzky estate—dark, rich, superbly blended. The Szell is bigger, more powerful in sound, and well conveyed, though not with so much eloquence as the Koussevitzky. As for the Toscanini, it is unduly *maestoso* throughout, a rare failing for this maestro. Good but not outstanding sound.

No. 4 in E minor. NBC, Toscanini, V LM 1713. NYPH, Walter, C ML 4472. LSO, Krips, L LL 208.

A noble effort by Toscanini in a work that has come to mean more and more to him and, through him, to us. It is a notably energetic, spacious, and full-blooded performance he offers here, and it is suitably reproduced. The Walter is one of the most successful of his recent recordings, but is rather too relaxed and gentle, too soft of outline, insufficient in tonal contrast, for the needs of the music. Good recording of Columbia's 30th Street studio type. The

Krips version has a measure of fine melodic statement, but the finale does not match the standard of the others. Fine sound.

Works for Orchestra and Voices

*Alto Rhapsody (Harzreise im Winter). Ferrier, LPO, Krauss, L LL 903 (*Brahms: Songs). Anderson, RCAO, Reiner, V LM 1146 (*Mahler: Kindertotenlieder).*

Both of these performances have their virtues, though if the late Ferrier had been spared to make a projected re-recording pending at the time of her death, those factors weighing against her would have been resolved. However, the sound borrowed from 78-rpm masters is rich and warmly rewarding, if not of the utmost fidelity. Anderson's concept is admirable, her delivery less satisfactory.

German Requiem, opus 45. VPH, Karajan, soloists, C SL 157 [2]. *RCAO, Shaw, soloists, V LM 6004* [2].

There is a preponderance of stylistic virtue on the side of Karajan, but neither version satisfies fully, the Columbia because it dates from early LP days and derives from 78's, the Shaw because it doesn't probe deeply enough into the musical values.

Miscellaneous

Hungarian Dances, Nos. 1, 3, 5, 6, 17, 18, 19, 20, 21. BPH, Van Kempen, 10" D DL 4078.

*Nos. 1, 5, 6, 7, 12, 13, 19, 21. PSO, Reiner, C ML 4116 (*Strauss: Southern Roses, Schatz Waltz, etc.).*

Of the various collections available, these offer the best value: the Van Kempen for excellent-sounding reproduction of hearty performances by the Berlin Philharmonic, the Reiner for less resonant but more volatile performances by the Pittsburgh Symphony as he molded it. The Strauss waltzes are also well played.

Serenade for Small Orchestra, No. 1 in D. LOS, Scherman, D DL 9651.

An endorsement without enthusiasm, for it is better in sound than either of two other versions, but not a remarkably successful statement of the music.

*Variations on a theme by Haydn. NBC, Toscanini, V LM 1725 (*Elgar: "Enigma" Variations). ACG, Van Beinum, L LL 735 (*Academic Festival and Tragic overtures). PHI, Markevitch, V LBC 1010 (*Tchaikovsky: Francesca da Rimini). NYPH, Toscanini, V LCT 1023 (*Beethoven: Symphony No. 1).*

Either by itself, or in combination with the glorious playing of the "Enigma," this is a Toscanini record few would want to be without. However, if the "Enigma" does not appeal as a coupling, the Van Beinum compendium of Brahms is suavely accomplished, with the characteristic sound of the great orchestra finely conveyed. At the price, the Markevitch version has attractions for its sound musicianship and adept engineering. The early Toscanini version with the New York Philharmonic-Symphony has no such aural substance as today's techniques provide, but it is a superb example of the remarkable rapport between maestro and men. The Beethoven No. 1 with it is the BBC collaboration, musically preferable to the late NBC one.

BRITTEN, BENJAMIN (1913-)

Diversions on a Theme for Piano and Orchestra. Rapp, BRS, Rother, U 7101 (**Strauss: Burleske*).

A little-known work of more than passing quality, well performed and successfully reproduced.

Peter Grimes: Sea Interludes (Four). ACG, Van Beinum, L LL 917 (**Young Persons' Guide to the Orchestra*). *LSO, Sargent, 10" C ML 2145* (**Lambert: Rio Grande*).

The Van Beinum (not to be confused with a similar venture originally issued on 78 rpm) is five years newer than the Sargent, and that much more vivid in sound. For that matter, the second side *Guide* is close to spectacular in quality. However, those who prefer the Lambert coupled on C ML 2145 will find the Sargent treatment of the *Sea Interludes* excellent, the sound more than good.

Serenade for Tenor, Horn, and Strings. Lloyd, Stagliano, Burgin, Bos 205 (**Songs*).

Members of the Boston Symphony orchestra comprise the ensemble well led by Burgin, and skillfully reproduced. Lloyd is as good a voice for these songs as Pears, for whom they were written, and Stagliano manages the difficult horn part expertly.

Symphony, opus 4 ("Simple"). MGS, Solomon, MGM E 3704 (**Ireland: Concertino Pastorale*).

A melodious, well-constructed work of Britten's twentieth year, performed with zest and plentiful style under the watchful direction of Solomon. Fine clear sound, a little close up.

*Variations on a Theme of Frank Bridge. PHI, Karajan, An 35142 (*Vaughan Williams: Fantasia on a Theme by Thomas Tallis). BNO, Neel, LL 801 (*Warlock: Capriol Suite).*

Karajan's orchestra is larger and better reproduced than Neel's, which does not necessarily guarantee more musical results. However, in a work whose effect depends as much on execution as this one, it adds up to more under the leadership of Karajan. The overside Vaughan Williams is more than a little showy and overphrased for my taste. The two Neel sides are both well reproduced, if not with the room resonance of the Karajan.

*Young Persons' Guide to the Orchestra. ACG, Van Beinum, L LL 917 (*Peter Grimes, Sea Interludes).*

A *ne plus ultra,* for the while anyway. See under *Peter Grimes.*

BRUCH, MAX (1838-1920)

*Concerto No. 1 in G minor. Milstein, PSO, Steinberg, Cap P 8243 (*Mendelssohn: Concerto). Menuhin, BSO, Munch, 10" V LM 122. Heifetz, LSO, Sargent, V LM 9007 (*Saint-Saëns: Sonata).*

Menuhin and Heifetz have no lack of violinistic resource at their disposal, but Milstein has quite enough, also something more: a conviction and devotion that makes his effort much more personal. In addition, Steinberg is at one with him in his view of the score, and the reproduction is decidedly good. The second-side Mendelssohn is hardly less successful, thus binding the bargain.

*Kol Nidrei. Casals, LSO, Ronald, V LCT 1028 (*Boccherini: Concerto).*

No contemporary version offers an eloquence equal to that of Casals, and a recommendation based on better sound may be resisted for the simple reason that there is no better sound than his. The Boccherini (q.v.) is, of course, a classic.

Scottish Fantasy. Heifetz, RCAO, Steinberg, 10" V LM 4.

Remarkably suave performance by Heifetz, with a strong assist from Steinberg, and admirable engineering in RCA's West Coast style.

BRUCKNER, ANTON (1824-1896)

Overture

*In G minor. VAO, Adler, SPA 24/5 [2] (*Symphony No. 9).*

Adler is a conscientious workman who knows his Bruckner. A

little more drive and power would add to the effect of the performance. However, the orchestra (a Viennese composite, disc-named "Philharmonia") does its work well, and the reproduction is consistently good, if not dazzling in tonal values. The Overture is rather short measure for a 12" LP side, slightly more than thirteen minutes.

Symphonies

No. 2 in C minor. LBS, Jochum, Urania 402 [2].

Fairly good sound, though the pickup is somewhat at a distance from the orchestra. It should be noted that the Jochum of this recording is Ludwig George, not the better known Eugen Jochum of Munich. Like most interpreters devoted to Bruckner, he manifests a strong love for the "master" and little inclination to effects, cheap or otherwise—few of them possible in this work, in any case.

No. 3 in D minor. VPH, Knappertsbusch, L LL 1044. VAO, Adler. SPA 301/2 (**Mahler: Symphony No. 10*).

The sumptuous-sounding, musically persuasive performance under Knappertsbusch's discerning direction has every advantage—including price—over the lesser effort of Adler. Were London to continue this repertory under the alternating leadership of Knappertsbusch and Van Beinum (see No. 7), it would have a highly desirable repertory of works.

No. 4 in E flat ("Romantic"). HPO, Van Otterloo, Ep SC 6001 [2] (**Mahler: Kindertotenlieder*). *VSO, Klemperer, Vox PL 6930.*

No amount of rolling sound is excessive for the special values in this score, and the fine reproduction of Van Otterloo's good performance has it in more abundance than the good reproduction of Klemperer's fine performance. The extra disc is an expense, of course, but the added space is integral in the fidelity values provided thereby. Also, the Mahler (Herman Schey is the baritone) is quite good.

No. 6 in A. VSY, Swoboda, W 5055/6 (**Two Psalms*).

Good value in Bruckner, incorporating the two Psalms, of which there is no other recording. Swoboda is painstaking rather than convincing, but the total enterprise is a worthy one.

No. 7 in E. ACG, Van Beinum, L LL 852/3 (**Franck: Psyché*).

Van Beinum provides the kind of leadership, and his great orchestra the kind of playing, that makes non-Brucknerites listen and learn.

One of the fine Bruckner performances now available, and magnificently reproduced. A more congruent fourth side would have been welcome, but the standard of performance remains high.

No. 8 in C minor. HPHO, Jochum, D DX 109 [3] (**Te Deum*).

Thoroughgoing direction by Jochum, and broadly spacious reproduction. The *Te Deum* is also handsomely done. According to best sources available, this is the same Jochum (Eugen) version that circulated on 78 rpm as DG Set 17.

No. 9 in D minor. VAO, Adler, SPA 24/5 [2] (**Overture in G minor*).

See entry under *Overture in G minor.*

In D minor, "opus Zero." SYM, Spruit, CH 1142.

The simplicities of this work appeal to my taste more than the cumbersome machinery of some of the later works, Spruit, who is otherwise unknown to me, directs a fine performance of the slow movement in particular. Fine sound.

Work for Orchestra and Voices

Te Deum. HPHO, Jochum, D DX 109 [3] (**Symphony No. 8*).

See entry under *Symphony No. 8.*

BRUNETTI, GAETANO (1740-1808)

Symphony in C minor. ICO, Jenkins, HS L 77 (**Giordani: Concerto for Piano; Valentini: Concerto for Oboe*).

A singularly ingratiating work of approximately 1775, played with more poise and better orchestral sound than others in this series. Fine reproduction.

Symphony in G minor. ICO, Jenkins, HS L 78 (**Viotti: Concerto for Piano and Violin*).

The foregoing remarks are equally applicable here, with the additional observation that Jenkins shows valuable traits as an interpreter in this record. Very good sound.

CAPLET, ANDRÉ (1878-1925)

Mask of the Red Death. Stockton, CAO, Slatkin, Cap P 8255 (**McDonald: From Childhood*).

Minor French impressionism, with a prominent harp part well played by the lady virtuosa. Good clean recording.

CARPENTER, JOHN ALDEN (1876-1951)

Adventures in a Perambulator. VSY, Swoboda, CH 1140.
Reasonably perceptive performance, though an American orchestra would make more of it. Good sound.

CASELLA, ALFREDO (1883-1947)

Scarlattiana. SCA, Col 1038.
Engaging arrangements of typically bright Scarlatti matter, minimized by poor reproduction and inferior processing.
*Italia. ORB, Kleinert, U RLP 7118 (*Serenade for Small Orchestra).*
On inspection, the seldom-heard *Italia* turns out to be a work of rather Straussian character, up to and including variations on "*Funiculì-Funiculà.*" It is very well played under the direction of Kleinert, and the quality of sound is good. The more recent *Serenade* (LRO, Kegel) is much busier, musically, and less satisfying. Acceptable recording.

CHABRIER, ALEXIS EMMANUEL (1841-1894)

Works for Orchestra (Collections)

España; Gwendoline Overture; Marche Joyeuse; Suite Pastorale; Fête Polonaise from Le Roi Malgré Lui. LAM, Fournet, Ep LC 3028.
Highly satisfactory style by Fournet, with the orchestral sound an exceptional example of the Epic technique. Some items are done better by specialists in the entries noted below, but the total is striking. Pierre Germain is the baritone in the *Fête Polonaise.*
España; Bourée Fantasque; Gwendoline Overture; Habanera; Marche Joyeuse. OCC, Fourestier, Vox PL 7650.
The points of difference from the preceding are not numerous enough to rate it as a collection worth having on its own, and the other values are all inferior.

Work for Orchestra

*España. OSR, Ansermet, 10" L LS 193 (*Marche Joyeuse; Ravel: Pa-*

vanne pour une Infante Défunte). *RPO, Beecham, 10" C AL 11.* (**Rossini: Cambiale di Matrimonio*).

Beecham's place of pre-eminence in this music has been usurped by Ansermet, owing in part to a more dashing recorded sound, but no less to his strong feeling for the idiom. The other pieces are extremely well played. Beecham's is good sound-reproduction, the Rossini overture being marked by uncommon horn-playing.

Suite Pastorale. OSC, Lindenberg, L LL 871 (**Bizet: Jeux d'Enfant, Fair Maid of Perth*). *CGO, Braithwaite, MGM 3000* (**Bizet: Fair Maid of Perth*).

Neither of these outdoes the Fournet effort on Epic, to which those inclined to a Chabrier miscellany are commended. However, if other considerations govern, I prefer the total value of the Lindenberg disc, while noting that the Braithwaite is quite as well performed.

Opera Excerpts (Orchestral)

Le Roi Malgré Lui: Danse Slave. OSC, Fournet, L LL 639 (**Ode à la Musique; Debussy: Damoiselle Élue*).

This excerpt from an opera is orchestral, but it also has a prominent part for the voice of Janine Micheau, who is not in best form here—also a part for Jean Mollien, tenor. Attractive music, well performed and clearly reproduced.

Le Roi Malgré Lui: Fête Polonaise. LAM, Fournet, Ep LC 3028.

See under *Collections* above.

CHAUSSON, ERNEST (1855-1899)

Poème for Violin and Orchestra. Francescatti, PHO, Ormandy, 10" C ML 2194 (**Saint-Saëns: Introduccion and Rondo Capriccioso*). *Heifetz, RCAO, Solomon; 10" V LM 7017* (**Conus: Concerto*). *Thibaud, LAM, Bigot, Vox PL 6450* (**Fauré: Ballade*).

Thibaud may be endorsed for style, and Francescatti for sound, with Heifetz somewhere in between. On the whole, the Francescatti with Philadelphia, though a little weighty for this music, is my preference.

Symphony in B flat, opus 20. SFS, Monteux, V LM 1181.

It is a by no means needed distinction for Monteux that he is a decided partisan for this music, which fares beautifully at his hands. Broad well-defined recording, though not in the high-fidelity category.

CHÂVEZ, CARLOS (1899-)

La Hija de Cólquide. MEX, Chavez, 10" D DL 7512.

The composer's participation speaks for the musical integrity of the performance. The recording is thinner than we now expect.

CHERUBINI, LUIGI (1760-1842)

Overtures

*Medea. BAM, Leitner, D DL 8509 (*Flotow: Overture to Martha; Thomas: Excerpts from Mignon; Weber: Invitation to the Dance; etc).*

The guiding principle of this miscellany would seem to be to include anything as long it doesn't go with what precedes. The Beethovenish overture is played in suitable style, but the recording is lacking in body.

*Portatore d'acqua (Wasserträger, or Water-Carrier). AUS, Gui, Rem 199-142 (*Rossini: Overtures to Siege of Corinth, Italian in Algiers; Wolf-Ferrari: Overtures to Secret of Suzanne, The Happy Deception).*

Coarse sound and foggy instrumental detail are blemishes on Gui's well-defined performance. However, the intrinsic interests of the material are considerable.

Symphony

*In D. NBC, Toscanini, V LM 1745 (*Beethoven: Septet, opus 20).*

An embracing performance by Toscanini, which means that little is left for any other interpreter to add on this particular subject. Clean recording, not too resonant.

Work for Orchestra and Violin

*Pater Noster (1834). LBO, Pougnet, Haas, 10" D DL 4081 (*Tartini: Sinfonia in A; Lully: Marche; etc.).*

An expressive oddity of unidentified origin, well played and properly recorded.

CHOPIN, FRÉDÉRIC (1810-1849)

Concertos

For Piano and Orchestra

No. 1 and No. 2. Badura-Skoda, VSO, Rodzinski, W WL 5308.

As an omnibus edition of the two works, the Badura-Skoda and Rodzinski effort is sound, musicianly, and beautifully reproduced. It would also have to be granted equality of accomplishment in No. 1 with Sandor and Brailowsky, though either Novaes or Rubinstein (see below) appeals more to me in the F minor. If Badura-Skoda could sustain his best level consistently, he would be a formidable Chopianist: he is inclined to let his fingers do their own thinking in the display passages.

No. 1 in E minor. Sandor, PHO, Ormandy, C ML 4651. Brailowsky, RCAO, Steinberg, V LM 1020. Uninsky, HPO, Van Otterloo, Ep LC 3012. Gulda, LPO, Boult, L LL 1001.

Sandor's tone and phrasing please me more in this work than Brailowsky's, but I would not quarrel with those who prefer the latter. There can be no quarrel with the statement that the Columbia sound is superior to the RCA here, as the Epic is to both. However, there is too much that is heavy and forced in that performance for me. Gulda's must be considered separately, for Boult uses the Balakirev version of the score, which makes it a rather different-sounding thing. Very beautiful sound here, and artful execution by Gulda, who does not, however, appeal to me as a Chopin player.

*No. 2 in F minor. Novaes, VSY, Klemperer, Vox PL 7100. Rubinstein, NBC, Steinberg, V LM 1046. Malcuzynski, PHI, Kletzki, An 35030 (*Fantasy in F minor).*

The science of recording is better exemplified by the Malcuzynski than by either of the others, just as the art of interpretation is superior in either the Novaes or the Rubinstein. In deftness and finesse—both qualities applicable to this work—Novaes is supreme here, though the Rubinstein has many virtues.

Miscellaneous

Les Sylphides. OSC, Désormière, 10" L LS 192.

For taste in direction and excellence of reproduction—also lack of conflicting material—this version is clearly superior to all others. Those who want more than this for their money are directed to V LBC 1011, in which Sargent directs the LPO in a conventional *Sylphides*, and Basil Cameron's version of Kodály's *Dances from Galanta* is appended.

CIMAROSA, DOMENICO *(1749-1801)*

*La Cimarosiana (arranged by Malipiero). ROO, Braithwaite, MGM 3013 (*Il Matrimonio Segreto overture; Respighi: Rossiniana).*

A thoroughly pleasant disc, well conducted by Braithwaite and acutely reproduced.

*Concerto for Oboe and Strings. Miller, SCO, Saidenberg, Mer 10003 (*Vaughan Williams: Concerto for Oboe). Goossens, LIV, Sargent, C ML 4782 (*Marcello: Concerto; Bach-Tovey: Concerto; etc.).*

Artistry abounds in both performances, with the advantage in recording with Miller. However, the combined offerings of the Goossens disc, especially the Marcello concerto, make it a must for any oboe-fancier.

*Il Matrimonio Segreto: Overture. ROO, Braithwaite, MGM 3013 (*Cimarosiana, etc.). LSO, Kish, 10" L LS 353 (*Gli Orazi; Gluck: Iphigénie en Aulide, Alceste overtures).*

Braithwaite's effort seems to me well worthy of the music, and the combination offering is desirable. Kish does not handle this matter as well, nor is there anything notable about the additional overtures on the disc.

*Gli Orazi ei Curiazi: Overture. LSO, Kish, 10" L LS 353 (*Matrimonio Segreto; Gluck: Iphigénie en Aulide, Alceste overtures).*

A work of brightly Cimarosian quality, faithfully performed. See comment on *Matrimonio Segreto* above.

CLEMENTI, MUZIO *(1752-1832)*

*Symphony in D, opus 18, No. 2. VDR, Fasano, V LHMV 2 (*Corelli: Concerto Grosso in D, opus 6, No. 4; Vivaldi: Concerto in F, for Oboe).*

This collection is of special note not only for its superior sound, but also for the opportunity provided to hear a work by Beethoven's illustrious contemporary, Clementi (as restored by Casella). It cannot be called earth-shaking in quality, but it has fine melodic flow and implacable musical dignity.

COATES, ERIC (1886-)

London; London Again (*Suites*). *SYM, Coates, C RL 3053.*

Coates is the best conductor known to me for his attractive works, and these are two of the best. The fidelity is not high, but neither is the price.

Three Elizabeths; Four Centuries (*Suites*). *NEW, Coates, L LL 753.*

Here the recording is all it should be, as Coates makes maximum point with his inventions.

CONUS, GEORGE (1862-1933)

Concerto in E minor. Heifetz, RCAO, Solomon, 10" V LM 7017 (**Chausson: Poème*).

Superlative playing by Heifetz of a work to which he has a long-standing devotion. The orchestral support is appropriate, the recording acceptable. The overside Chausson is not my preference in that category, but it is a fine performance nevertheless.

COPLAND, AARON (1900-)

Ballet Music

Appalachian Spring. NSO, Mitchell, W WL 5286. (**El Salón México; Billy the Kid; Fanfare for the Common Man*). *BSO, Koussevitzky, V LCT 1134* (**El Salón México*).

Mitchell's compilation is generous in scope and well reproduced, though other performances of individual works may please more. The Koussevitzky is now dimmer in sound, but the quality of the playing merits continuing interest.

Billy the Kid. RCAO, Bernstein, V LM 1031 (**Gershwin: An American in Paris*). *BTO, Levine, Cap P 8238* (**Schuman: Undertow*).

Bernstein's fine performance, amply reproduced, appeals to me more, especially as his *American in Paris* is outstandingly good. Those who prefer the coupling with the Schuman score will find Levine's effort more in the ballet spirit, and ably managed as such. Good sound. Both are full-length treatments of the score, in contrast with the Mitchell version on W 5286 (q.v.) and the Stokowski-Philharmonic on 10" C ML 2167.

Rodeo. BTO, Levine, 10" Cap L 8198.

Another in the excellent series of Ballet Theatre Orchestra recordings sponsored by Capitol. Note that it is also available in a 12" disc, coupled with Bernstein's *Fancy Free* score (Cap P 8196).

Concerto

*For Clarinet and Orchestra. Goodman, COL, Copland, C ML 4421 (*Quartet for Piano and Strings).*

Deft performance by the musician for whom it was written, and well reproduced.

Film Music

*Our Town. LOS, Scherman, 10" D DL 7527 (*Thomson: Plow That Broke the Plains).*

Not the utmost that can be made of this work, but a reasonable approximation of its sound. The suitable coupling adds interest.

*The Red Pony. LOS, Scherman, D DL 9616 (*Thomson: Louisiana Story excerpts).*

The remarks above are applicable here also.

Works for Orchestra

*Music for the Theater. MGO, Solomon, MGM 3095 (*Weil: Kleine Dreigroschenmusik).*

Perceptive treatment by Solomon of a work that was ahead of its time when first heard in the '20's. Skillful playing, well reproduced.

*El Salón México. COL, Bernstein, 10" C ML 2203 (*Milhaud: Création du Monde). NSO, Mitchell, W WL 5286 (*Appalachian Spring, etc.). BSO, Koussevitzky, V LCT 1134 (*Appalachian Spring).*

Bernstein's vivid evocation of the Mexican dance hall is compactly coupled with the equally well-reproduced Milhaud work. A part of the Copland omnibus noted above, Mitchell's performance is thoroughly good, particularly in sound. Koussevitzky's pioneering effort has its interests, though ear appeal is not one.

Symphony No. 3. MIN, Dorati, Mer 50018.

A strong work, compellingly directed by Dorati and strikingly well recorded. One of the best in the notable sequence from Minnesota.

Work for Orchestra and Speaker

*A Lincoln Portrait. NYPH, Rodzinski, 10" C ML 2042 (*Gould: Spirituals).*

An enduring tribute to the kind of work Rodzinski did with the Philharmonic during his tenure, with the narration well managed by Kenneth Spencer. Good sound for its time, though not outstanding now.

CORELLI, ARCANGELO (1653-1713)

Concerto

*For Oboe and Orchestra. Pierlot, PPO, Leibowitz, Oc 29 (*Gluck: Concerto for Flute; Haydn: Toy Symphony).*

All the works are worthy, and Pierlot is an excellent oboist, as Rampal is an excellent flutist in the Gluck work. However, there is little of the needed delicacy or finesse in the backgrounds supervised by Leibowitz, and the quality of reproduced sound is not more than acceptable.

Concerti Grossi

Opus 6 (Complete). TCSO, Eckertsen, Vox PL 7893 [3].

This enterprise may be likened to a flashlight probing the tunnels of a forgotten mine, now and then revealing a vein of precious metal but not going much beyond the surface. The participation of such soloists as Daniel Guillet, Frank Miller, and Edwin Bachman suggests that, for the purposes of the occasion, NBC has come to mean Nothing But Corelli. Eckertsen is a young American who rides his hobby with energy and enthusiasm, but not too much judgment of pace. In sum, sound but rather impersonal performance, efficiently reproduced.

Opus 6, Nos. 1, 2, 7, 8, 9. SC, V LM 1776.

This inspired band of devotees (operating on the theory that every man can be his own concertmaster, for it has no conductor) provides not only superbly phrased and tonally pulsating performances of Nos. 1, 2, 7, and 9, but also the best available playing of No. 8, the "Christmas" Concerto. In addition to the impassioned, orderly statement of musical content, the reproduction is all it should be.

*Opus 6, No. 8: "Christmas" Concerto. VDR, D DL 9649 (*Torelli: Concerto in forma di Pastorale, etc.).*

A performance in the manner of that above, but not so good, nor so well reproduced.

*Opus 6, No. 12. SAX, Liersch, U RLP 7113 (*Telemann: Suite in D).*

Rather thick, heavily accented playing, not more than passably well reproduced.

Miscellaneous

*Suite (arranged by Pinelli). PHO, Ormandy, 10" C ML 2054 (*Handel: Water Music, Concerto in D).*

Early LP sound, and not suitable in any case for Corelli.

Apothéose de Lully Quatrième Concert Royal. OLO, Désormière, OL LD 1.

Limited sound, but expert performance.

*Pièces en Concerto. SCH, Fournier, Münchinger, L LL 687 (*Boccherini: Concerto).*

Sensitive interpretation, well reproduced.

*La Sultane (arranged by Milhaud): Overture and Allegro only. NYPH, Mitropoulos, 10" C AL 16 (*Travis: Symphonic Allegro).*

Not my idea of appropriate style, and less than desirable with the incongrous coupling.

COUPERIN, LOUIS (1630-1665)

*Concert dans le goût Theàtral. WIES, Weyns, Cap P 8111 (*Telemann: Tafelmusik).*

Delightful music, musicianly performance. The sound is fair.

COWELL, HENRY (1897-)

Saturday Night at the Firehouse. VAO, Adler, SPA LP 47 (*North, Antheil, Jacobi, etc.*).

One in a series of brief works by Americans, in a folkish vein well served by Adler.

Symphony No. 4. ERO, Hanson, Mer 40005 (**Hovhanness: Concerto No. 4*).

Excellent reproduction of a well-prepared performance.

CRESTON, PAUL (1906-)

Symphonies Nos. 2 and 3. NSO, Mitchell, W 5272.

Creston's muscular kind of writing (Stravinsky and Sibelius are among the suggested antecedents) is firmly flexed under Mitchell's understanding direction. The recording suffers from less than the best acoustical surroundings, but is otherwise well managed.

DEBUSSY, CLAUDE (1862-1918)

Ballet Music

La Boîte à Joujoux. RIAS, Perlea, Rem 199-159.

The humors and weaknesses of this score are well understood by Perlea, who does as much as can reasonably be done with both. Clear, well-balanced sound.

Opera Excerpts (Orchestral)

Pelléas et Mélisande (*Suite*). CO, Leinsdorf, C ML 4090 (**Sonata No. 2 for Flute, Viola, and Harp.*)

The appearance of qualified, contemporary full versions of *Pelléas* has rather diminished the interest of this enterprise. However, the interludes are thoughtfully performed and effectively reproduced.

Works for Orchestra

Danses Sacrée et Profane. ACMS, Van Beinum, 10" L LS 621 (**Ravel: Introduction and Allegro*).

Van Beinum's participation as conductor makes this legitimately a part of this survey, and it is a record that belongs in any representative collection. The playing is superb, the recording outstandingly good. As much applies to the Ravel on side two.

Images (Complete). SFS, Monteux, V LM 1197.

Superior interpretative art, and fine, clean recording. All details may not be as distinct as in the best recent reproductions, but it is excellent of its type.

*Images: Ibéria only. PHO, Ormandy, C ML 4434 (*La Mer).*

What we have here, in effect, is the first side of the foregoing, with *La Mer* on side two instead of *Gigues* and *Rondes de Printemps*. I prefer the Monteux style in *Ibéria*, and the Ormandy *La Mer* is not outstanding. For those who want a judgment anyway on this *Ibéria*, it is notable for fine orchestral execution and well-balanced reproduction.

*Jeux (Poème Dansé). OSR, Ansermet, L LL 992 (*Debussy-Ansermet: Six Épigraphes Antiques).*

Ansermet's service to Debussy is even more conspicuous in his perceptive orchestration of the *Épigraphes Antiques* than in his devoted but not wholly successful effort to vitalize Debussy's minor *Jeux*. Fine sound in both.

*Marche Ecossaise. ONA, Inghelbrecht, An 35103 (*Nocturnes, L'Après-midi d'un faune).*

This entertaining oddity gets the benefit of the same precision and good tonal sense lavished by Inghelbrecht on the longer, better-known pieces, and the sound is decidedly good. However, there is less personal expression in the major works than in the performances of them noted below.

*La Mer. NBC; Toscanini, V LM 1221 (*Mendelssohn: A Midsummer Night's Dream music). OSR, Ansermet, L LL 388 (*Ravel: Ma Mère l'Oye). PHI, Karajan, An 35081 (*Ravel: Rhapsodie Espagnole).*

The unique power of Toscanini's conception of this music is not as well honored by the recording as is Ansermet's more traditional treatment; however, each second side is outstanding in its category—which may be a factor of influence. Karajan's domination of the orchestra per se is the salient fact of his Debussy, and it makes a big splash of sound, if not exactly what the composer intended. Hence, for a combination of fine sound and poetic thought, turn to Ansermet; for the most rousing musical experience, choose Toscanini.

*Nocturnes (Complete). OSR, Ansermet, L LL 530 (*Ravel: Rhapsodie*

Espagnole). *HIS, Stokowski, V LM 1154* (**Clair de Lune; L' Après midi d'un faune*).

With so fine a version of the three nocturnes as Ansermet's available—or in its own style, so well-sounding a one as the Stokowski—there seems little reason for settling for the pair traditionally offered record-buyers (with *Sirènes* omitted). Ansermet's is purer in style, beautifully played and reproduced; Stokowski's is more played with, and is over-recorded in some details of richness.

Nocturnes: Nuages, Fêtes only. PHO, Ormandy, C ML 4020 (**Respighi: Pines of Rome*).

One of the earliest LP's, and now entitled to honorable retirement. See comment above.

Prélude a l'après-midi d'un faune. OSR, Ansermet, 10" L LD 9031 (**Ravel: Alborado del Gracioso*). *HIS, Stokowski, V LM 1154* (**Clair de Lune; Nocturnes*).

Substantially speaking, the version of Ansermet adds less that is extraneous to Debussy than any other, and is the best reproduced of all. If one prefers the Stokowski treatment, it may best be procured directly from the maker, rather than via the more synthetic Kostelanetz. Good sound, a little throbby.

Printemps. RPO, Beecham, V LM 9001 (**Sibelius: Tapiola*).

A dubbing, pre-tape, but quite successful inasmuch as the original was excellent in sound. Beecham could hardly do more for a work that does not quite repay his all-out effort.

Work for Orchestra and Solo Instruments

Fantasy for Piano and Orchestra. WES, Jacquinot, Fistoulari, MGM 3069 (**Poulenc: Aubade Concerto Choréographique*).

A work of limited interest, but well served by the performers. The recording is bright, somewhat thin, but acceptable. The two sides are complementary in interest.

Rhapsody for Saxophone and Orchestra. PPO, Mulé, Rosenthal, Cap L 8231 (**Ibert: Concertino*).

An excellent effort by all the French talent involved, including the engineers. Mulé's special skill is equally evident on side two.

Works for Orchestra and Voices

La Damoiselle élue. PHO, Sayão, Ormandy, C ML 4075 (**Ravel: Con-*

*certo for Left Hand). OSC, Micheau, Fournet, L LL 639 (*Chabrier: Ode à la Musique).*

It may seem perverse to prefer the American enterprise to the French—especially when the former is one of the early LP entries—but it combines a singularly suitable sense of the work's character with a vocalist who charms the ear with her sound. Fuller sound on the London, but not as much musical satisfaction.

Arrangements

*Six Épigraphes Antiques (arranged by Ansermet). OSR, Ansermet, L LL 992 (*Jeux).*

Were one unaware that these were originally piano pieces, one would accept them unquestioningly as genuinely orchestral Debussy, so well has Ansermet done his work. Much of the result, of course, derives from his skill as an orchestral colorist and from the reflection of that skill in the recording.

DELIBES, LÉO (1836-1891)

Ballet Music

Coppélia. OSC, Désormière, 10" L LS 183. ROO, Lambert, C ML 4145.

The sequence here is strictly alphabetical, because there is nothing but virtue in either performance. If a distinction must be made, the Lambert has slightly more lift in a rhythmic sense, and his total of fifteen excerpts is more than Désormière provides. London has the edge in recording.

Sylvia. OSC, Désormière, 10" L LS 184.

Nothing presently available can compete with the brightness and zest of this playing or with its satisfying sound.

DELIUS, FREDERICK (1863-1934)

Works for Orchestra (Collections)

Brigg Fair; On Hearing the First Cuckoo in Spring; Walk to Paradise Garden; Song of Summer. LSO, Collins, L LL 758.

Dance Rhapsody No. 1; Summer Night on the River; A Song Before Sunrise; On Hearing the First Cuckoo in Spring; When Twilight Fancies; Intermezzo and Serenade. RPO, Beecham, V LHMV 1050.
*On Hearing the First Cuckoo; Summer Night on the River. CAO, Slatkin, Cap P 8182 (*Excerpts from Hassan and Irmelin).*

As an inspection of the three entries above will show, a combination of the Beecham and Collins discs (alphabetized, let it be noted, in order of the first entry on each) will provide the greatest diversity of Delius with the least duplication. No mention need be made now of the Beecham prowess in regard to the music of his longtime friend and colleague: the reproduction of his work is uniformly good. Collins has a warm feeling for this idiom, and the reproduction of his work is excellent. Slatkin is thoroughgoing and not very enlivening, the reproduction good but not outstanding.

Works for Orchestra

Eventyr; North Country Sketches. RPO, Beecham, C ML 4637.

Finely colored pastels, beautifully reproduced.

*Over the Hills and Far Away. RPO, Beecham, 10" C ML 2133 (*Bizet: Fair Maid of Perth).*

One of the best of the Delius pieces—evocative, ear-caressing—given a poetic realization by Beecham and his excellent men. Fine sound.

*Paris, The Song of a Great City. LSO, Collins, L LL 923 (*In a Summer Garden; Summer Night on the River).*

Thoughtful attention to Delius's long and loving tribute to every man's "other" home, enhanced by superb reproduction. The two shorter works are also affectingly played.

Work for Orchestra and Solo Instruments

*Caprice and Elegy. CAO, Slatkin, Cap P 8182 (*On hearing the First Cuckoo, etc.).*

Eleanor Aller is the able violoncellist in this melodic conceit, which might have been the point of beginning for the song called "*When Day Is Done*"...save that it was not written till 1930. Good instrumental detail in the recording.

Work for Orchestra and Voices

A Mass of Life. RPO, Beecham, vocal soloists, C SL 197 [2].

One of the major efforts of Beecham's long life of musical effort, and among the most compelling instances of his affection for the art and his devotion to its highest standards. The generally excellent soloists are Mmes Raisbeck and Sinclair, Messrs. Craig and Boyce. Fine, resonant sound in a spacious framework, and suitable textual matter.

*Appalachia. RPO, Beecham, chorus, C ML 4915 (*Koanga, Closing Scene).*

Beecham makes a remarkably substantial thing of the sometimes thin texture of this score, which has, nevertheless, considerable poetic essence. Both it and the subjoined scene from *Koanga* are very well reproduced.

Opera Excerpts (Orchestral)

*Hassan: Intermezzo and Serenade. CAO, Slatkin, Cap P 8182 (*On Hearing the First Cuckoo, etc).*

See entry under Collections, above.

Irmelin: Prelude. CAO, Slatkin, Cap P 8182.

As above.

DELLO JOIO, NORMAN (1913-)

*Concerto for Harp and Orchestra. Vito, LOS, Scherman, C ML 4303 (*Diamond: Romeo and Juliet music).*

Not the most assured kind of execution in accent and intonation; rather muffled recording.

*Triumph of St. Joan Symphony. TLO, Whitney, C ML 4615 (*Villa-Lobos: Erosion, Origin of the Amazon River).*

Clean articulation, purposefully reproduced, of what seems a better-realized work than the foregoing.

DE NARDIS, CAMILLO (1857-)

Scene Abbruzzesi (Suites 1 and 2). SCA, Argento, Col LPS 1037.

Melodic pieces in the vein of Massenet's *Scènes Alsaciennes*, well played and tolerably reproduced save for some awkward splices.

DIAMOND, DAVID (1915-)

*Music for Shakespeare's Romeo and Juliet. LOS, Scherman, C ML 4303 (*Dello Joio: Concerto for Harp).*

Well-organized performance, clearly reproduced, though with little embellishing brightness or resonance.

DITTERS VON DITTERSDORF, KARL (1739-1799)

Concerto

*For Harp and Orchestra. ORB, Haarth, U 7110 (*Hoffmann: Concerto for Mandolin).*

A rather anonymous kind of music, arranged from a work not for harp and only accidentally suited to it. Good, steady performance, with an unexpected amount of vibrance in the reproduction.

Symphonies

*In A minor. FRO, Kloss, Ly 26 (*Prince Louis Ferdinand: Rondo, opus 13).*

Interesting music, suggestive of the better among the lesser-known works of Mozart, or the *Sturm und Drang* Haydn. Strong direction by Kloss, and generally acceptable reproduction, though the resonant surroundings are poor.

*In E flat. ZRO, Dahinden, CH 1227 (*Symphony in F minor).*

*In F minor (The Rescue of Andromeda by Perseus). WIN, Dahinden. CH 1227 (*See above).*

This work, with its reposeful introductory slow movement in the manner of Gluck, is the more rewarding of the two. Egon Parolari plays the lengthy oboe solo beautifully, and the reproduction in both instances is excellent.

DOHNÁNYI, ERNEST VON (1877-)

*Ruralia Hungarica. LPO, Schuechter, MGM 3019 (*Kodály: Háry János).*
Energetic direction by Schuechter, and highly efficient reproduction. The coupled side is equally good.

Suite in F sharp, opus 19. LAP, Wallenstein, 10" D DL 6006.
Acute direction by Wallenstein, and better sound than in the 78-rpm predecessor, though well short of proper fidelity. The Sargent (C ML 2172) is decidedly inferior in the latter respect.

*Symphonic Minutes. BAV, Graunke, U 7066 (*Borodin: Symphony No. 1).*
Excellent orchestral playing under Graunke's potent direction, and large masses of sound in the reproduction.

*Variations on a Nursery Theme. Jacquinot, LPO, Fistoulari, MGM 3004 (*Strauss: Burleske).*
Jacquinot's fluency and good taste and the excellent reproduction of piano and orchestra make a recommendation almost mandatory. However, it is well to remember that the collaboration of Cyril Smith and Sir Malcolm Sargent gave more zest to this work on C ML 4146, should they be granted a second effort with better reproduction.

DONIZETTI, GAETANO (1797-1848)

*Don Pasquale: Overture. NBC, Toscanini, 10" V LRM 7028 (*Weber: Overtures to Oberon, Der Freischütz).*
Brief but magical interlude, with some superb solo playing very well reproduced.

*La Fille du Régiment: Overture. OBCO, Rother, U RLP 7057 (*Don Pasquale; Rossini: Overtures to Barber of Seville, William Tell; Verdi: Overtures to Forza del Destino, Aïda).*
Well-routined performance, rather poorly reproduced.

DUKAS, PAUL (1865-1935)

*L'Apprenti Sorcier. DSO, Paray, Mer MG 50035 (*Fauré: Pelléas et Mélisande music; Roussel: Spider's Feast). NBC, Toscanini, V LM 1118 (*Saint-Saëns: Danse Macabre; Smetana: Moldau). PHO, Ormandy,*

*10" C AL 26 (*Debussy: L'Après-midi). PHI, Markevitch, An 35008 (*Falla: Dances from Tricorne; Prokofiev: Classical Symphony; etc.).*

Till the appearance of the Paray, the Toscanini blend of incisiveness and orchestral virtuosity was clearly superior to the alternative versions, but this is a work for which Paray has a strong and special feeling, admirably carried out by his men, and sharply, vigorously reproduced. A choice would rest largely on the associated works, well played in all instances. If *The Sorcerer's Apprentice* is wanted with least encumbering matter, the Ormandy is splendidly played and well reproduced. The Markevitch is also a worthy piece of work, excellent in sound.

*La Peri. WES, Fistoulari, MGM 3062 (*D'Indy: Istar). OCC, Sebastian, U 7097 (*Fauré; Pelléas et Mélisande).*

Either of these is acceptable if not distinguished, with a preference related to the attractiveness of the second side. Both are well reproduced.

DVOŘÁK, ANTONIN (1841-1904)

Concertos

For Piano and Orchestra

In G. Wührer, VSY, Moralt, Vox PL 7630.

Not the most characteristic Dvořák (Brahmsian inclinations prevail), but well performed and acutely reproduced.

For Violin and Orchestra

In A minor. Kulenkampff, BPH, Jochum, Cap P 8052. Oistrakh, USSR, Kondrashin, Van 6016.

Neither of these qualifies, for reasons that obviously have nothing to do with the skill of the violinists involved. However, the sound is too far from current expectations to be acceptable. A Milstein or Menuhin version would be welcome.

For Violoncello and Orchestra

In B minor. Casals, CPH, Szell, V LCT 1026. Janigro, VSO, Dixon, W 5225. Piatigorsky, PHO, Ormandy, C ML 4022.

The place of honor remains with Casals largely in tribute to the power and conviction of his solo effort, for the orchestral values are but dimly recalled in the pre-war recording. As between the newer ones, I incline to the fine-sounding collaboration of Janigro and Dixon, as much for the latter's lyric feeling as the former's poetry. The Piatigorsky is in a more dramatic, virtuoso style, set off by the similar inclinations in the orchestral accompaniment.

Overture Cycle

*Amid Nature; Carnaval; Otello. VSO, Swoboda, CH 1141 (*Notturno for Strings).*

Workmanlike performances throughout, and very well reproduced, with Swoboda's rather good ideas about the music not accompanied by enough persistence to produce sufficient shading and emphasis from his players. The *Otello* is of particular interest.

Overtures

*Carnaval. LBS, Jochum, U LP 7094 (*The Jacobin; Smetana: Libussa). NYSO, Smallens, 10" D DL 4034 (*Berlioz: Beatrice and Benedict).*

The truly joyous spirit of this music is not present in either of these performances, though the playing under George Ludwig Jochum is more artistic than the machine-made precision of the summer Philharmonic. For those to whom the rest of the Czech repertory included appeals, this will be the choice. The Urania sound is big and a little distant from the microphone; the Decca is smaller, but not much better managed.

*Husitska. BPO, Fiedler, 10" V LM 1 (*Smetana: Moldau).*

This has been a stanch credit to Fiedler since 78-rpm days, and is welcome in the newer form. However, the pairing could be improved, for there are several performances of Smetana superior to this.

Scherzo

*Scherzo Capriccioso, opus 66. VSY, Swoboda, W 5029 (*Symphony in E flat, 1873).*

An engaging work, well turned by Swoboda. An early entry in the

Westminster catalogue, it represents an aspiration toward current sound standards rather than an achievement of them.

Serenades

In D, opus 44. LBE, Haas, 10" D DL 7533.

Delightful music in the spirit, if not the style, of a Mozart divertimento, lovingly played and admirably reproduced.

Slavonic Dances

Complete Set, opus 46 and 72. CPH, Talich, U 604 [2].

One of the glories of the post-war catalogues: a reprise, in contemporary brightness of sound, of the tangy, flavorsome performances long considered the model for this repertory. Rather than mentioning any alternative collections—none of which begins to match this standard—I note that opus 46 may be obtained separately on U 7076, as opus 72 may be on 7079. Further, it is hard to imagine a musical taste to which this homespun artistry would not appeal.

Slavonic Rhapsodies

Nos. 2 and 3, opus 45. BAM, Lehmann, 10" D DL 4018.

The Bambergers' aptitude for this music may be better understood if it is mentioned that they are almost entirely former members of a Czech orchestra who migrated, over a period of time, to the Bavarian community. I would trade all this, however, for the kind of non-national sympathy Beecham manifested in C Set X 55 of old. But let us be grateful for what we have. Excellent sound.

*No. 2, opus 45. VSY, Swoboda, W 5008 (*Rimsky-Korsakov: Symphonietta on Russian Themes).*

A more personal style of performance by Swoboda than Lehmann provides above, but not materially superior—in fact, not as well reproduced.

*No. 3, opus 45. HPO, Dorati, Ep 3015 (*Smetana: Moldau; Mussorgsky-Ravel: Pictures).*

A high-fidelity prize winner (Grand Prix du Disque, 1953) which does not return as much musical pleasure as the more modest effort of Lehmann (q.v.).

Suites

*In D ("Czech"), opus 39. WIN, Swoboda, CH 1157 (*Quartet "American").*

A work in the composer's most ingratiating folkish vein, sympathetically directed by Swoboda. The string sound is somewhat gritty, but otherwise appropriate in size and timbre.

*The Jacobin. ORB, Kretschmar, U LP 7094 (*Carnaval Overture; Smetana: Libussa).*

A medley of excerpts from an opera of 1888, with occasional suggestions of Dvořák's melodic aptitude, but not much else. Big-sounding, rather steely-stringed reproduction of a vigorous performance.

Symphonies

No. 1 in D. CO, Leinsdorf, C ML 4269.

Hardly a scintillant specimen of recording science, but the performance is creditable to Leinsdorf's brief period of control in Cleveland.

No. 2 in D minor. PHI, Kubelik, V LHMV 1029. HRS, Schmidt-Isserstedt, L LL 778.

A work with what might be described as embarrassing riches of reminiscence, with the first movement dominated by what amounts to variations on the slow movement of Brahms's B flat Concerto, and a slow movement steeped in Wagnerisms. Of the two performances, the Kubelik is more forward-moving, though the Schmidt-Isserstedt is also excellent, and a shade better reproduced.

No. 3 in F. LRO, Schüler, U 7-11.

More substance here than might be suspected from the score's obscurity, performed with real fervor under Schüler's perceptive direction. Powerful sound, a little steely.

No. 4 in G. NYPH, Walter, C ML 4119. ACG, Szell, L LL 488. PHI, Kubelik, V LHMV 1014. CIN, Johnson, Rem 199-168.

Walter's grand effort, energetic yet warmly colored, retains its superiority over any of those of the younger men, though it is not more than a good example of LP recording. Szell's combines fine orchestral discipline with good sound in better balance than either the Kubelik or the Johnson. The latter is impressively recorded for a disc in its price class, but the leadership lacks sparkle or real sympathy with the style of the music.

No. 5 in E minor ("New World"). NBC, Toscanini, V LM 1778. HPO, Dorati, Ep LC 3001. CHO, Kubelik, Mer 50002. DNO, Malko, V LBC 1005.

Even the hifi diehards must admit here that Victor's fidelity to the proclamative eloquence of Toscanini, which reproduces the aura of a performance as few others of his discs do, gives this music greater breadth and stature than the sounding cymbals of Dorati and the tinkling brass of Kubelik. In terms of musical content, the RCA should sell for twice what it does—fortunately, it doesn't. Malko's is excellent for the moderate cost.

*In E flat (1873). VSY, Swoboda, W 5029 (*Scherzo Capriccioso).*

A work of Dvořák's thirty-first year, with much promise of things to come, as well as some reminiscences of things that have been. Swoboda knows it thoroughly, and the sound is first-class.

Symphonic Poems

*Golden Spinning Wheel; Midday Witch. CPH, Talich, U 7073 (*Two Waltzes, opus 54, Nos. 1 and 4).*

Minor Dvořák, of typical melodic charm (especially *The Midday Witch*), realized with expectable finesse by Talich. Good sound throughout.

*Legends, opus 59. LOS, Scherman, C ML 4920. ORB, Lehmann, U 7010 (*Wood Dove).*

Credit Scherman with the enterprise inherent in being the first American conductor to discover these ingratiating works, perhaps through Lehmann's pioneering venture. He does them quite as well, and with the blessing of more even reproduction of his orchestra than Lehmann enjoys. Ordinarily, the presence of an additional work on another record would enhance its attractions, but the *Wood Dove* is the weakest of the works involved, Lehmann's performance of it not persuasive.

Arrangements

Waltzes, opus 54 (arranged by Jan Seidel). CZS, Jeremiaš, Mer 10030.

Suitable transcriptions, sympathetically directed by Jeremiaš.

The original recording sounds to be 78-rpm, and though the dubbing is skillful, the total sound is clear but without much body.

Work for String Orchestra

*Notturno, opus 40. VSO, Swoboda, CH 1141 (*Overture Cycle).*
A welcome dividend on the collection mentioned previously, and well reproduced.

EASDALE, BRIAN (1909-)

*The Red Shoes. PHI, Mathieson, 10" C ML 2083 (*Lambert: Horoscope).*
The lively film score, reproduced as heard on the sound track.

ELGAR, SIR EDWARD (1857-1934)

Concertos

For Cello and Orchestra. Pini, LPO, Van Beinum, 10" L LS 95.
Excellent work by Pini, well supported by Van Beinum. Not the best ffrr, but good sound nevertheless.
For Violin and Orchestra. Heifetz, LSO, Sargent, V LM 1090.
Silky, suave violin-playing by Heifetz, and very much to the point of this work. Sargent is a helpful associate, and the recording is very good, if not specifically high-fidelity.

Works for Orchestra

*Cockaigne Overture. LPO, Van Beinum, L LL 43 (*Wand of Youth).*
Musicianly work by Van Beinum, but not in the most notable tradition of Elgar. Good sound.
*Froissart; In the South. ORL, Pflüger, U LP 7136 (*Britten: Soirées Musicales).*
Both overtures are full of the Elgarian orchestral mannerisms, though not with as productive musical ideas as in other works. The performances are energetic enough, but without illumination of whatever purpose might have animated Elgar in these instances. Big, rather toneless reproduction. The overside Britten (ORB, Kleinert) does not compare with the competing version.

Pomp and Circumstance marches, Nos. 1 and 4. LSO, Sargent, 10" L LD 9057.

Not the best treatment this music has had on records, susceptible to improvement in both direction and reproduction.

Symphony No. 1 in A flat. LPH, Boult, V LHMV 1036.

Boult is a thoroughgoing Elgarian, and the sound is well suited to the material.

*Variations on an Original Theme ("Enigma"). NBC, Toscanini, V LM 1725 (*Brahms: Variations on a Theme). LSO, Sargent, L LL 740 (*Purcell: Suite).*

Toscanini's treatment is of a breadth and substance rarely heard in this music, performed with sweeping virtuosity by the orchestra, and strongly reproduced. The Sargent is much more "normal" in its stresses, and that much less affecting. Excellent sound.

*The Wand of Youth (Suite). LPO, Van Beinum, L LL 43 (*Cockaigne Overture). PHI, Sargent, C ML 4793 (*Walton: Façade).*

The choice between these is narrow, and may be resolved by the pairing of Elgar items on the Van Beinum disc, the superiority of other versions of *Façade* to Sargent's.

Work for String Orchestra

*Introduction and Allegro, opus 47. NEW, Collins, L LD 9062 (*Serenade).*

As noted in his treatment of Delius, Collins has a fine hand with English music. This pairing accounts well for the two works for string orchestra, both beautifully reproduced.

ENESCO, GEORGES (1881-)

Roumanian Rhapsodies, Nos. 1 and 2. HIS, Stokowski, 10" V LRM 7043.

Beautiful execution by the excellent orchestra, vividly reproduced.

*Roumanian Rhapsody, Nos. 1. LAP, Wallenstein, 10" D DL 4012 (*Smetana: Moldau).*

Lively performance, brightly reproduced. The second-side *Moldau* is not as good.

*Roumanian Rhapsody, No. 2. OCC, Enesco, 10" Rem 149-52 (*Smetana: Moldau).*

A coupling with Rem 149-47, on which Enesco conducts his Rhapsody No. 1, would be valuable for documentary purpose, if no other. However, the couplings in both cases with performances directed by other hands lessens their interest.

FALLA, MANUEL DE (1876-1946)

Ballet Music

El Amor Brujo. HBS, Merriman, Stokowski, V LM 1054 (**Borodin: Prince Igor Dances*). *MAD, Seone, Freitas Branco, W 5238* (**Retablo de Maese Pedro*). *OSC, Iriarte, Argenta, An 35089* (**Retablo de Maese Pedro*).

The Stokowski is far from a perfect product—too many microphones producing too many eerie effects are an obvious liability—but the orchestral playing is excellent, and Merriman's voice and style are highly apropos. The overside, as noted in its place, stands up well. The newer version under the direction of Freitas Branco is vigorous and mechanically well balanced, but the voice of Seone is only occasionally suited to the music. Those attracted to the Argenta by the conductor's name and its recent date of issue should know that it is at least five years old, and shows it.

Tricorne (*Complete Ballet*). *OOC, Prulière, Martinon, U LP 7034. OSR, Danco, Ansermet, L LL 598.*

Martinon's vigor and feeling for the material are decidedly attractive; the voice of Prulière is suitable. The sound is big and well balanced. Ansermet's effort is typically meticulous, perhaps a shade too refined for the subject in hand. Danco's singing is good, but not a factor of much value in such a work as this.

Tricorne (*Suite of Dances*). *PHI, Markevitch, An 35008* (**Dukas: L'Apprenti Sorcier; Prokofiev: "Classical" Symphony; etc.*). *STS, Golschmann, Cap P 8257* (**Prokofiev: Chout*). *LSO, Jorda, L LL 445* (**Nights in the Gardens of Spain*). *NYPH, Mitropoulos, C AL 44* (**La Vida Breve: Interlude and Dance*).

As regards the ballet material, the four versions are very close in quality, all of recent date and very well reproduced. As a totality, I prefer the Markevitch disc, for the fine service to Dukas and Prokofiev as well as Falla. Golschmann's is one of his best efforts to date on record, though inclined to orchestral display. Curzon is the fine soloist in *Nights in the Gardens of Spain*, which accompanies the Jorda interpretation, and the Mitropoulos excerpts from *Vida Breve* are expertly done. If it is just a good version of the dances that is wanted, the last will satisfy at a reasonable cost.

Concerto

*For Harpsichord. CHAM, Kirkpatrick, Mer 10012 (*Rieti: Partita).*
The associated ensemble hardly qualifies this for the orchestral category, but for completeness, reference may be made to Kirkpatrick's excellent musicianship and the fine collaboration of the Schneider-led ensemble. Good but not outstanding sound.

Work for Orchestra and Solo Instrument

*Nights in the Gardens of Spain. Curzon, NEW, Jorda, L LL 445 (Tricorne dances). Novaes, PRO, Swarowsky, Vox PL 8520 (*Grieg: Concerto). Rubinstein, STS, Golschmann, V LM 1091 (*Mozart: Concerto No. 23).*
This work is hardly so familiar that one can state a conviction about how it ought to be performed. However, it seems to me not well served by the soloist-accompanist relationship of Rubinstein to Golschmann, though Rubinstein performs more flashily than either Curzon or Novaes. Of the other conductors involved, I am more impressed with Jorda's handling of the orchestral text than with Swarowsky's, and as the London recording is also superior, the issue is resolved in favor of Curzon. For those attracted by the Novaes coupling, it may be described as a thoroughly good sampling of her art, well reproduced.

Opera Excerpts (Orchestral)

*La Vida Breve: Interlude and Dance. NYPH, Mitropoulos, C AL 44 (*Tricorne: Three Dances).*
Good, rhythmic effort by Mitropoulos, uncommonly well reproduced.

FAURÉ, GABRIEL (1845-1924)

Ballade for Piano and Orchestra. Long, OSC, Cluytens, An 35013

(*Ravel: Concerto in G). G. Casadesus, LAM, Rosenthal, Vox PL 6450 (*Chausson: Poème).

Soundwise, as well as musically, the advantage is with Long and Cluytens. However, there is something to be said for the Vox coupling with Thibaud's version of the *Poème.*

*Dolly. LSO, Fistoulari, MGM 3098 (*Poulenc: Les Biches).*

Apt direction by Fistoulari, good sound.

*Elégie for Violoncello and Orchestra. Michelin, USO, Hupperts, CH 1162 (*Lalo: Concerto).*

Uncommonly beautiful cello-playing, and resonantly reproduced.

*Pavane, opus 50. LAM, Martinon (*Dukas: L'Apprenti Sorcier; Honegger: Pastorale d'Été; Roussel: Festin de l'Araignée).*

If the other contents of this disc were as little duplicated and as well played as this one, Martinon would have a winner. However, the other literature (with the exception of the Honegger) exists in more attractive form elsewhere, and a recommendation is thus tentative. However, if the *Pavane* is the item desired, the others will give reasonable pleasure. Excellent sound.

*Pelléas et Mélisande. DSO, Paray, Mer MG 50035 (*Dukas: L'Apprenti Sorcier; Roussel: Spider's Feast). OCC, Sebastian, U 7097 (*Dukas: La Peri).*

Paray has a somewhat more sensitive hand on the strings of his orchestra than Sebastian, but the advantages and disadvantages are within a narrow range of difference. Both are well recorded, the Urania in closer proximity to the microphone.

FIELD, JOHN (1782-1837)

*Suite (arranged by H. Harty). LIV, Sargent, C RL 3043 (*Boccherini-Françaix: Scuola di Ballo).*

Not a good likeness of orchestral sound as presently preferred, but excellent performance at an advantageous price.

FOSS, LUKAS (1922-)

*Parable of Death. Zorina, LOUI, Whitney, C ML 4859 (*Martinu: Intermezzo; Milhaud: Kentuckiana).*

Expert ensemble work, well reproduced.

FRANÇAIX, JEAN (1912-)

*Concertino for Piano and Orchestra. Francaix, BPH, Borchard, 10" Cap L 8051 (*Serenade).*

A lively work, ably managed by the composer and his associates. Not the best sound. Eugen Jochum is the conductor of the overside *Serenade.*

*Emperor's New Clothes. SAX, Striegler, U 7122 (*Nicodè: Carnival Scenes).*

In its Frenchified form, *Le Roi Nu* "comes off," one might say, quite agreeably. Admirable orchestral performance, well reproduced. Jean Louis Nicodé of the companion side is a German composer of Berlin birth, despite the French name. His Richardisms (Wagner-Strauss) are competently performed (ORL, Weber) and reasonably well reproduced.

FRANCK, CÉSAR (1822-1890)

Works for Orchestra

*Le Chasseur Maudit. RPO, Beecham, C ML 4454 (*Rimsky-Korsakoff: Coq d'Or).*

Enlivening treatment by Beecham of a work for which he has a strong feeling. Bright, spacious reproduction.

Psychè. ACG, Van Beinum, 10" L LD 9081.

Van Beinum uses the amended, and customary, version without voices. It is a splendid example of the orchestra's qualities, beautifully reproduced. (Those who prefer his version of the Bruckner No. 7 will find this as the fourth side.)

*Redemption: Prelude to Part II. OCS, Sebastian, U 7061 (*Berlioz: Three excerpts from Damnation of Faust, Funeral March for the Last Scene of Hamlet).*

Atmosphere or creative thought are not the strong attributes of of this performance. Clean sound, but without the resonance wanted.

*Symphony. VPH, Furtwängler, L LL 967. DSO, Paray, Mer 50023. OSC, Munch, L LL 464. HPO, Van Otterloo, Ep 3019. VSO, Rodzinski, W WL 5311 (*Le Chasseur Maudit). ROB, Leinsdorf, V LBC 1001.*

The paradoxes of Furtwängler being as numerous as they are, it need hardly surprise that his *authorized* version (an unauthorized one was circulated in the early LP era) is the most impressive of all. The sound is one of the best on any record. Paray's fine-grained treatment is reasonably well reproduced, the personal one of Munch from Paris less well. Of top quality in sound, but not otherwise, is the Van Otterloo. The Rodzinski interests me for its excellent blend of musical elements. Though it does not have the special flavor of those previously endorsed, with the additional piece it is a worthy investment. In its price category, the Leinsdorf is outstanding.

Works for Orchestra and Piano

*Les Djinns. OCC, d'Arco, Sebastian, U URLP 7099 (*Saint-Saëns: Carnival of the Animals*).

Rather steely sound of both piano and orchestra is a detriment here. Technically, d'Arco is a capable pianist, Sebastian well posted on the problems of the work.

*Symphonic Variations. Gieseking, PHI, Karajan, C ML 4536 (*Mozart: Concerto No. 23). Lympany, PHI, Süsskind, V LHMV 1013 (*Schumann: Etudes Symphoniques). Casadesus, PHI, Weldon, C ML 4298 (*D'Indy: Symphony on a Mountain Air*).

As the orchestra in all cases is the Philharmonia, it is evident that there will be little to choose among the discs on that ground. Moreover, the recording is substantially equal. However, Gieseking has long seemed to me to have more to say about this music than any other contemporary, and he is aided here by proper sound and a vitalizing conductor. The Lympany piano tone is the best I have heard from her, and Casadesus's expert, if not too zestful, playing is linked to his beautiful version of the D'Indy score.

FREDERICK THE GREAT (1712-1786)

*Concerto for Flute and Orchestra, No. 3. Wanausek, VAO, Adler, SPA 23 (*Quantz: Concerto No. 17*).

Expert playing by Wanausek, of Vienna, of a lively work capably reproduced.

GABRIELI, GIOVANNI (1557-1612)

*Canzone for Double String Orchestra. SCH, Münchinger, 10" L LS 686 (*Telemann: Concerto for Viola and Orchestra).*

Throbbing, beautifully sonorous sound is the singular distinction of this disc, one of the Stuttgarters' best.

GERSHWIN, GEORGE (1898-1937)

Concerto

*For Piano and Orchestra, in F. Levant, NYPH, Kostelanetz, C ML 4879 (*Rhapsody in Blue; American in Paris). Pennario, PSO, Steinberg, Cap P 8219.*

Style and authority are all on the side of Levant, though there is a bigger sound on the Capitol disc. With the additional material now offered, the former is a far more advantageous buy.

Works for Orchestra

*An American in Paris. RCAO, Bernstein, V LM 1031(*Copland: Billy the Kid). NBC, Toscanini, V LM 9020 (*Prokofiev: "Classical" Symphony). SYM, Gershwin, 10" V LPT 29 (*Rhapsody in Blue).*

Practically speaking, there is only one valid performance of the *American in Paris*—Bernstein's. He pulls it along, and together, valuable attributes in any performance. Toscanini's is vivid and energetic, but not really Gershwin. Gershwin's, of course, is—what can be heard of it.

*Cuban Overture. SYM, Kostelanetz, C ML (*Songs of Gershwin).*

Lively performance, well reproduced.

*Porgy and Bess (arranged by Bennett). HBP, Green, 10" D DL 4051. MIN, Dorati, Mer 50016 (*Gould: Spirituals).*

Green has the happiest feeling for this music of any contemporary, coupled with sound of reasonable quality. Dorati's performance is not as suitable, though brilliantly conveyed.

Works for Orchestra and Solo Instrument

*Rhapsody in Blue. Levant, PHO, Ormandy, C ML 4879 (*Concerto in*

*F; An American in Paris). Gershwin, Whiteman, 10" V LPT 29 (*An American in Paris).*

The four or five other available performances add nothing to the light shed on this work by the longtime preferred interpreters of Gershwin's music—himself and Levant. The early performance by the composer has its curiosity value within a very limited sound range. Levant's vitality and fluency are well supported by Ormandy, with very good sound (Academy of Music). The additional items of this disc are variable, the *Concerto* excellent, the *American in Paris* (conducted by Rodzinski) animated enough, but pre-dating LP, and hence of secondary sound quality.

*Second Rhapsody. SYM, Levant, Gould, 10" C ML 2073 (*Variations on "I Got Rhythm").*

Not the best Gershwin, but second-best Gershwin is better than most other persons' best. Bright sound, a little shallow in resonance.

*Variations on "I Got Rhythm." SYM, Levant, Gould, 10" C ML 2073 (*Second Rhapsody).*

A piece of much ingenuity, which should be better known. Levant plays it with his usual fluency, and the sound is of the same order as that above.

GHEDINI, GIORGIO (1892-)

Concerto for Two Celli ("L'Olmeneta"). Mazzacurati, Gusella, SCA, Ghedini, Col LPS 1039.

Decidedly absorbing work by the Italian composer known here for his *Concerto del Abattro.* The instrumental forces are able, the composer's direction persuasive. Clear recording, rather harsh in the climaxes.

GIORDANI, TOMMASO or GIUSEPPE

*Concerto for Piano and Orchestra, in C. Bussotti, ICO, Jenkins, HS L 77 (*Brunetti: Symphony in C minor; Valentini: Concerto in C for Oboe).*

A work of charm and ingenuity, though by which of two Mozartian contemporaries (brothers) is unknown. Not the least attractive element is the rippling finger work of Bussotti, well partnered by Jenkins. Excellent sound.

GLAZUNOV, ALEXANDER (1865–1936)

Ballet Music

Raymonda. PRO, Rosenthal, Cap P 8184

Rosenthal's apt direction and the excellent reproduction make more of this score than one would believe to be in it. Well worth investigation by anyone partial to the Tchaikovsky idiom.

*Raymonda: Grand Valse only. PHI, Malko, V LBC 1022 (*Seasons excerpts; Prokofiev: Love for Three Oranges suite; etc.).*

Well-paced performance by Malko, rich sound at a reasonable price. The *Seasons* excerpts include *Winter*, the "Waltz of the Cornflowers" from *Summer*, and the "Bacchanale" from *Autumn*. Very good value.

The Seasons (Suite). FNS. Désormière, Cap P 8157.

The conductor's well-known skill with both Russian music and ballet music are admirably supported by the recording.

*The Seasons: Excerpts. PHI, Malko, V LBC 1022 (*Grand Valse from Raymonda, etc.).*

See entry above under *Raymonda*.

Concertos

*For Saxophone and Orchestra. Abato, SYM, Pickering, Ph 103 (*Ibert: Concertino da Camera).*

Not the most flavorsome Glazunov, but very well played and excellently reproduced. For the curious, the conductor, Pickering, is also the maker of the widely used pickup cartridge. (He was a horn-player before he became an audiophile.)

*For Violin and Orchestra. Oistrakh, USSR, Kondrashin, Per 598 (*Beethoven: Concerto). Milstein, RCAO, Steinberg, V LM 1064 (*Mozart: Adagio).*

Oistrakh's conception is more subjective, the conductor more attentive to details of orchestration than in performance commonly heard here. As Oistrakh's violinistic skill is superlative, I find it more interesting than the Milstein, well played as that is in a conventional way. Neither is well recorded, though the Oistrakh is in the better category of Russian effort.

Works for Orchestra

*Moyen Âge (Suite). IND, Sevitzky, V LBC 1062 (*Haydn: Symphony No. 73).*

The price bracket is more appropriate than the former Red Seal rating, but the music is still poor Glazounow, the playing not distinguished. Raw sound.

*Scènes de Ballet, opus 52. BSI, Samosud, Per SPL 596 (*Valses de Concert, Nos. 1 and 2).*

Ingratiating music, well directed. Recording is fair. The same applies to the reverse side.

*Stenka Razin. OSR, Ansermet, L LL 1060 (*Rimsky-Korsakov: Antar).*

This is hardly a deathless masterpiece (it consists largely of embattled variations on the familiar "Song of the Volga Boatmen"), but its clanking panoply of orchestral effects provides excellent occupation for Ansermet's orchestra and the recording engineers. Both perform in fine style.

Symphony No. 4 in E flat. STC, Rachmilovich, 10" Cap L 8027.

Sound work by Rachmilovich, fairly well reproduced.

*Symphony No. 7. ORB, Lederer, U 7088 (*Miaskovsky: Lyric Concertino).*

Poorly pitched reproduction (everything sounds slightly off center) of a not overcareful performance.

Valses de Concert, Nos. 1 and 2. BSI, Samosud, Per SPL 596.

See above, under *Scènes de Ballet.*

GLIÈRE, REINHOLD (1875–

Ballet Music

*The Red Poppy. VSO, Scherchen, W WAL 210 [2] (*Ilya Mourometz).*

Highly effective direction by Scherchen, eminently well reproduced.

Concertos

*For Harp and Orchestra. Dulova, USSR, Gauk, Per 567 (*Rimsky-Korsakov: Symphony No. 3).*

Musically, this is as interesting when the harp is not playing as when it is—which suggests that the problem has baffled even the resourceful Glière. Reasonably good performance, distant pickup, not too much fidelity.

*For Horn and Orchestra, opus 91. Polek, BSI, Glière, CE 3001 (*Glinka: Jota Aragonesa; Prokofiev: Gypsy Fantasy from Stone Flower).*

Old-fashioned but agreeable work, played with impressive facility by the Russian hornist. Tolerable sound, in an outmoded "studio" tradition.

Symphony

No. 3 "Ilya Mourometz." VSO, Scherchen, W WAL 210 [2] *(*Red Poppy). PHO, Stokowski, V LCT 1106.*

The Scherchen is one of the master performances of the LP era to date, and sumptuously reproduced. Stokowski's is mentioned not merely to identify it as a much-slashed condensation of the original, but also to remark it as one of the most powerful examples of his personal style in conjunction with the great orchestra. Tubby sound, of a bygone studio type.

GLINKA, MICHAEL (1803–1857)

Works for Orchestra

Jota Aragonesa. USSR, Samosud, CE 3001 (Glière: Concerto for Horn, etc.).

Reasonably listenable performance, with what sounds like auditorium recording of not too good quality.

*Kamarinskaya. PHI, Süsskind, MGM E 3045 (*Rimsky-Korsakov: Concerto for Piano, Overture to May Night, etc.).*

An incidental but far from minor attraction of the collection whose total contents are stated under Rimsky-Korsakov's *May Night: Overture.* The basic ideas are Glinka's, but the all-important elaboration of them, orchestrally, is among Rimsky's important contributions to Russian music. Stellar sound.

*Valse-Fantasie. PHI, Malko, V LBC 1021 (*Tchaikovsky: Serenade for Strings).*

A work of uncommonly delicate texture, beautifully comprehended by Malko, and superlatively executed by the virtuoso orchestra. Very satisfactory sound.

Opera Excerpts (Orchestral)

*Russlan and Ludmilla (Suite). LSO, Fistoulari, MGM E 3053 (*Berlioz: Trojans at Carthage suite). Overture only. OSC, Ansermet, L LL 864 (*Prokofiev: "Classical" Symphony; Moussorgsky: Night on Bald Mountain; etc.).*

Fistoulari adds to his rather routine playing of the Overture a charming sequence of Oriental and Fairy dances, and a March of the Wizard. The Overture as offered by Ansermet is certainly a brighter, more invigorating experience. MGM's sound is good, but the London is better.

GLUCK, CHRISTOPH WILLIBALD VON (1714-1787)

Ballet Music

Don Juan. VSY, Moralt, W 5028.

The attractive material is only moderately well served by Moralt, but is a way of hearing it, at least. Clear recording, but not as good as Westminster has done more recently.

Concerto

*For Flute and Orchestra. Rampal, PPO, Leibowitz, Oc 29 (*Corelli: Concerto for Oboe; Haydn: Toy Symphony)*

Most of the honors here belong to the flutist, an instrumentalist of taste and fine technical craft. However, the accompaniment is dull in pace and lacking in rhythmic animation. Not particularly good sound.

Overtures

*Alceste. BPH, Furtwängler, 10" Cap H 8130 (*Beethoven: Cavatina from Quartet No. 13). LSO, Kisch, 10" L LD 9035 (*Iphigénie en Aulide).*

The gravity and weight of the Gluck conception are more powerfully conveyed by Furtwängler, but the two sides of the Kisch disc are both better reproduced.

*Iphigénie en Aulide. LSO, Kisch, 10" LD 9035 (*Alceste).*
See above.

GOEB, ROGER (1917-)

*Symphony No. 3. HIS, Stokowski, V LM 1727 (*Bartók: Sonata for Two Pianos and Percussion).*
A work of more than casual interest, performed with verve and fine tonal quality under Stokowski's apt direction.

GOLDMARK, KARL (1830-1915)

Concerto for Violin and Orchestra, opus 28. Rybar, VSY, Swoboda, W 5010.
Rybar is a proficient violinist, and the direction of Swoboda is appropriate. Good sound.

Symphony ("Rustic Wedding"). RPO, Beecham, C ML 4626.
One of the best post-war recordings by Beecham, superbly performed and reproduced with resonant fullness.

GORDON, GAVIN (1901-)

*Rake's Progress. ROO, Lambert, C ML 4229 (*Prokofiev: Cinderella).*
Sound work by Lambert, acceptably reproduced.

GOTTSCHALK, LOUIS M. (1829-1869)

*Cakewalk. PHO, Ormandy, C ML 4616 (*Gould: Fall River Legend).*
Lively Americana, well reproduced.

GOULD, MORTON (1913-)

Ballet Music

*Fall River Legend. NYPH, Mitropoulos, C ML 4616 (*Gottschalk: Cakewalk).*

Mitropoulos gives proper service to Gould, and the orchestra plays well for him.

*Interplay (with piano). Gould, ROB, C ML 4218 (*Spirituals; Cowboy Rhapsody; American Salute; New China March; Russian Cavalry March). De Groot, HPO, Van Otterloo, Ep 3021 (*Spirituals).*

Gould is fortunate in virtually all his recording interpreters, including himself. The Epic sound is brilliant, the Columbia almost as good. Preference here would be largely involved with reverse-side repertory.

Concertos

*Mediterranean. Gould, ROP, 10" C AL 36 (*Legend).*

The comment above is equally applicable here. Good sound.

*Tap Dance Concerto. Daniels, ROP, Gould, 10" C ML 2215 (*Family Album).*

Unseen, the percussive foot-taps provided by Daniels are a little pointless, but the whole is well reproduced.

Works for Orchestra

*Family Album. ROP, Gould, 10" C ML 2215 (*Tap Dance Concerto).*

Not the most engaging of Gould's work, to which he gives the best of his own good efforts as conductor.

*Latin-American Symphonette. ERO, Hanson, Mer 40002 (*Barber: Adagio).*

Hanson performs a handsome service for his younger colleague, and the reproduction is on the brilliant side.

*Philharmonic Waltzes. NYPH, Stokowski, 10" C ML 2167 (*Quickstep; Griffes: White Peacock).*

Stokowski states the case for these entertaining pieces persuasively, and the sound is gratifying.

*Spirituals. NYPH, Rodzinski, 10" C ML 2042 (*Copland: A Lincoln Portrait). Van Otterloo, HPO, Ep 3021 (*Interplay). MIN, Dorati, Mer 50016 (*Gershwin: Porgy and Bess).*

All of these performances are capable ones, with the Dutch orchestra powerfully reproduced, the Minnesota one somewhat overreproduced. In the aggregate, the coupling with Rodzinski's performance of Copland strikes me as the best value.

GOUNOD, CHARLES (1818-1893)

Faust: Ballet Music. *OTN, Fourestier, V LBC 1016 (*Tchaikovsky: Swan Lake). OTN, Fournet, Ep LC 3030 (*Delibes: Sylvia, Coppélia; Rabaud: Marouf). ROO, Braithwaite, MGM 3052 (*Tchaikovsky: Aurora's Wedding).*

The values among these are hardly so different as to warrant much discussion. The Fourestier is the most reasonable in price and, though inferior to the Fournet in sound, as good as any other in performance. Braithwaite's effort is good, and up to standard reproductively.

GRAINGER, PERCY (1882-)

Works for Orchestra (Arrangements)

*Country Gardens; Shepherd's Hey; Molly on the Shore; Mock Morris; Early One Morning; Handel in the Strand; Irish Tune from the County Derry. HIS, Stokowski, V LM 1238 (*Mozart: Sleight Ride; Schubert: Tyrolean Dances; Sibelius: Berceuse; etc.).*

The Grainger side is beautifully performed and warmly reproduced.

GRANADOS, ENRIQUE (1867-1916)

*Orientale; Andaluzia; Rondalla Aragonesa. PHI, Schuechter, MGM 3018 (*Turina: Danzas Fantásticas).*

Well-flavored performances of these Spanish dances by Schuechter, brightly reproduced.

GRÉTRY, ANDRÉ (1741-1813)

*Céphale et Procris (Suite). INR, André, 10" Cap L 8135 (*Dukas: (*L'Apprenti Sorcier).*

André's abilities as elsewhere demonstrated hardly prepare one for the finesse and detail of his interpretation here. The sound is not sensational, but reasonably satisfactory.

GRIEG, EDVARD (1843-1907)

Concerto

*For Piano and Orchestra. Novaes, PRO, Swarowsky, Vox PL 8520 (*Schumann: Concerto). Lipatti, PHI, Galliera, C ML 4525 (*Schumann: Concerto). Schiøler, DNO, Tuxen, 10" Mer 15012. Dorfmann, ROB, Leinsdorf, V LBC 1043 (*Mendelssohn: Concerto in G minor).*

Every one of the above is an excellent performance of Grieg's ingratiating work, and the standard of sound throughout varies from good to excellent. The most spirited performance is Lipatti's, but as a recording it is the least good of the four, though well worth a place in any collection. The Novaes musicianship gives beautiful service to Grieg (as well as Schumann), as does Dorfmann, whose Mendelssohn, on side two, is outstanding in its category, despite the economy price. Schiøler may be honored for a very sturdy version, powerfully reproduced.

Incidental Music

Peer Gynt (Stage Sequence). OPH, Grüner-Hegge, Mer 10148.

This collection of thirteen excerpts from the twenty-three written by Grieg for Ibsen's drama differs from the total of the two familiar suites by the addition of a prelude to the whole, the "Norwegian Bridal Procession" (orchestrated by Halvorsen), the singing of the Saeter girls in the hills, the "Arabian" march, and Solveig's final lullaby. The conducting is affectionate though with less than the ultimate refinement of some versions of the separate suites hereafter mentioned. Eva Prytz is the able soprano, and the recording is first-class.

*Peer Gynt (Suites Nos. 1 and 2). HO, Barbirolli, V LBC 1017 (*Strauss: Rosenkavalier Suite). LPO, Cameron, L LL 153. BPO, Fiedler, 10" V LM 7002. HPO, Van Otterloo, Ep LC 3007.*

The obvious advantage of combining the two suites on a single disc is a boon of LP, to which RCA adds good measure at low cost in its highly worthwhile Barbirolli effort. However, it should also be noted that the Suite No. 2, well played as it is, is conducted by Robert Irving (LSO). London's Cameron is afforded the best sound, though Fiedler's has its customary ring. The Epic-

Van Otterloo is somewhat overstressed in both performance and recording.

*Peer Gynt (Suite No. 1). PHO, Ormandy, 10" C AL 35 (*Alfven: Midsummer Night's Vigil).*

For those who desire Suite No. 1 only, this is a finely turned effort, admirably reproduced. With it is the Alfven whimsy, equally well done.

Peer Gynt (Suite No. 2). See entry under Suites 1 and 2 above.

*Sigurd Jorsalfar. CGO, Hollingsworth, MGM 3072. (*Humperdinck: Hansel und Gretel suite).*

The brightest version now available, and acutely reproduced.

Works for Orchestra

*Lyric Suite, opus 54. DSTR, Tuxen, 10" L LS 849 (*Reesen: Himmerland).*

A prime example of nationalistic feeling warmly translated into musical expression. Beautiful sound.

*Norwegian Dances, opus 35. VSO, Litschauer, Van 430 (*Sibelius: Rakastava).*

Vienna is hardly the place one would look for sturdy Norwegian sympathies, but Litschauer's attention to musical detail and the fine reproduction of the orchestra's excellent sound make for a highly enjoyable disc.

Symphonic Dances. DNO, Tuxen, Mer 10132.

More evidence of the sympathy attested to by Tuxen in the *Lyric Suite*, as noted above. Not as good recording, but suitable.

Work for String Orchestra

Holberg Suite. BNO, Neel, 10" L LS 173.

Neel's vigorous feeling for this music and the fine sound of his excellent ensemble leave little doubt of favor to it.

GRIFFES, CHARLES (1884-1920)

*Poem for Flute and Orchestra. CHAM, Baker, Saidenberg, 10" D DL 4013 (*Foote: Night Piece).*

Finespun tones by Baker, pungently recorded.

*The White Peacock. NYPH, Stokowski, 10" C ML 2167 (*Gould: Philharmonic Waltzes).*

Stokowski's tonal painting is highly appropriate to the vista, and brightly reproduced.

HANDEL, GEORGE FREDERICK (1685-1759)

Concerti Grossi

Opus 6 (Complete Set, Nos. 1-12). CHAM, A. Busch, C SL 158 [4]. *BAM, Lehmann, D DX 126* [4]. *BNO, Neel, Nos. 1-2: 10" L LS 206; 3-4: 10" L LS 207; 5-6: 10" L LS 396; 7-8: 10" L LS 543; 9-10: 10" L LS 585; 11-12: 10" L LS 870.*

I should like to think there is something of more promise in the phonographic future of these works, for none of the entries is wholly satisfactory. Busch (Adolf) has, perhaps, the best approach, with the leading parts very well played by himself, Ernest Drucker (violins), Hermann Busch (cello), and M. Horszowski (clavier), but the sound is rough and scratchy; Boyd Neel has the sound, but also a rather impersonal way of going about this enterprise, while Lehmann's more spirited performances are also somewhat thin and unresonant. (In this last version the principals are Otto Büchner and Franz Berger, violins, Hans Melzer, cello, and Karl Richter, clavier.) On the whole, one might acquire individual works of preference in the Neel versions, and wait for something more satisfying in the total sequence.

Opus 6, No. 5 in D, No. 6 in G minor. LPO, Weingartner, C ML 4676.

Weingartner's aristocratic sense of line and his admirable sense of pace are very welcome in these works. The sound has a fuzz of age on it, but is by no means bad.

*Opus 6, No. 7 in B flat (arranged by Schoenberg). JSO, Janssen, C ML 4406 (*Bach-Mozart: Adagios and Fugues, K. 404A, etc.).*

If Handel had been Schoenberg (perish the thought!), he might have written something as disjointed and non-reposeful as this "transformation," as schizophrenic a work as I know. All sorts of things happen, mostly non-Handelian. Careful performance, clean, slightly brittle reproduction.

Concertos

For Orchestra

*Opus 3, Nos. 1-6. VSO, Prohaska, BG 505/6. (*Alexanderfest Concerto).*

These eminently Handelian works are especially worth knowing for the variety and resource of the instrumentation, in which flutes, oboes, bassoons, and solo strings are combined in a beguiling gamut of possibilities. The players of them are not so artful as one would wish, but Prohaska beats a brisk Handel, and the reproduction is highly satisfactory.

*Alexanderfest. VSO, Prohaska, BG 505/6 (*See above). JSO, Janssen, Cap P 8137 (*Oboe Concerto in B flat; Haydn: Concerto for Horn in D).*

Janssen uses an adaptation by F. Ronchini with stress on two cellos. However, the Prohaska performance is not only livelier and more authentic, but also better reproduced.

In B flat and F. CCM, Friisholm, HS 1049.

The two works, for strings and winds, are attributed to 1746, and if not the most majestic Handel, provide the opportunity to hear excerpts from *Esther, Messiah, Belshazzar, Semele,* etc., in a new guise. Businesslike playing, fairly well reproduced.

For Oboe and Orchestra

*No. 3 in G minor, No. 4 in E flat. Kamesch, CHAM, Kuyler, Oc 25 (*Concertos for Organ, Nos. 13 and 14). No. 3 in G minor only. Goossens, LIV, Cameron, C ML 4782 (*Concertos by Cimarosa, Marcello, Bach-Tovey, etc.).*

The Vienna recordings of the Kamesch performances are louder and more veritable then the English reproduction, pre-war, of Goossens, but the effort to hear what the latter is doing is more than repaid. It is high art, and as such incomparable. The Austrian effort is dutiful and rather dull.

*In B flat. Gassman, JSO, Janssen, Cap P 8137 (*Alexanderfest Concerto; Haydn: Concerto for Horn, in D).*

The oboe-playing of Gassman, especially in the slow movement, is excellent. Clean, rather dead recording. The work is identified as No. 9 in the catalogue of Max Seiffert.

For Organ and Orchestra

Opus 4, Nos. 1-6: Kraft, PRO, Reinhardt, Vox PL 7132 [2]. *Nos. 1 and 2: Demessieux, OSR, Ansermet, L LL 695.*

Specialists in music of the baroque may find pleasure in these works and their performance, but the wheezy, uncertain pitch of the instrument used by Kraft is neither more nor less pleasant (just different) than the much bigger one favored by Demessieux. In each case, notes follow one another like so many elephants tail to tail—to no more aesthetic outcome. The London processing is better.

Opus 7, Nos. 1-6. Kraft, PRO, Reinhardt, Vox PL 7202 [2].

This is an altogether more agreeable prospect than the foregoing, with a better pickup of the organ (in better tune, if it is the same one, as it sounds to be) and rather more attentive work all around.

Nos. 13-16. Hoelderlin, PRO, Reinhardt, Vox PL 7802 [2]. *Nos. 13, 14. Leonhardt, CHAM, Kuyler, Oc 25 (*Concerti for Oboe, in G minor and E flat).*

The improvement in this sequence from Stuttgart continues here, with an engaging performance of the B flat (No. 13) concerto known as "The Cuckoo and the Nightingale." The organ is a bit distant, but the total sound is pleasant. Leonhardt's squeaky instrument is something to avoid.

For Organ (Harpsichord) and Orchestra

Nos. 13 in F, 14 in A, 19 in D minor. Pelleg, ZRO, Goehr, HdS L 3.

So far as the musical content of the work known as "The Cuckoo and the Nightingale" is concerned, it strikes me as better served here than in the versions with organ. Pelleg is an excellent harpsichordist, Goehr his usual competent self. No. 19 is identified as a work also originally for organ, but not published until 1797. First-class recording.

For Viola and Orchestra

In B minor, G minor, B flat. Vardi, CHAM, Str 617.

Aside from identifying the B minor as the edition of Henri Casadesus, the information offered about these works is meager. That is regrettable, for Vardi draws a superb sound from his instrument and administers it with taste and imagination. The accompanying orchestra could do with more than the leadership he provides, but the results are uniformly musical. Good sound, a little dull in resonance.

Works for Orchestra

Overture Suite. LBE, Haas, 10" D DL 4070.

Doubtless a better Handelian than I could identify this material, for which the label offers no clarifying information. However, I have full admiration for the excellent playing of the little group led by Haas and for its finely sonorous reproduction.

*Royal Fireworks. ACG, Van Beinum, L LL 760 (*Handel-Harty: Water Music). BPH, Lehmann, D DL 9696 (*Schubert: Symphony in B minor).*

Both the sound and the quality of thought in the Van Beinum performance are superior to those in the Lehmann. Moreover, the *Water Music* is a more desirable disc partner than another "Unfinished." (Lehmann plays one more Handel movement than Van Beinum.)

*Water Music (Complete). HEW, Hewitt, HSL 107. BPH, Lehmann, D DL 9594. Suite (arranged by Harty) ACG, Van Beinum, L LL 760 (*Royal Fireworks).*

Thanks to the fine effort of Hewitt and the splendid playing of his assorted wind virtuosi, I have conquered a long-standing preference for the Harty suite. There is little doubt that the original twenty sections embody considerable great music omitted in Harty's matched-pearl necklace of six. However, Lehmann does not get nearly as much out of the sequence as Hewitt, and the Parisian recording is also superior. It is, in fact, a sonorous pleasure on its own. Van Beinum plays the familiar sequence with considerable artistry and the distinction of reproduction noted above.

Works for Orchestra (Arrangements)

*The Faithful Shepherd. RPO, Beecham, C ML 4374 (*Haydn: Symphony No. 93).*

A favorite compilation by Beecham, played with the authority of yesterday and the good sound of today.

The Great Elopement. *RPO, Beecham, V LHMV 1030 (*Mozart: Divertimento in D, K.131).*

The flowing, ample measures are, in Beecham's arrangement, a beautiful addition to the literature, warmly played, spaciously reproduced.

Jephtha. *SAL, Fekete, Mer MG 10066 (*Haydn: Symphony in C).*

Fekete's self-compiled suite takes its name from the opening *Jephtha* overture, to which are joined one excerpt each from *Solomon, Judas Maccabeus,* and *Athalia.* The orchestral sound is not distinguished, the reproduction disposed to shrill highs and insubstantial bass.

HANSON, HOWARD (1896-)

Centennial Ode. *RSO, Hanson, Eas 1.*

A properly ceremonial work (for the University of Rochester) well performed and suitably reproduced.

Concerto for Piano and Orchestra, in G, opus 36. *Firkusny, RSO, Hanson, C ML 4403 (*Grieg: Holberg Suite).*

Self-promotion is hardly a vice, especially when conveyed through so agreeable a work as this, and with so able an artist as Firkusny as soloist. Good, but not prize, sound.

Symphony No. 2 ("Romantic"). *ERO, Hanson, C ML 4638 (*MacDowell: Concerto No. 2).*

This is at least the second recording by Hanson of this work, and he is well in command of its problems. Good sound.

Symphony No. 3. *BSO, Koussevitzky, V LCT 1153 (*Harris: Symphony No. 3).*

The vitalizing force of Koussevitzky can still be felt in this performance of 1940, in which the Sibeliussy quality is more evident than ever. The recording, originally regarded as "loud," now sounds quite realistic.

Symphony No. 4. *ERO, Hanson, Mer 40004 (*Harris: Symphony No. 3).*

A recent addition to the Hanson catalogue, better reproduced than most of the preceding.

HARRIS, ROY (1898-)

Symphony No. 3. *ERO, Hanson, Mer 40004 (*Hanson: Symphony No. 4).*

A friendly service to his colleague by Hanson, and one of a distinctly good group of recordings by Mercury.

HARRISON, LOU (1917-)

*Suite for Violin, Piano, and Orchestra. A. and M. Ajemian, Stokowski, V LM 1785 (*Weber: Symphony on Poems of William Blake).*

Stokowski's "orchestra," in this instance, is a small ensemble of ten or so, with which the Ajemians collaborate beautifully under the conductor's skillful direction. Fine sound.

HAYDN, FRANZ JOSEF (1732-1809)

Concertos

For Cembalo and Orchestra

*In G. E. Heiller, CHAM, A. Heiller, HS LP 1014 (*Concerto for Violin, in G).*

A genial work of no special distinction, played rather too quietly for the best results. Fair sound, good balance.

For Flute and Orchestra

*In D. CHAM, Shceck-Wenzinger, U URLP 7031 (*Telemann: Overture in D).*

No guarantee is offered that this is by Haydn. However, the key of performance is definitely C, not D. Otherwise it is routine work, not more than tolerably recorded.

For Harpsichord and Orchestra

*In D. Landowska, CHAM, Bigot, V LCT 1029 (*Mozart: Concerto No. 26 in D). Nef, LAM, Colombo, OL 50007 (*J. C. Bach: Symphonies in D and E). Roesgen-Champion, LAM, Goldschmidt, Vox PL 6320 (*Concerto for Oboe in C). Heiller, VSO, Litschauer Van VRS 454 (*Concerto in E flat for Trumpet).*

Landowska's spirited way with this music is as old as this recording, whose lack of decibel count is hardly serious. The Nef has more substance in the strings, though her harpsichord produces a more fragile sound than Landowska's, and is not well balanced. However, it is more decisive, energetic playing than the Roesgen-Champion. Heiller's capable playing is best reproduced of all, but her status as an artist is not yet in the classification of those with whom she is contending. In no case do the phrases have the sparkle and point of Landowska's.

For Horn and Orchestra

*In D (1762). Koch, VSY, Heiller, HS LP 1038 (*Concerto in E flat, for Trumpet).*

All the elements in this sprightly work are comprehended with skill, including Koch's artful work with the *corno da caccia* writing. Finely mellow, well-balanced sound.

*In D (No. 2). A. Brain, JSO, Janssen, Cap P 8137 (*Handel: Concerto for Oboe, in B flat, Alexanderfest Concerto).*

The Hollywood branch of the Brain family performs in expectable style (utilizing, however, what sounds like a conventional French horn). Janssen's orchestral direction is too angular for my taste, the reproduction no more than serviceable.

For Oboe and Orchestra

*In C. Pierlot, LAM, Goldschmidt, Vox PL 6320 (*Concerto for Harpsichord, in D).*

A work of singular interest, by turns martial and plaintive, as though it might have been written originally for wind band. Pierlot is an excellent oboist, the orchestra is well directed, and the recording is good, in the French studio style.

For Organ and Orchestra

In C (1756), in C (1760). A. Heiller, VSY, Gillesberger, HS L 1043.

The clear, well-focused sound of the organ of the Franziskanerkirche in Vienna is a decided asset in these performances. Heiller uses its bright sound to the best advantage, and the recorded quality is first-class.

For Piano and Orchestra

*In F. Roesgen-Champion, OSC, Goldschmidt, Per SPL 556 (*C. P. E. Bach: Concerto in C minor).*

A work of much interest, though not known to me in any other form. Roesgen-Champion and Goldschmidt both earn more esteem here than elsewhere. Good, serviceable recording, though the strings are a little thin.

For Trumpet and Orchestra

*In E flat. Eskdale, VSO, Litschauer, Van VRS 454 (*Concerto for Harpsichord in D). Wobitsch, VSY, Heiller, HS LP 1038 (*Concerto for Horn in D).*

Wobitsch is a thoroughly capable trumpeter, but Eskdale plays this work as though he owns it—which, in a manner of speaking, he does, as his pioneering recording in the thirties acquainted this generation with the virtues of the music. The soaring purity of his sound is beautifully reproduced in Vanguard's customary manner. Those who prefer a coupling with the horn oddity to another version of "the" D major *Concerto for Harpsichord* will find the Haydn Society issue highly satisfactory in all respects, lacking only the sovereign authority of Eskdale.

For Violin and Orchestra

In A. Bertschinger, CHAM, Heiller, 10" HS L 1017.

This work has been so thoroughly reconstructed that its identity with the original of Haydn would be more accident than documentation. At best its qualities are modest, with limited technical difficulties and no approach to profundity. Good, straightforward performance.

*In C. Stern, CHAM, Zakin, C ML 4301 (*Mozart: Sonata No. 26). Goldberg, PHI, Süsskind, D DL 8504 (*Handel: Sonata No. 4 in D).*

Each of these performances has its virtues, with the Stern somewhat better in sound.

*In G. Bertschinger, CHAM, Heiller, HS LP 1014 (*Concerto for Cembalo in G).*

As in the case of the other violin concertos, Haydn conveyed little that was personal in this G major. A pleasant occasional piece which could do with a little more impact than is provided by the present players. Fine reproduction.

For Violoncello and Orchestra

*In D. Feuermann, SYM, Sargent, C ML 4677 (*Schubert: Arpeggione Sonata). Fournier, PHI, Kubelik, V LHMV 1043 (*Saint-Saëns: The Swan, etc.). Janigro, VSO, Prohaska, W WL 5126 (*Boccherini: Concerto in B).*

Both Fournier and Janigro are superior artists, but the sensitivity and finesse of Feuermann are something to treasure, whether or not the sound is all it might be. If that is a strong consideration, I propose the Fournier on behalf of his lively style in this work and Kubelik's advantageous leadership. Both it and the Westminster are fine in sound.

Symphonies

*No. 1 in D. VSY, Sternberg, HS 1001 (*Nos. 13 and 28).*[1]

These and other early issues in the Haydn Society sequence are marked by scholarship in the use of authentic ensembles as prescribed by Haydn, but the performances are mechanical, lacking in flexibility or nuance. Also, the recording emphasizes clarity of sound at the expense of resonance or proper bass.

*No. 6 in D ("Le Matin"). CHAM, Litschauer, HS 1025 (*No. 21).*

An improvement on the foregoing, both in aesthetic and acoustic qualities. Hardly first-rate, however.

*No. 7 in C ("Le Midi"). CHAM, Litschauer, HS 1016 (*No. 8). ASO, Randolf, Rem R 199-71 (*Mozart: Symphony No. 33). PHO, Ormandy, C ML 4673 (*No. 45, "Farewell").*

The combination on the Haydn Society disc of "*Le Midi*" and its successor "*Le Soir*" obviously makes it the sensible choice. However, the version by Randolf (a name not known even as a name) is surprisingly well played and decently recorded, for those who might prefer the economy pairing. Needless to say, the Philadelphia is the best played and suavest sounding, but Ormandy's

[1] *EDITOR'S NOTE:* The common practice being to combine two or more Haydn symphonies on a disc, the second-side reference to Nos. 13 and 28, for example, identifies two other works by Haydn.

muscular style and the undue size of the ensemble are counts against it.

*No. 8 in G ("Le Soir"). CHAM, Litschauer, HS 1016 (*No. 7).*
See preceding entry.

*No. 12 in E. SYM, Loibner, Ly 36 (*Nos. 23, 29, 30).*
Clean, efficient execution, the generally good sound suavely reproduced. However, little effort is expended on dynamics, contrasts of mood, or finesse in phrasing. In short, what is offered is good, though it leaves more than a little lacking. The works are hardly exceptional Haydn, but they add to a comprehension of his development.

*No. 13 in D. VSY, Sternberg, HS 1001 (*Nos. 1, 28).*
For comment on Sternberg, see No. 1.

*No. 21 in A. CHAM, Litschauer, HS 1025 (*No. 6).*
This is hardly a sonorous treat. The playing is heavy and not too accurate in pitch, the reproduction clear but without much resonance.

*No. 22 in E flat ("Der Philosoph"). LBE, Haas, D DL 9561 (*Concerto in F). VSY, Sternberg, HS 1009 (*No. 35).*
Haas and company are the preference here, though it is a better effort for Sternberg than some of the preceding ones.

*No. 26 in D minor. CHAM, Heiller, HS 1019 (*No. 36).*
The subtitle "*Lamentazione*" actually bears, according to the unsigned annotation, on the Passion of Christ, with opposing Pilatus and Christus themes. It is a most unusual work, and beautifully accounted for here.

*No. 28 in A. VSY, Sternberg, HS 1001 (*Nos. 1, 13).*
See Symphony No. 1.

*No. 29 in E, 30 in C. CHAM, Loibner, Ly 36 (*Nos. 12, 23, 30).*
See Symphony No. 12.

*No. 31 in D ("Hornsignal"). VSY, Sternberg, HS 1002 (*No. 34).*
One of the earliest Haydn Society recordings, and recommended only with the considerable reservations noted in re No. 1.

*No. 34 in D minor. VSY, Sternberg, HS 1002 (*No. 31).*
See above.

*No. 35 in B flat. VSY, Sternberg, HS 1009 (*No. 22).*
As in the case of "*Der Philosoph,*" a little better than the other early discs by Sternberg.

*No. 36 in E flat. CHAM, Heiller, HS 1019 (*No. 26).*
This is not quite the introspective equivalent of its disc mate, but it is an expressive work, with the solo string parts (violin, Edith

Steinbauer, cello, Frieda Krause-Litschauer) well played. When properly compensated, the sound is much improved.

*No. 42 in D. CHAM, Litschauer, HS 1026 (*No. 47).*

A transitional work, with a slow movement of full, songful Haydnesque expressiveness. Appropriate treatment by Litschauer, and decidedly better recording than in earlier items from this source.

*No. 43 in E flat ("Mercury"). DSTR, Wöldike, HS 1041 (*No. 50).*

A convincing demonstration of competence in Haydn by Wöldike. In both proportions and sound the reproduction is close to ideal.

*No. 44 in E minor ("Trauer"). DSTR, Wöldike, L LL 844 (*No. 48). VSO, Scherchen, W WL 5206 (*No. 49). RIAS, Fricsay, D DL 9614 (*Mozart: Symphony No. 35 in D, K.385).*

The interest of the conductors listed is ample indication of the quality of this work, its position as perhaps the first wholly mature symphony in the long sequence. The more puzzling, then, is it to find Scherchen, the high priest of Haydn, switching the minuet and adagio in order to put the "*Trauer*" movement second! Wöldike's treatment is not so intense, but preferable and, needless to say, not inclined to such unconventionalities. Fricsay does a thoroughly good performance without special feeling for the style. Excellent reproduction all around.

*No. 45 in F sharp minor ("Farewell"). PHO, Ormandy, C ML 4673 (*No. 7). SCH, Münchinger, L LL 525 (*Wagner: Siegfried Idyll).*

The kind of virtuosity the Philadelphia Orchestra commands, and that Ormandy utilizes to such good advantage in this work, are highly suitable to its patterns (especially the horn solo of the finale). Münchinger's ensemble also does its work well, on a smaller scale. The Columbia recording is superb, the London very good.

*No. 47 in G. CHAM, Litschauer, HS 1026 (*No. 42).*

An uncommonly sonorous work, handsomely managed by the recorders.

*No. 48 in C ("Maria Theresa"). DSTR, Wöldike, L LL 844 (*No. 44).*

Finely vigorous treatment by Wöldike of a work notable for Handelian trumpets in the allegros, horns and oboe in the adagio. Ideal sound.

*No. 49 in F minor ("La Passione"). VSO, Scherchen, W WL 5206 (*No. 44). HOL, Newstone, HS L 1052 (*No. 73).*

Scherchen commands more of the subtleties of orchestral coloration to animate this tricky work than his younger competitor. On the other hand, Newstone's paired "Hunt" symphony is preferable to Scherchen's No. 44 ("*Trauer*," q.v.). Both are well recorded.

*No. 50 in C. DSTR, Wöldike, HS 1041 (*No. 43).*

A work of quality, beautifully played by the Danish musicians. Very good sound.

*No. 52 in C. VSO, Heiller, HS 1039 (*No. 56).*

Two songful works deserving of wider circulation conducted by Heiller in a manner to suggest that, of the lesser-known Viennese conductors, he has the best feeling for this style. Admirable sound.

*No. 53 in D ("Imperial"). VSY, Sacher, Ep LC 3038 (*No. 67). HIS, Stokowski, V LM 1073 (*Liszt: Les Préludes).*

Although Sacher is not the orchestral technician Stokowski is, he knows his way around Haydn. Both works are soundly played and well reproduced. The Stokowski performance is very adroit, but the second side *Préludes* is a smaller inducement than Sacher's paired symphony.

*No. 54 in G. CHAM, Swarowsky, Ly 32 (*No. 70; Mozart: Paris overture, K.311a).*

The strings of this ensemble are quite capable, the brass and tympani less productive of pleasure. Swarowsky's manner is thoroughgoing, the end product pleasurable. Fairly good recording.

No. 55 in E flat ("The Schoolmaster"). VSY, Scherchen, W WL 5066 (No. 104).

One of the more volatile Haydn scores, which would profit from a lighter touch than Scherchen provides. His treatment is methodical, but not very enlivening. Good sound.

*No. 56 in C. VSY, Heiller, HS 1039 (*No. 52).*

See entry under No. 52.

*No. 60 in C ("Il Distratto"). GFO, Gui, V LHMV 1064 (*Mozart: Symphony No. 38 in D).*

A masterful work, though of no performance history at all in this country. Gui's direction is decidedly apropos, and the fine ensemble (substantially the Royal Philharmonic) is splendidly reproduced.

*No. 61 in D. DSTR, Wöldike, HS 1047 (*Mozart: Concerto for Clarinet).*

A work of particular euphony, strongly delivered by Wöldike, and beautifully reproduced.

*No. 64 in A. VSY, Swoboda, W WL 5023 (*No. 91).*

Swoboda's choice of material is much to his credit, but not his treatment of it. The recording is not of the sort that made Westminster's reputation.

*No. 67 in F major. VSY, Sacher, Ep LC 3038 (*No. 53).*

Sacher handles this chugging work, in the manner of the "Farewell," with style, and the reproduction is notably good for detail as well as for total sound.

*No. 70 in D. CHAM, Swarowsky, Ly 32 (*See No. 54).*

As in the paired work, the balance is often faulty on behalf of the tympani. The slow movement and finale are notable for contrapuntal ingenuities, well managed by Swarowsky.

No. 73 in D ("Hunt"). HOL, Newstone, HS L 1052 (No. 49).

Freed from the oppressive competition of Scherchen, Newstone's sensitivity and purpose amount to more that is complementary to this work than to *"La Passione."* Excellent orchestral playing, especially in the finale based on *La Fedeltà premiata.* Fine reproduction.

No. 77 in B flat, No. 78 in C minor. SYM, Swoboda, CH 30.

No. 77, with its slow movement reminiscent of Mozart's *"Il mio tesoro,"* deserves better than Swoboda gives it. No. 78 fares better, though here too the slow movement is rushed. Acceptable recording.

*No. 80 in D minor. VSY, Scherchen, WL 5050 (*No. 103).*

A particular beauty among the works rescued from oblivion by Dr. Alfred Einstein, with a slow movement of sterling qualities. Scherchen plays it to near-perfection, but the recording is only passable.

*No. 82 in C ("The Bear"). VSY, Sternberg, HS 1008 (*No. 85).*

A creditable effort for Sternberg, and reasonably well reproduced. The work invites a conductorial master hand, however, which Sternberg is not yet.

Nos. 83 in G minor ("The Hen") and 84 in E flat. CHAM, Heiller, HS 1015.

One of the poorer products of this agency, interpretatively limited and dull in tone quality.

*No. 85 in B flat ("The Queen of France"). MGMO, Solomon, MGO E 3109 (*K. P. E. Bach-Steinberg: Concerto in D). VSO, Baltzer, HS 1008 (*No. 82).*

Despite its esteem, prior to the Haydn revival, this fine work fares poorly in both performances. The recent MGM is dismally engineered, with shrill strings and cutting woodwinds, the Haydn Society afflicted with other ills. Solomon's performance is the better of the two.

No. 87 in A. VSO, Swarowsky, HS 1018 (**No. 89*).

A sparkling little work, though No. 2 in the Paris sequence rather than the last, as the B & H placement would suggest. Diligent performance, clear but not too sonorous reproduction.

No. 88 in G. BPH, Furtwängler, D DX 119 [2] (**Schubert: Symphony in C, No. 7*). *DSTR, Busch, V LHMV 1019* (**Mozart: Symphony in C, No. 36*). *VSO, Scherchen, W WL 5178* (**No. 93*).

Inasmuch as none of these is positively wonderful (though all are superior to the unmentioned playings of Ormandy and Toscanini), the preferable procedure would be to acquire Furtwängler's generally good, excellently reproduced version, incident to his magnificent Schubert C major. The Busch is hearty, a shade coarsely reproduced, the Scherchen overdone in virtually all respects.

No. 89 in F. VSO, Swarowsky, HS LP 1018 (**No. 87*).

A little-known counterpart of the preceding work, and, like it, commissioned by a merchant named Tost. It is not so spacious a work, but one of fine materials and workmanship. Lively performance, well reproduced.

No. 91 in E flat. VSO, Swoboda, W WL 5023 (**No. 64*).

A "big" work, as its position on the brink of the London symphonies would suggest, and barely known. Swoboda exposes it, so to speak, but the opportunities it contains are not developed fully. Too much top in the recording, too little bottom. Plenty of clarity, however.

No. 92 in G ("Oxford"). CO, Szell, C ML 4268 (**No. 101*). *LSO, Krips, L LL 780* (**Mozart: Symphony No. 40 in G minor*). *VSO, Scherchen, W WL 5137* (**No. 94*).

A clear line of distinction may exist among these works, but it is too thin to be traced by me. All are excellent, with Szell's the most spirited, Krips's the best-sounding, and Scherchen's the most probing. Equating one thing and another (including the qualities of the musicians involved), the order above is win, place, and show—each by less than a nose.

No. 93 in D. RPO, Beecham, C ML 4374 (**Handel: Faithful Shepherd*). *VSO, Scherchen, W WL 5178* (**No. 88*). *ASO, Singer, Rem 199-110* (**Schubert: Symphony No. 3*).

In refinement and elegance, Beecham holds a slight but audible advantage over Scherchen, though the latter's performance is of the first class. Tonally, the two are excellent in different styles, with the Vienna sound cleaner but a little coarser than the English. Singer's economy-price performance is decidedly good in style (what better-known conductor does this pseudonym cover?) and very decently reproduced.

*No. 94 in G ("Surprise"). RPO, Beecham, C ML 4453 (*No. 103). ACG, Van Beinum, L LL 491 (*Mozart: Symphony No. 33). VPH, Furtwängler, V LHMV 1018 (*Mozart: Kleine Nachtmusik). BPH, Schmidt-Isserstedt, Cap P 8038 (*Mozart: Kleine Nachtmusik). VSO, Scherchen, W WL 5137 (*No. 92). NBC, Toscanini, V LM 1789 (*Mozart: Symphony No. 40 in G minor).*

The preference previously allotted to Schmidt-Isserstedt is regretfully withdrawn in view of the *status quo* as sound of that otherwise admirable effort. In any case, the versions of Beecham, Van Beinum, and Furtwängler add more vigor of thought and finesse of orchestral detail to Haydn's concept than S-I did, and all are uncommonly fine recordings, the Furtwängler being an especially faithful likeness of the great Vienna Philharmonic. Scherchen makes a ponderous thing of this first movement, Toscanini an impossibly impersonal one. Neither is redeemed by what follows.

*No. 95 in C minor. VSY, Scherchen, W WL 5045 (*No. 100).*

Not since the pre-war Harty recording has there been a suitable treatment of this superior work and its fine slow movement in particular. Inasmuch as the overside "Military" is a notable phonographic occurrence, further words may be spared.

*No. 96 in D ("Miracle"). ACG, Van Beinum, L LL 854 (*No.* 97). *VSO, Scherchen, W WL 5111 (*No. 98). VPH, Walter, V LCT 6015* [2] *(*Mahler: Symphony No. 9).*

The issue between Van Beinum and Walter was resolved in the former's favor when both were represented by 78-rpm issues. Van Beinum's new performance substantially outdistances the dubbed Walter, and gives me more pleasure, in its orchestral nuances and subtleties, than the excellent Scherchen. However, if a choice is determined by a preference in second sides, either of these will satisfy.

*No. 97 in C. VSY, Scherchen, W WL 5062 (*No. 102). ACG, Van Beinum, L LL 854 (*No. 96).*

Remarkably successful close-up microphoning gives the Scherchen a dimension of realism not heard in the fine-sounding but more conventional Van Beinum. In musical treatment, the virtues are equal, and high, in both instances.

*No. 98 in B flat. VSO, Scherchen, W WL 5111 (*No. 96).*

Thoughtful, effective work by Scherchen in a score too seldom heard. Good sound.

*No. 99 in E flat. VSO, Scherchen, W WL 5102 (*No. 101, "Clock"). LSO, Kisch, 10" L LS 171.*

Neither of these is a match for the earlier version of Beecham (C Set 264), no longer available, but the brusque Scherchen does not, at least, perpetrate the solecism of Kisch in splitting the slow movement over two sides. For the impatient, Scherchen will suffice.

*No. 100 in G ("Military"). VSY, Scherchen, W WL 5045 (*No. 95). LPO, Van Beinum, L LP 339 (*No. 104).*

Not only in his divining of Haydn's purpose in the instrumentation of this work, but also in his feeling for its totality, Scherchen is far ahead of any competitor, including the usually able Van Beinum. The Westminster recording, with its sweet woodwinds and thunderous drums, is one of the notable accomplishments on LP.

*No. 101 in D ("Clock"). NBC, Toscanini, V LM 1038 (*Mozart: Symphony No. 35). PHO, Ormandy, C ML 4268 (*No. 92). VSO, Scherchen, W WL 5102 (*No. 99). ASO, Busch, Rem 199-149 (*Beethoven: Symphony No. 8).*

Unquestionably the most absorbing performance among these is Toscanini's, but the tight, dead sound is more of self-punishment than most will willingly endure in these days of opulence and warmth in such matters. Ormandy's is very well accomplished, with somewhat more flexibility and lightness than Scherchen's. Sound in both cases is excellent. At the price, Busch's well-phrased performance is attractive.

*No. 102 in B flat. VSY, Scherchen, W 5062 (*No. 97).*

This performance is a tribute to the consistency of Scherchen rather than to his best capacities as a conductor of Haydn. It rouses some curiosity as to a reissue of the well-remembered Koussevitzky (V Set 529). It wouldn't measure to this standard tonally, but it might probe deeper emotionally.

*No. 103 in E flat ("Drum Roll"). VSY, Scherchen, W WL 5050 (*No. 80). RPO, Beecham, C ML 4453 (*No. 94). LPO, Solti, 10" L LS 124.*

The Scherchen and Beecham versions will be automatic acquisitions for those who also indulge Haydnesque fancy for the No. 80 in D minor and the "Surprise." However, the preference here is clearly for Scherchen, who performs perceptively and with ideal assistance from the engineers. Solti's poised interpretation is marred by a break in the slow movement.

*No. 104 in D ("London"). VSY, Scherchen, W WL 5066 (*No. 55). LPO, Beecham, C ML 4771 (*Schubert: Symphony No. 5). BSO, Munch, V LM 9034 (*No. 94).*

The Beecham sounds quite persuasive until one measures its good pre-war reproduction against the much better post-war reproduction of Scherchen. Stylistically, the latter is as good in his gruffer way as Beecham in his more elegant one. All the values are superior to those in the Munch.

*Toy Symphony. SYM, Leibowitz, Oc 29 (*Gluck: Concerto for Flute). SYM, Weingartner, C ML 4776 (*Mozart: Symphony No. 39, etc.).*

The processing of the Weingartner is rather poor, inclining one to the brighter sound of the Leibowitz.

*Symphony in C. SAL, Fekete, Mer MG 10066 (*Handel: Jephtha Suite).*

A work of dubious authenticity, but with a worthwhile slow movement. The performance is energetic, the processing rather shrill.

Sinfonia Concertante

*In B flat, opus 84. PRO, Reinhardt, Vox PL 7390 (*Concerto for Cello).*

A richly textured, carefully elaborated work for small orchestra and solo violin (Reinhold Barchet), oboe (Friedrich Milde), bassoon (Hugo Gehring), and cello (Siegfried Barchet). The spirited playing is not always exact in pitch, but the processing is satisfactory.

HERBERT, VICTOR (1859-1924)

Pan Americana; American Fantasy; Irish Rhapsody. PHP, Ormandy, 10" C AL 21.

Lively batoneering by Ormandy, brilliantly reproduced.

HÉROLD, LOUIS (1791-1833)

*Zampa: Overture. NBC, Toscanini, 10" V LRM 7014 (*Humperdinck: Hansel and Gretel Prelude; Liadov: Kikimora).*

A reminder, lest this be overlooked, that it is one of Toscanini's most dashing performances, played in a manner to out-*Zampa* all *Zampas*. Very good sound.

HINDEMITH, PAUL (1895-)

*Concert Music for Strings and Brass. PHO, Ormandy, C ML 4816 (*Mathis der Maler).*

Excellent articulation under Ormandy's direction, good firm sound. Also, the paired side is a preferable version in its category.

The Demon (Ballet-Pantomime). SCA, Caracciolo, Col LPS 1036.

An oddity of 1924, of which neither the conducting nor the reproduction is magnetizing. However, the sounds are distinguishable, for those interested in this phase of Hindemith's career.

*Kammermusik No. 4, opus 36, No. 3. Rybar, WIN, Swoboda, W 5074 (*Theme and Four Variations).*

Musicianly effort all around, but the recording is not up to later Westminster standards.

*Kammermusik, opus 24, No. 1. LOS, Scherman, 10" D DL 7529 (*Stravinsky: Suites pour Petit Orchestre).*

Effective work by Scherman, bright in sound.

*Mathis der Maler. PHO, Ormandy, C ML 4816 (*Concert Music for Strings and Brass). BPH, Hindemith, 10" Cap L 8003.*

Among current versions, Ormandy's is outstanding for justice of treatment and richness of sound (likewise the overside). Hindemith's own performance has considerable value, but it is a pre-war recording, of the mid-thirties, and accordingly limited.

*Noblissima Visione. PHO, Ormandy, C ML 4177 (*Symphonic Metamorphosis on Theme by Weber).*

Columbia's prevailing thoughtfulness in combining works of this composer on the same disc is a boon here, adding Szell's spirited performance of the *Symphonic Metamorphosis* to the *Noblissima Visione* (also identified as the score for the ballet *St. Francis*). Better sound in Philadelphia than Cleveland, but both are good.

*Der Schwanendreher. Primrose, CHAM, Pritchard, C ML 4905 (*Walton: Concerto for Viola).*

A sumptuous performance by Primrose and superb English recording do something but not everything to alleviate the grit-in-the-teeth taste of this music. When the composer grants the instrument a consecutive line to sing, Primrose does it peerlessly.

Symphonic Metamorphosis on a Theme by Weber. CO, Szell, C ML 4177 (*Nobilissima Visione*). CHO, Kubelik, Mer 50024 (*Schoenberg: Five Pieces*).

My preference for the Szell version coupled with Ormandy's treatment of the overside work has been registered under the title of the latter. Kubelik's vitality is coupled with brilliant sound, but the overside, though well played, is less attractive. (The Hindemith is also available on Mer 50027, in team with the *Concerto Grosso* of Bloch.)

Symphony in E flat. JSO, Janssen, C ML 4387.

Dull-sounding studio recording does not enhance the appeal of a work whose design hardly warrants the amount of musical resource employed.

Theme and Four Variations. ZS, Foss, 10" D DL 7501. Holletschek, VSY, Swoboda, W 5074 (*Kammermusik No. 4*). Aller, CAO, Slatkin, Cap P 8230 (*Shostakovich: Concerto in C minor*).

This is the work sometimes also described as *The Four Temperaments*. The Foss-Zimbler Sinfonietta endeavor strikes me as the most acceptable, not only for inherent musical virtue, but also becasue it eschews extraneous matter. The vital factor in a choice among the others is preference in pairings, for both performances of Hindemith are competent without being exceptional. The sound values are about even.

HOFFMANN, JOHANN (1730-1793)

Concerto in D. Lindner-Bonelli, LRO, Pflüger, U LP 7110 (*Dittersdorf: Concerto for Harp*).

A work of Mozartian suggestions, with a mandolin solo part utilized much in the manner of the accompaniment to the *serenata* in *Don Giovanni.* Effective performances, reasonably well reproduced.

HOLST, GUSTAV (1874-1934)

The Planets. LPP, Boult, W 5235.

Boult's latest version of this work is an even more notable service to Holst than his earlier one, and one of the remarkable recordings of the LP era. Some of the climaxes are astonishing.

St. Paul Suite. BNO, Neel, 10" L LS 94 (*Grace Williams: *Fantasia*).
An enthusiasm of long standing with Neel, and broadly reproduced.

HONEGGER, ARTHUR (1892-)

*Concertino for Piano and Orchestra. Jacquinot, PHI, Fistoulari, 10" MGM E 122 (*Milhaud: Concertino). Levant, COL, Reiner, 10" C ML 2156 (*Debussy: L'Après-midi, etc.).*

Levant has some interesting ideas on this music, but the balance of orchestra and piano is inferior to that in the Jacquinot, as is the total sound.

*Concerto da Camera. LACS, Byrns, Cap P 8115 (*Strauss: Duet Concertino).*

Excellent solo playing by the flute (Cleghorn) and the English horn players, and bright reproduction.

King David. ORD, Honegger, W WAL 204 [2].

Long awaited, this is also less than what was hoped for, with too much prominence for some voice parts, not enough orchestral resonance, etc. Honegger does well, but hardly brilliantly, by his fine work.

*Pastorale d'Été. LAM, Martinon, Ep 3058 (*Dukas: L'Apprenti Sorcier; Fauré: Pavane; Roussel: Le Festin de l'Araignée).*

This and the Fauré *Pavane* are the distinctive items of this collection, for the clean, musicianly treatment that makes them welcome in the absence of other performances does not suffice in the Dukas and Roussel works. Fine sound throughout.

Symphonie Liturgique. DPH, Stoschek, U LP 7090.

A curious-sounding affair, dull in sound and without much revelation of the composer's purpose.

*Symphony No. 2 for Strings and Trumpet. MGS, Solomon, MGM 3104 (*Rivier: Symphony No. 2).*

This does not equal, in richness or dramatic force, the performances heard from the BSO and Munch, but it is clearly, cleanly played and reproduced.

*Symphony No. 5. BSO, Munch, V LM 1741 (*Roussel: Bacchus et Ariane).*

One of the most notable additions by Munch to his American catalogue, and successfully reproduced.

HOVHANESS, ALAN (1911-)

*Concerto No. 1 ("Arevakal"). ERS, Hanson, Mer 40005 (*Cowell: Symphony No. 4, etc.).*

A typical functioning of Hovhaness's special kind of muse, aptly propounded by Hanson. Live sound.

HUMPERDINCK, ENGELBERT (1854-1921)

*Hansel und Gretel: Overture, Dream Pantomime, CGO, Hollingsworth, MGM 3072 (*Grieg: Sigurd Jorsalfar).*

Nicely turned performances by Hollingsworth, cleanly reproduced.

*Hansel und Gretel: Overture only. NBC, Toscanini, 10" V LRM 7014 (*Hérold: Zampa overture; Liadov: Kikimora).*

Much the best recorded Humperdinck, broadly reproduced.

*Hansel und Gretel: Dream Pantomime only. LPO, Collins. 10" L LD 9025 (*Strauss: Rosenkavalier waltzes).*

Sumptuous sound and warmly melodic phrasing are the virtues of Collins as a conductor of Humperdinck. The Strauss is reasonably good, but not of the same quality.

IBERT, JACQUES (1890-)

Concerto

*For Flute and Orchestra. Graf, WIN, Desarzens, CH 1109 (*Martin: Concerto for Winds, Percussion, Strings).*

Bright, fluent performance by the excellent Graf, with appropriate assistance by the orchestra. Good sound.

Concertino

*Concertino da Camera. Mulé, PPO, Rosenthal, 10" Cap L 8231 (*Debussy: Rhapsody).*

As a saxophonist, Mulé has few superiors, and Rosenthal's collaboration is first-rate. Good sound.

Works for Orchestra

Capriccio. *VSY, Swoboda, W 5061 (*Divertissement, etc.).*
An engaging conceit, reasonably well managed by Swoboda. The recording is rather undernourished.

Divertissement. *OSC, Désormière, L LL 884 (*Chopin: Les Sylphides).*
*CAO, Slatkin, Cap P 8270 (*Saint-Saëns: Carnival of the Animals).*
Sparkling music-making under Désormière's knowing direction, aptly reproduced. The combination with his fine *Sylphides* is a decided asset. Slatkin's direction is not so persuasive, and the recording is marred by hifi overemphasis on individual instruments.

Escales. *HIS, Stokowski, V LM 151 (*Sibelius: Swan of Tuonela; Granados: Intermezzo; etc.).*
The color values in these works are brilliantly managed by Stokowski, and the sound is decidedly good.

Suite Elizabethiane. *VSY, Swoboda, W 5061 (*Capriccio, Divertissement).*
Emmy Loose is the vocalist and the music is well worth knowing. However, the *Divertissement*, which occupies much of the disc, is better performed on another record.

INDY, VINCENT d' (1851-1931)

Works for Orchestra

Istar, Symphonic Variations. *WES, Fistoulari, MGM E 3062 (*Prelude to Fervaal; Dukas: La Peri).*
Not the ideal solution to any of the problems posed by this disc, but at least interesting matter throughout. Clear recording.

Symphony on a French Mountain Air. *Casadesus, NYPH, Munch, C ML 4815 (*Franck: Variations Symphoniques).*
A high degree of mutual understanding is the special interest in this collaboration. The recording is a factor neither of advantage nor of disadvantage.

Symphony No. 2 in B flat. *SFS, Monteux, V LCT 1125.*
A new edition of this work is in order, and Monteux is the man to do it. His purpose here is abundantly evident, despite sound that does not conform to current standards.

Opera Excerpt (Orchestral)

Fervaal: Introduction to Act I. *WES, Fistoulari, MGM E 3062* (**Istar, etc.*).
See entry under *Istar.*

IPPOLITOV-IVANOV, MICHAEL (1859-1935)

Caucasian Sketches. PHI, Malko, V LBC 1019 (**Saint-Saëns: Danse Macabre; etc.*). *PHI, Schuechter, 10" MGM E 137. OSC, Désormière, L LL 440* (**Tchaikovsky: Sleeping Beauty*).
None of these is triumphant in finesse or spirit, which inclines me to recommend the Malko for its reasonable price. The MGM's Schuechter is capable, the music well reproduced without extraneous matter. The Désormière is not as attractive as some of his other efforts.

IRELAND, JOHN (1879-)

Concertino Pastorale. MGS, Solomon, MGM E 3074 (**Britten: Simple Symphony*).
Ireland's engaging work is deftly managed by Solomon, and well reproduced.

IVES, CHARLES (1874-1954)

Symphony No. 2. VPA, Adler, SPA 39.
Hardly the most spirited performance imaginable, and rather dead on the acoustic end.
Symphony No. 3. NGO, Bales, WCFM 1.
A rather ambitious task for Bales, and not too well served by his recording resources.

JACOBI, FREDERICK (1891-1952)

Concerto for Violin. Gertler, SYM, Jacobi, SPA 78 (**Concertino for Piano*).

Gertler is a notably good violinist (see Berg Concerto), as Irene Jacobi, the soloist in the overside work, is a good pianist. Sound values not brilliant.

JAMES, PHILIP (1890-)

Symphony No. 1. VPA, Adler, SPA 38.
Something for the library, if not the home. The recording is an improvement on earlier SPA efforts.

JANÁČEK, LEOŠ (1854-1928)

*Sinfonietta for Orchestra. LRO, Neumann, U LP 7030 (*Rossini-Respighi: Rossiniana).*
A work for which an appropriate word would be "peculiar," as it projects a strong musical impulse without the craftsmanship to bind the ideas together. Sharp, edgy recording, especially of the brass.

*Taras Bulba. VSY, Swoboda, W WL 5071 (*Suite for String Orchestra).*
The early work for strings is a much more ingratiating piece of music than either of the more ambitious works included in this compilation. A particularly brisk, well directed performance (with the WIN ensemble), very well reproduced.

JOHNSON, HUNTER (1906-)

*Concerto for Piano and Chamber Orchestra. Kirkpatrick, Hull, CH 1189 (*Honegger: Symphony for Strings).*
Vigorous exposition by soloist and conductor, cleanly reproduced. As much applies to the overside Honegger, though it lacks tonal richness.

*Letter to the World (Dance Suite). CHAM, Hull, CH 1151 (*Vaughan Williams: Flos Campi).*
Vigorous direction by Hull, and satisfactory performance. The recording is well balanced, but dull in sound.

JOLIVET, ANDRÉ (1905-)

Concerto for Piano and Orchestra. Descaves, OTCE, Bour, WL 5239

(**Concerto for Trumpet, Piano, and Strings; Andante for Strings*).

Lucette Descaves is a well-qualified pianist, as Serge Baudo is in the overside work (Roger del Motte, trumpet), and Bour is obviously devoted to the work of his countryman. Clear, not very resonant sound.

KABALEVSKY, DMITRI (1904-)

Concertos

For Cello and Orchestra. Shafran, USSR, Kabalevsky, Van VRS 6005 (**Glazounow: Concerto for Violin*).

A magnificent cellist, Shafran plays the melodious if rather derivative work splendidly. Better than average USSR sound. The coupled instrumentalist is David Oistrakh in one of the numerous pairings of his superior playing of Glazounow.

For Violin and Orchestra. Oistrakh, USSR, Kabalevsky, Van VRS 6002 (**Khrennikov: Much Ado About Nothing*).

A stronger work than the preceding, and masterfully played by Oistrakh. Sound orchestral work under the composer's direction, tolerable reproduction.

Opera Excerpts (Orchestral)

Colas Breugnon (Suite). PHI, Schuechter, MGM E 3112 (**Prokofiev: The Gambler excerpts*).

Not much of a musical gain is effected by the addition to the racy overture of a "*Fête populaire*," "*Fleau publique (la peste)*," and "*Insurrection*." Lively but not outstanding direction by Schuechter, and typically crisp MGM microphoning.

Work for Orchestra

The Comedians. BPO, Fiedler, V LM 1106 (**Anderson: Classical Juke Box*). *NYPH, Kurtz, C ML 4083* (**Lecocq: Fille du Mme. Angot suite*).

A virtual toss-up, with merits about even in performance and reproduction. The second-side Lecocq is well worth having.

KALINNIKOV, VASILI (1866-1901)

Symphony No. 1 in G minor. USSR, Rachlin, W WL 5136.

Agreeable music, well performed. However, the sound from the Russian tape is far from the Westminster standard, though skillfully doctored.

Symphony No. 2 in A. BSI, Rachlin, Per 566.

The melodic charm of this score is considerable, but so are its repetitions. Persuasive performance, rather poorly reproduced.

KAY, ULYSSES (1917-)

*Concerto for Orchestra. OTLF, Perlea, Rem R 199-173 (*Lockwood: Concerto for Organ and Brasses).*

The resonance of the recording tends to blur somewhat the lines of the complicated texture. Playing and direction are excellent.

KHATCHATURIAN, ARAM (1903-)

Ballet Music

Gayne (Suites Nos. 1 and 2). NYPH, Kurtz, C ML 4030.

An adequate solution to the *Gayne* problem, assuming it is a problem. Vigorous performance, well reproduced.

Concertos

For Piano and Orchestra. Lympany, LPO, Fistoulari, L LL 692. Kapell, BSO, Koussevitzky, V LM 1006.

The collaboration of the K's has its interests historically, but the Lympany performance is thoroughgoing and much more vividly reproduced.

For Violin and Orchestra. Igor Oistrakh, PHI, Goossens, An 35100. David Oistrakh, SYM, Gauk, Mer 10000.

Whatever else may be said about Khatchaturian's stylized trickery, it is the only work in this volume to attract father and son as interpreters. Thanks to the superb English recording and the subtle hand of Goossens with the orchestra, Prince Igor comes off better than King David.

*For Violoncello and Orchestra (1946). Posegga, LRO, Kempe, U 7119 (*Shostakovich: Concerto for Piano, opus 35).*

The kind of flair to make this music appealing is lacking in this performance. The orchestra tends to blanket the solo instrument.

Incidental Music

Masquerade (Suite). OSC, Blareau, 10" L LD 9100.
French lightness may not be most of what is wanted in this music, but the results seem to me superior to those otherwise available, especially in sound.

Symphony

No. 2. NPH, Khachaturian, Col CRLP 136.
Khachaturian pleads his case vigorously, if not with persuasive effect on this listener. The recording is thin, lacking the body currently deemed desirable.

KHRENNIKOV, TIKHON (1913-)

Much Ado About Nothing (Incidental Music). USSR, Stassevich, Van VRS 6002.
As far as style is concerned, Khrennikov could be Kabalevsky and vice versa, but the relationship, in either case, to Shakespeare, is rather casual. Reasonably good sound.

KODÂLY, ZOLTÂN (1882-)

*Dances from Galanta. ORB, L. G. Jochum, U URLP 7014 (*Psalmus Hungaricus).*
Adroit performance by the Linz Jochum (see Bruckner), beautifully reproduced on a large, resonant scale.

*Háry János (Suite). PHI, Schuechter, MGM E 3019 (*Dohnányi: Ruralia Hungarica). PHI, Solti, D DL 9518 (*Dances from Galanta).*
An excellent performance of the Kodály, as Schuechter was credited also with in the Dohnányi. If, for any reason, the coupling is unappealing, the Solti performances are both first-class.

*Psalmus Hungaricus. ORB, Krebs, Rother, U URLP 7014 (*Dances from Galanta).*
A proper companion piece to the *Dances from Galanta* noted above. The recording is not quite so good, but it passes.

*Te Deum. VSY, Swoboda, W 5001 (*Theater Overture).*
The qualities in this work are considerable; Swoboda's effort is

commendable. The sound, as in the item below, is not fully conveyed.

Theater Overture. VSY, Swoboda, W 5001.

Suitable performance by Swoboda, but, as the very first in Westminster's series, less than ideally recorded.

KORNGOLD, ERICH (1897-)

*Concerto for Violin and Orchestra. LAP, Heifetz, Wallenstein, V LM 1782 (*Lalo: Symphonie Espagnole).*

Splendid fiddling by Heifetz, and generally good technical work all around. The music, however, is mostly on the other side.

KŘENEK, ERNST (1900-)

*Symphonic Elegy. NYPH, Mitropoulos, C ML 4524 (*Schoenberg: Erwartung).*

Dazzling performance by the Philharmonic's strings, cogently directed by Mitropoulos. Fine recording.

KUPFERMAN, MEYER (1926-)

*Little Symphony. VSO, Litschauer, Van VRS 434 (*Swanson: Short Symphony).*

I am not persuaded that Litschauer wholly understands the idiom of this work, which does not come off as well as it has in some live performances. Good enough sound.

LALO, ÉDOUARD (1823-1892)

Ballet Music

*Namouna (Suite 1). LAM, Fournet, Ep LC 3049 (*Le Roi d'Ys overture; Norwegian Rhapsody).*

An appealing package of Lalo, carefully selected, well wrapped, and attractively served.

Concertos

*For Cello and Orchestra. Nelsova, LPO, Boult, L LL 964 (*Saint-Saëns: Concerto No. 1). Michelin, HAAR, Verheij, CH 1162 (*Fauré: Elégie).*

Nelsova's suave sound and the energetic direction of Boult are well honored by the effective reproduction. Michelin also plays well, but his sound is not so well conveyed.

For Violin and Orchestra. Solovieff, VSO, Swoboda, CH 1143.

Solovieff's playing is both energetic and tasteful, the recording suitably balanced.

Overture

*Le Roi d'Ys. LAM, Fournet, Ep 3049 (*Namouna Suite No. 1; Norwegian Rhapsody). BSO, Munch, V LM 1700 (*Ravel: Rhapsodie Espagnole, La Valse; Berlioz: Beatrice and Benedict, etc.).*

Fournet has congruity in repertory and resonance in sound on his side, but the Munch performance is more flavorsome and broadly phrased.

Work for Orchestra

*Norwegian Rhapsody. LAM, Fournet, Ep 3049 (*Namouna Suite No. 1, etc.).*

This is the most vigorous performance in the sequence, and a desirable addition to the Lalo literature.

Work for Orchestra and Solo Instrument

Symphonie Espagnole. Menuhin, OCC, Fournet, V LM 1011. Heifetz, RCAO, Steinberg, 10" V LM 127. Campoli, LPO, Van Beinum, L LL 763.

Menuhin is mentioned first because his well-played version includes all five movements of the work. However, the Heifetz is more dazzling in detail, more exuberant in sum, though the recording is weighted on the side of the soloist. For a combination of suavity and beautifully polished sound, the Campoli-Van Beinum is outstanding.

LAMBERT, CONSTANT (1905-1951)

*Concerto for Piano and Nine Players. Pressler, Bloomfield, MGM 3081 (*Berners: Piano Pieces).*

A work of the early thirties, liberal in its jazz allusions, and ending, perversely, with an elegiac tribute to Philip Heseltine (known also as Peter Warlock). Not the smallest attraction of the issue is the virtuoso group of players, which includes Harry Glantz, trumpet, Janos Starker, cello, Saul Goodman, percussion, and Augustin Duques, clarinet. Excellent recording.

*Horoscope. PHI, Lambert, 10" C ML 2083 (*Easdale: Red Shoes).*

The later version by Irving (L LL 771) has some sound values not found in Lambert's own, but this is otherwise preferable.

*Rio Grande. PHI, Lambert, 10" C ML 2145 (*Britten: Sea Pieces from Peter Grimes).*

What many consider Lambert's most successful work, splendidly presented by the composer and warmly reproduced.

LECOCQ, ALEXANDRE (1832-1918)

*La Fille du Mme. Angot (Suite). NYPH, Kurtz, C ML 4083 (*Kabalevsky: Comedians).*

Kurtz has a bright hand for music such as this, and the crisp playing is well reproduced.

LIADOV, ANATOL (1855-1914)

*Baba Yaga. ORB, Schartner, U 7117 (*Arensky: Silhouettes; Amirov: Caucasian Dances).*

The playing is satisfactory, but the recording does not have the color values to do Liadov's concept justice.

*Kikimora. NBC, Toscanini, 10" V LRM 7014 (*Hérold: Overture to Zampa; Humperdinck: Prelude to Hansel and Gretel).*

A highly atmospheric, remarkably well controlled performance, and, like the other material of this disc, soundly reproduced.

LISZT, FRANZ (1811-1886)

Concertos

For Piano and Orchestra

Nos. 1 and 2. Farnadi, VSO, Scherchen, W 5168. Frugoni, PRO, Swarowsky, Vox PL 8390.

Both performers are more concerned with musical values than with personal display, which is not invariably the case with interpreters of these works. Farnadi has a more active sense of Lisztian style than Frugoni, and her recording is decidedly more brilliant. Likewise I prefer the work of Scherchen to that of Swarowsky.

*No. 1 in E flat. Arrau, PHO, Ormandy, C ML 4665 (*Hungarian Fantasy). Schiøler, DNO, Dobrowen, V LHMV 1031 (*Beethoven: Sonata 23). Cherkassky, PHI, Fistoulari, V LBC 1041 (*Consolation No. 3; Don Juan Fantasy).*

Preferences in music of this kind are largely personal and not subject to much objective recommendation. However, of the numerous versions currently available, the Arrau-Ormandy is the most powerfully in the virtuoso tradition and well reproduced, the Schioler-Dobrowen the most musical and the best reproduced, and the Cherkassky-Fistoulari the most interesting in approach (somewhat slower than customary) and very good value for the price.

*No. 2 in A. Malcuzynski, PHI, Süsskind, An 35031 (*Sonata in B minor). Casadesus, CO, Szell, C ML 4588 (*Weber: Concertstück).*

Malcuzynski's way with this music has been admired for half a dozen years, and it profits here from much better sound than in its previous version. The Casadesus performance is not as flavorsome or as well reproduced, but the second-side *Concertstück* is the best available.

Rhapsodies

*Nos. 1 and 2. PHO, Ormandy, C ML 4132 (*Grieg: Peer Gynt Suite No. 1).*

Ormandy's qualifications for interpreting this music are first-rate, and the sound of the virtuoso orchestra is well reproduced. No versions of the individual Rhapsodies now available are of consequential interest.

No. 12. BAV, Nick, D DL 4000 (**Hungarian Rhapsody No. 2*).

A rather routine playing of this work, creditably reproduced.

Symphonies

Dante. LAP, Wallenstein, D DL 9670. VPA, Adler, SPA 44. OCC, Sebastian, U 7103.

The standards in this work are elusive, and not made more firm by the performances now available. Wallenstein's is reasonable and well recorded; the others are of comparable musical value, but not as good mechanically.

Faust. OCC, Sebastian, U 606 [2] (**Mazeppa*).

This doesn't conform to the expectable standards in this work, and patience may be cautioned. The recording is good.

Symphonic Poems

Ce qu'on entend sur la montagne. MTO, Stroble, Mer MG 10008.

Who Joseph Stroble is, I do not know, but he is an expert on this odd and provocative work. It is powerfully played, and surprisingly well reproduced.

Hungaria. MPH, Dolzycki, Mer MG 10058.

The musical content hardly merits two sides of an LP, especially as the recording is strident and full of irritating distortion.

Hunnenschlacht. PSL, Dixon, W L 5269 (**Les Préludes; Mazeppa; Orpheus*).

Good brisk work by Dixon, and expertly played by the orchestra, whose leader, David McCallum, is also leader of the Royal Philharmonic. Excellent recording of all the works included, mention of which will be found in the appropriate places.

Mazeppa. PSL, Dixon, W L 5269 (**Les Préludes; Mazeppa; Orpheus; etc.*).

As in the instance of *Hunnenschlact*, Dixon is full of a fine flair and enthusiasm for his subject, and has ample technique for realizing those virtues. Superb sound.

Orpheus. PSL, Dixon, W WL 5269 (**Mazeppa, etc.*).

As this is substantially the same orchestra which, as the Royal Philharmonic, made the previous best version under Beecham, it is far from an unfamiliar task for them. To this, Dixon adds ample energy of his own. Like the others on the generous disc (see above), a fine-sounding reproduction.

*Les Préludes. BSO, Monteux, V LM 1775 (*Scriabin: Poem of Ecstasy). PSL, Dixon, W WL 5269 (*Mazeppa; Orpheus; etc.). PHI, Galliera, An 35047 (*Tchaikovsky: Capriccio Italien). HIS, Stokowski, V LM 1073 (*Haydn: Symphony No. 83). ACG, Mengelberg, C RL 3039 (*Tchaikovsky: Romeo and Juliet).*

Although a fair number, these are less than half the versions now available. However, each has a distinction worth considering. The Monteux is perhaps the best performance I have ever heard, marvelously played and vividly reproduced. The Dixon is well played, beautifully reproduced, and—with three other works—an excellent value. Beyond these, the Galliera shows the Philharmonia as a truly great orchestra, and the Stokowski attests to this conductor's personal powers, in particularly high gear. As for the Mengelberg, it is a musical antique now available at costume-jewelry rates.

*Prometheus. OSC, Münchinger, 10" L LD 9153 (*Mephisto Waltz).*

Typically "rhetorical" Liszt, which might be another part of the *Faust Symphony*, though it has one element of interest: a climbing bass scale (just before the fugal section) which could be a reference to a device employed by Beethoven in his *Prometheus* music and, more prominently still, in the variations finale of the *Eroica* derived from that source. Münchinger's direction is persuasive, the London recording not as good as the house standard.

Works for Orchestra and Piano

*Hungarian Fantasy. Kilenyi, ASO, Prohaska, Rem R 199-61 (*Mozart: Concerto No. 23). Arrau, PHO, Ormandy, C ML 4665 (*Concerto No. 1).*

Despite the improbabilities of cost, the cheaper Kilenyi disc is more idiomatically played than the Arrau, and, aside from less rich orchestral tone, better recorded.

*Rhapsodie Espagnole. Petri, MIN, Mitropoulos, C RL 3040 (*Chopin: Preludes complete). Bachauer, NEW, Alec Sherman, V LM 9000 (*Mozart: Concerto No. 26).*

Busoni's transcription has two satisfactory exponents in Petri and Mitropoulos, and at the advantageous price the recording may be rated better than the point of origin would suggest. The more recent Bachauer is doubtless better in sound, but is not otherwise preferable.

*Todtentanz. Brailowsky, RCAO, Reiner, V LM 1195 (*Franck: Variations Symphoniques). Jacquinot, PHI, Fistoulari, 10" MGM E 182 (*Rimsky-Korsakov: Concerto).*

Brailowsky's virtuosity and Reiner's exposition of the orchestral score, plus excellent engineering, make for a performance well superior to the alternate listed. However, for the price-conscious, the MGM is worth its cost.

Miscellaneous

*Mephisto Waltz. OSC, Münchinger, 10" L LD 9153 (*Prometheus). NYPH, Rodzinski, 10" C ML 2057 (*Enesco: Roumanian Rhapsody No. 1).*

Congruent repertory and substantially superior recording are the advantages offered by the Münchinger disc. The Rodzinski is not particularly distinguished as a performance, and the recording is pre-LP.

LOCATELLI, PIETRO (1693-1764)

*Concerto da Camera for Clavier and Orchestra, in E flat. CHAM, Litschauer, Van VRS 418 (*Respighi: Trittico Botticelliano).*

Something of the same situation as noted below, with the added intrusion of a piano where a harpsichord would be more appropriate. However, the music is of such health and virility as to attract nevertheless. Clear sound, a little coarse.

Concerto Grosso (F minor); Trauersymphonie. VSY, Swoboda, W WL 5030.

Both of these works have very good musical reasons for being perpetuated, but Swoboda is hardly the man with the stylistic flair to make them vital. The results, then, are rather colorless, though the design of the patterns does emerge. Excellent string sound.

LOEFFLER, CHARLES M. (1861-1935)

*A Pagan Poem. PPO, Rosenthal, Cap P 8188 (*Scriabin: Poem of Ecstasy).*

Rosenthal's sympathy for the French idiom serves him well here. Very good sound.

LOUIS FERDINAND OF HOHENZOLLERN (1772-1806)

*Rondo for Piano and Orchestra. Graef, FRO, Kloss, Ly LL 26 (*Dittersdorf: Symphony in A minor).*

Melodious music in the manner of the lesser early Beethoven works, acceptably played and well reproduced.

LUIGINI, ALEXANDRE (1850-1906)

*Ballet Egyptien. BPO, Fiedler, V LM 1084 (*Massenet: Le Cid ballet music).*

Although rather short measure for a 12" LP side (barely twelve minutes), Fiedler's tasteful treatment and the fine sound of the Pops orchestra are hard to resist.

MacDOWELL, EDWARD (1861-1908)

Concertos for Piano and Orchestra, Nos. 1 and 2. Rivkin, VSO, Dixon, W 5190.

Rivkin plays both works with steady control and thorough understanding, well supported by Dixon's able direction and excellent technical means. The individual versions of the more familiar Concerto No. 2 are not as good.

Suite No. 2 (Indian). ERO, Hanson, Mer 40009.

On a rehearing, in adequate orchestral sound, it is remarkable how much the "Indian" influence of MacDowell resembles the "Negro" influence in Dvořák. Most sympathetic performance, well engineered, though the hall is not advantageous.

MAHLER, GUSTAV (1860-1911)

Symphonies

No. 1 in G ("Titan"). PRO, Horenstein, Vox PL 8050. ORB, Borsamsky, Van VRS 436. The same, U RLP 7080. PSO, Steinberg, Cap P 8224.

Considering the diverse points of origin, there is surprisingly little variation in these performances, with all the conductors well gaited to the task. Preference on the basis of orchestral sound and its reproduction goes to Horenstein, whose Vienna players are beautifully reproduced. The Borsamsky tape fares somewhat better on Vanguard than on Urania. Steinberg's excellent effort is marred by distant microphoning, lack of sound at a reasonable volume level.

No. 2 in C minor ("Resurrection"). VSY, Klemperer, soloists, Vox PL 7010 [2].

The noble spirit and grand proportions of this performance are one of a not too numerous number of LP's by Klemperer, considering his stature as a conductor. The recording is clear, but afflicted by a tonal shrillness typical of the early LP processing. The singers are good, especially Rössl-Majdan in "*Urlicht.*"

No. 3 in D minor. VPA, Adler, SPA 20/1/2 (**Fourteen Youth Songs, with Piano*).

This is one of the more diffuse and lengthy of the Mahler symphonies, diligently if not persuasively presented by Adler. The quality of sound is good, well balanced, and ample in quantity. For those interested, Rössl-Majdan sings the songs very well; the reproduction of her voice and of the piano played by Herbert Haefner is excellent.

No. 4 in G. NYPH, Walter, Halban, C ML 4031. ACG, Van Beinum, Ritchie, L LL 618.

Van Beinum's performance is recorded with more clarity and orchestral justice, but Walter's is reasonably represented, his superior understanding of this score self-apparent. Also, Halban is more a stylist in the vocal music than Ritchie.

No. 5 in C sharp minor. VSO, Scherchen, W WAL 207 [2] (**Symphony No. 10*). *NYPH, Walter, C SL 171* [2] (**Eight Songs*).

The margin between these performances is slight indeed, with Scherchen slightly more incisive in the dramatic passages, Walter more masterful in the lyrical. As the Westminster is slightly but perceptibly the better recording, I would prefer to have the unduplicated Symphony No. 10 (what there is of it) on the fourth side rather than the songs (Halban and Walter), which are elsewhere available.

No. 6 in A minor. VPA, Adler, SPA 59/60.

One of the weakest works of Mahler, not made more attractive by the powerful but rather strident sound of the strings and brass.

No. 7 in B minor. VSO, Scherchen, W WAL 211 [2]. *ORB, Rosbaud, U RLP 405* [2].

Through both his own effort and those of the collaborating engineers, Scherchen achieves substantially better results than Rosbaud. However, I would not commend it to anyone but devoted Mahlerites.

No. 8 in E ("Symphony of a Thousand"). VSY, Scherchen, C SL 164 [2].

Despite the sponsorship of Columbia, this is a rather second-class "actual performance" tape, poorly balanced for the microphone, and with more than a modicum of uncertain vocal work. Scherchen is in characteristic command, but little else is characteristic of his work.

No. 9 in D major. VSY, Horenstein, Vox PL 7600 [2]. *VPH, Walter, V LCT 6015* [2] (**Haydn: Symphony No. 96*).

Horenstein's version is a decade newer, at least, and accordingly superior in sound. However, Walter's pre-war public performance of July 16, 1938 is considerably improved in the LP form, and possesses substantial interest.

No. 10 in F sharp major (Adagio only). VSO, Scherchen, W WAL 207 (**Symphony No. 5*).

Although the impulse of this movement peters out before the end, it is good enough to be of interest to admirers of the composer. Excellent sound.

Works for Orchestra and Voices

Kindertotenlieder. Ferrier, VPH, Walter, 10" C ML 2187. Schey, HPO, Van Otterloo, Ep SC 6001 [2] (**Bruckner: Symphony No. 4*). *Anderson, SFS, Monteux, V LM 1146* (**Brahms: Alto Rhapsody*).

The subtlety and sureness of the late Ferrier's performance are more than can be approached, let alone equaled, by the others indicated. Moreover, Walter directs the orchestra with complete command, and the sound is beautifully appropriate. Schey sings well, in a not too cultured way, and Van Otterloo's direction is of much the same generalized competence. The conception of Anderson has much to be said for it, but her vocal control is far from what it ought to be. Excellent direction by Monteux and well-balanced sound.

Das Klagende Lied. VSO, Fekete, soloists, chorus, Mer MG 10102.

Despite its obscurity, this "dramatic cantata" contains more genuine music than some of Mahler's more celebrated scores. The performance, by both orchestra and soloists (Ilona Steingruber, Sieglinde Wagner, and Ernst Majkut), is reasonably good, the reproduction clear if shrill on the high end.

Das Knaben Wunderhorn (13 Songs). Poell, Sydney, VSO, Prohaska, Van RS 412/13 [2].

A collection that will do very well until an improbable superior appears, this has the solid virtues of good direction by Prohaska, excellent reproduction, and solid, if not spectacular, vocal work by Poell and Sydney. Included are *"Revelge," "Der Schildwache Nachtlied," "Der Tambourg'sell," "Trost im Ungluck," "Lied des Verfolgten im turm,"* sung by Poell, and *"Das Irdische Leben," "Wer Hat Dies Liedlein Erdacht," "Verlorne Muh," "Wo Hat die schonen Trompeten blasen," "Des Antonius von Padua fischpredigt,"* and *"Urlicht,"* sung by Sydney.

*Lieder aus der Jugendzeit. Felbermayer, Poell, VSO, Prohaska, Van VRS 421 (*Rückertlieder).*

Robert Heger and Lothar Windsperger are responsible for the orchestrations by which these engaging songs qualify for consideration here. They are very much in Mahler's style, as is the singing of the bright-voiced Felbermayer, somewhat less so that of the gruffer Poell. Fine sound. (Included are *"Scheiden und Meiden," "Fruhlingsmorgen,"* and *"Ich ging mit Lust durch einen grunen Wald"* by Felbermayer, and *"Hans und Grethe"* by Poell.)

*Lieder eines fahrenden gesellen. Brice, PSO, Reiner, C ML 4108 (*Bach: Excerpts from Mass in B minor, etc.). Metternich, ORB, Ludwig, U RLP 7016 (*Kindertotenlieder).*

The distinguishing factors of the Columbia disc remain Reiner's faultless conducting and the richness of the Brice voice. However, she does not always use it effectively, and the lack of resonance in the sound is a disadvantage. Metternich is, in this recording, not yet the singer he has since become, though the sound is superior. The recording is of the radio tape type, meaning clean but not very well balanced. (The vocalist in the overside *Kindertotenlieder* is the lugubrious Lorri Lail.)

*Rückertlieder (Five). Felbermayer, Poell, VSO, Prohaska, Van VRS 421 (*Lieder aus der Jugendzeit). Three. Ferrier, VPH, Walter, L LL 625/6 (*Lied von der Erde).*

The qualities of performance noted here are similar to those in the reverse side, with the additional fact that Poell makes very lethargic business of *"Ich bin der Welt abhanded gekommen"* and *"Liebst du um Schonheit."* Felbermayer is more listenable in *"Fruhlingsmorgen."* Ferrier sings *"Ich bin der Welt," "Ich Amet' Einen Lindenduft,"* and *"Um Mitternacht"* very expressively. Fine sound.

*Das Lied von der Erde. Ferrier, Patzak, VPH, Walter, L LL 625/6 (*Rückertlieder).*

One of the great recordings of this or any era, with wholly qualified interpreters working harmoniously under the direction of a conductor thoroughly attuned to the score. Superb orchestral playing and reproduction.

*Es sungen drei Engel. Felbermayer, VSO, Prohaska, Van VRS 421 (*Lieder aus der Jugendzeit; Rückertlieder).*

A charming derivation from the finale of the Third Symphony, converted to its present form by Joseph Woss. Fine performance and recording.

MALIPIERO, G. FRANCESCO (1882-)

*Concerto for Violin and Orchestra. Kirmse, LRO, Kleinert, U RLP 7112 (*Rakov: Violin Concerto).*

A searing emphasis on highs is not an embellishment of a work full of ear-tingling clashes on its own. The playing is competent, however.

*Symphony No. 7. RIO, Mitropoulos, Cet 50044 (*Bach: Chaconne).*

Poor reproduction is a failing of this performance also. However, the work has substance and style.

MARCELLO, BENEDETTO (1686-1739)

*Concerto for Oboe and Strings, in C minor. Goossens, PHI, Süsskind, C ML 4782 (*Cimarosa: Concerto; Bach-Tovey: Concerto; etc.). Reversy, OSR, Ansermet, 10" L LS 591 (*Vivaldi: Concerto for Bassoon).*

The fine art of Goossens and its integration with an excellent group of Philharmonia players have been admired for several years. Their appearance in this form is doubly welcome. The sound is good, though not as crisply oboistic as that of Reversy.

His elegant performance does not have the individuality of Goossens's, but has virtually everything else one would desire.

MARTIN, FRANK (1890-)

Concerto for Harpsichord and Orchestra (1952). *Nef, CHAM, de Froment, 10" OL DL 53001.*

Good engineering gives distinctive value to the combination of harpsichord and small orchestra. Nef's performance is expert (the work was written for her), as is the orchestra's.

Concerto for Winds, Percussion, Strings. WIN, Desarzens, CH 1109 (**Ibert: Concerto for Flute*).

First-class instrumental execution, deftly integrated by Martin, and very well reproduced.

Petite Symphonie Concertante. OSR, Ansermet, L LL 390 (**Stravinsky: Baiser de la Fée*).

Rather tenuous music, but well performed and reproduced.

MARTINŮ, BOHUSLAV (1890-)

Concerto Grosso. VSY, Swoboda, W 5004 (**Strauss: Macbeth*).

Energetic performance, rather thin in string sound.

Concerto for String Quartet and Orchestra. WIN, Swoboda, W 5079 (**Partita; Serenade*).

Swoboda goes about his work convincingly, but the sound is diffuse, aurally unpleasant.

Intermezzo. LOUI, Whitney, C ML 4859 (**Foss: Parable of Death*).

Whitney has a live hand for this music, and it is well recorded.

Partita; Serenade. WIN, Swoboda, W 5079 (**Concerto*).

Substantially the same results as in the Concerto noted above.

MASSENET, JULES (1842-1912)

Ballet Music

Le Cid. ROO, Braithwaite, MGM E 3016 (**Scènes Alsaciennes*). *BPO, Fiedler, V LM 1084* (**Luigini: Ballet Egyptien*). *LSO, R. Irving. 10" L LD 9089.*

For a Massenet collation, the Braithwaite serving is agreeable, with the *Le Cid* matter including not only the seven sections also covered by Fiedler, but a "Moorish Rhapsody" from Act III. The quality of sound is about the same. For those who are interested only in *Le Cid*, Irving's performance is vigorous, the sound decidedly better than the others.

Incidental Music

*Les Erinnyes. OTN, Cluytens, Vox PL 8100 (*Saint-Saëns: Suite Algérienne).*

This is probably the first full recording ever of this music, whose distinction remains the perversely popular *"Elégie,"* here rendered in its instrumental form by an unidentified but highly able cellist. Good performance throughout and satisfactory sound.

*Phèdre: Overture. OOC, Wolff, 10" L LD 9020 (*Saint-Saëns: La Princesse Jaune).*

Powerful direction by Wolff, reproduced with clarity and fine definition.

Works for Orchestra

*Scènes Alsaciennes. LAM, Fournet, Ep LC 3053 (*Scènes Pittoresques).*

The perfection of this combination is another expression of the taste, musical skill, and engineering resource that have gone into its making. In a word, just what a record should be.

*Scènes Alsaciennes. ROO, Braithwaite, MGM E 3106 (*Le Cid: Ballet Music).*

Braithwaite works well at this music, and the sound is better than on the reverse side.

Scènes Pittoresques. LAM, Fournet, Ep LC 3053.

See first entry under *Scènes Alsaciennes.*

McDONALD, HARL (1899-)

Builders of America; Children's Symphony. COL, McDonald, 10" C ML 2220.

The composer is an effective interpreter of his own work, profiting, in *Builders of America*, from the participation of Claude Rains as narrator. Good sound.

*From Childhood (Suite). CAO, Stockton, Slatkin, Cap P 8255 (*Caplet: Mask of the Red Death).*

As in the coupled work, Miss Stockton performs skillfully and the sound is highly satisfactory.

MENASCE, JACQUES DE (1905-)

*Concerto for Piano and Orchestra, No. 2. De Menasce, VSO, Appia, Van VRS 442 (*Divertimento on a Children's Song; Suite for the Piano).*

Excellent technical work all the way, including the composer's own piano performance and the reproduction thereof. The Divertimento is a particularly pleasant piece.

MENDELSSOHN, FELIX (1809-1847)

Concertos

For Piano and Orchestra

*No. 1 in G minor. Dorfmann, ROB, Leinsdorf, LBC 1043 (*Grieg: Concerto). Frugoni, VSO, Moralt, Vox PL 7440 (*Overtures, opus 27, 32).*

Dorfmann's fluency and skill are adornments of this work, as is Leinsdorf's energetic direction. Very good sound in this, especially in view of the modest cost. Frugoni's work is also satisfactory, if one is interested in the second-side overtures.

*No. 2 in D minor. Wührer, VSO, Moralt, Vox PL 6570 (*Songs without Words).*

Musicianly work by all parties involved, and well-balanced reproduction.

For Two Pianos and Orchestra

In A flat. Frugoni, Taddei, VSY, Moralt, Vox PL 7400.

*In E. Frugoni, Mrazek, PRO, Swarowsky, Vox PL 8350 (*Capriccio Brillant, opus 22).*

Both works are well worth acquaintance, despite their obscurity. The performances are excellent, whether the second pianist is Taddei or Mrazek. Frugoni manages the *Capriccio Brillant* with fine spirit, and the recording throughout is excellent.

For Violin and Orchestra

*In D minor. RCAS, Menuhin, V LM 1720 (*Concerto in E minor).*

This youthful work has some remarkable qualities, fully expounded by Menuhin. The overside version of the familiar E minor is equally well done, in terms of Menuhin's capacities. However, there are other versions (see below) which are more appropriate.

*In E minor. Milstein, PSO, Steinberg, Cap P 8243 (*Bruch: Concerto in G minor). Heifetz, RPO, Beecham, 10" V LM 18. Kreisler, LPO, Ronald, V LCT 1117 (*Mozart: Concerto in D). Szigeti, LPO, Beecham, 10" C ML 2217. Borries, BPH, Celibidache, V LBC 1049 (*Symphony No. 4 in A, "Italian").*

The considerable cream in this crop is served in several sorts of containers, but all are excellent in terms of time and price. The newest and best in the sequence is the Milstein, performed with zest and clarity against the fine backdrop arranged by Steinberg. Heifetz performs with his own incomparable resources, though the partnership with Beecham is not wholly happy. I should not like to overlook the economy-priced Borries, which is beautifully played and soundly reproduced. Szigeti's is a durable work of musical thinking, as Kreisler's is of musical feeling and—insofar as his fingers permitted in the late 1920's—of physical execution. The LP processing of both is creditable.

Incidental Music

A Midsummer Night's Dream (Complete). BBC, Sargent, Old Vic Company, V LM 6115 [3].

"Complete" here means the spoken text of Shakespeare's play in the voices of Robert Helpmann, Moira Shearer, Stanley Holloway, *et al*, with the incidental music in full as created by Mendelssohn for a Prussian monarch in 1841. There are slight deviations from textual accuracy, but they are hardly of account beside the opportunity to hear, at will, the matchless music of Shakespeare and the unsurpassed poetry of Mendelssohn. I would not cite Sargent as an animator of these patterns in the class of a Toscanini or a Beecham, but he does his work with more animation, perhaps, than one would expect, and the recording is first-class.

*A Midsummer Night's Dream. NBC, Toscanini, V LM 1221 (*Debussy: La Mer). ROB, Reiner, V LM 1724 (*Debussy: Petite Suite; Ravel:*

Tombeau de Couperin). *CO, Rodzinski, C RL 3047* (**Beethoven: Symphony No. 1*).

Although the Toscanini version does not seem to have the unqualified endorsement even of RCA Victor (which has underwritten a later venture by Reiner), it stands as a miraculous vivification of the composer's thoughts, even if not perfectly reproduced. Among its pleasures are the finale with female chorus, magically done. Reiner's collection is limited to the Overture, Scherzo, Intermezzo, Nocturne, and Wedding March, all well done. At a lower price, the Rodzinski is a reasonable value, but not overwhelmingly attractive.

A Midsummer Night's Dream: Overture. BPH, Fricsay, 10" D DL 4006 (**Weber: Oberon*).

Energetic direction by Fricsay, well played and reproduced.

Overtures

Calm Sea and Prosperous Voyage. BPH, Lehmann, 10" D DL 4015 (**Fingal's Cave*). *VSY, Moltkau, Vox PL 7440* (**Die Schöne Melusine; Concerto No. 1*).

As a compact pairing, the Lehmann performances are musical and well phrased. The recording is better than the alternative available.

Fingal's Cave (Hebrides). GSO, Ludwig, V LBC 1028 (**Sibelius: Finlandia; Elgar: Pomp and Circumstance; Weber: Invitation to the Dance; etc.*). *BPH, Lehmann, 10" D DL 4015* (**Calm Sea and Prosperous Voyage*). *RPO, Beecham, 10" C AL 7* (**Roy Blas*).

Leopold Ludwig is a conductor otherwise unknown to me, but he manages this work with fine skill, and it is broadly reproduced. As part of a miscellany more miscellaneous than most, it commands interest for musical as well as monetary reasons. The characteristics of the Lehmann disc are as noted above. Beecham's remake does not find him in happiest vein, and the recording is not more than moderately good.

Ruy Blas. RPO, Beecham, 10" C AL 7 (**Fingal's Cave*).

Not the best Beecham or Mendelssohn. A Monteux reissue would be welcome.

Die Schöne Melusine. VSY, Moltkau, Vox PL 7440 (**Concerto No. 1; Calm Sea*).

Moltkau's graceful performance is hardly sufficient cause for buying this disc, but it rounds out a usable collection of Mendelssohn.

Symphonies

No. 1 in C minor. SPO, Van Hoogstraten, Ren X 28.

A work of Mendelssohn's fifteenth year, done with spirit, but ineptly reproduced.

*No. 3 in A minor ("Scotch"). NYPH, Mitropoulos, C ML 4864 (*Symphony No. 5).*

Both performances (side two is the "Reformation") are among the best Mitropoulos has done for the microphone, and the reproduction ranks high in Columbia's catalogue. In view of the double value proffered, it takes precedent over any other issue.

*No. 4 in A ("Italian"). HO, Barbirolli, V LBC 1049 (*Concerto in E minor). LSO, Krips, L LL 930 (*Schumann: Symphony No. 4 in D minor). BSO, Koussevitzky, 10" V LM 20.*

For the best contemporary sound and a performance of vigor and suavity, the Krips is my preference. However, the Barbirolli is very well conceived and is reproduced with justice, if a little echoey. Taken together with the excellent version of the Concerto, it is a robust value, especially at the price. The Koussevitzky performance is miraculous in its precision and orchestral definition. However, concepts of proper orchestral weight and abundance of reproduced sound have altered considerably since this was made.

*No. 5 in D minor ("Reformation"). NYPH, Mitropoulos, C ML 4864 (*Symphony No. 3, "Scotch"). LAP, Wallenstein, D DL 9726 (*Beethoven: Symphony No. 8).*

Wallenstein's estimate of this work is sound, but not more so than that of Mitropoulos, whose orchestra is decidedly better reproduced. Moreover, the coupled "Scotch" surpasses any other.

Works for Orchestra and Piano

*Capriccio Brilliant. Frugoni, PRO, Swarowsky, Vox PL 8350 (*Concerto for Two Pianos, in E).*

Spirited, well-phrased performance by Frugoni, with both piano and orchestra splendidly reproduced.

*Rondo Brilliant, opus 29. Lympany, PHI, Menges, V LHMV 1025 (*Concerto No. 1).*

Accurate performance, well reproduced.

MENOTTI, GIAN-CARLO (1911-)

*Sebastian (Suite). ROB, Mitropoulos, 10" C ML 2053 (*Mascagni, Puccini, Wolf-Ferrari: Intermezzos).*

Mitropoulos's affinity for M's includes Menotti as well as Mendelssohn, and the recording is reasonably good. However, the pairing with excerpts from *Cavalleria, Manon Lescaut,* and *Jewels of the Madonna* does not come under the category of "inevitable."

MESSAGER, ANDRÉ (1853-1929)

*Les Deux Pigeons (Ballet). OOC, Blareau, 10" L LS 647 (*Chabrier: Fête-Polonaise and Danse Slave, from Le Roi Malgré Lui).*

The French version of music to read by, pleasantly done by Blareau and handsomely engineered.

MESSIAEN, OLIVIER (1908-)

*L'Ascension (Four Symphonic Meditations). NYPH, Stokowski, C ML 4214 (*Vaughan Williams: Symphony No. 6).*

As a conductor with an organist's sense of mass sound, Stokowski is highly successful with this composer with an organist's sense of coloration. Excellent sound.

MEYERBEER, GIACOMO (1791-1864)

Les Patineurs. LSO, Irving, 10" L LD 9105.

A Lambert version of this ballet he arranged would be a boon, but, lacking it, Irving's work is idiomatic and wide-range in recorded sound.

MIASKOVSKY, NIKOLAI (1881-1950)

*Concerto for Violin and Orchestra, in D minor. Oistrakh, SYM, Gauk, Per SPLP 539 (*Prokofiev: Concerto No. 1).*

New patterns in which Oistrakh demonstrates his abundant virtuosity are the principal distinctions of this work. However, the recording is miserably dull, the surface scratch from the dubbed 78's obviously audible.

*Lyric Concertino. ORB, Guhl, U 7088 (*Glazunov: Symphony No. 7).*

The attractive Russianisms of this work are reasonably well rendered, though the solo instruments (flute, clarinet, horn, bassoon, and harp) are not as audible as they should be. Hardly polished performance, but well reproduced.

*Symphony No. 21 in F sharp minor. PHO, Ormandy, C ML 4239 (*Bartók: Concerto No. 3).*

A dividend for purchasers of what I consider the preferable version of the Bartók No. 3, which will appeal for its own sound structure and apt interpretation.

MILHAUD, DARIUS (1892-)

Ballet Music

*La Création du Monde. COL, Bernstein, C ML 2203 (*Copland: El Salón México).*

A completely agreeable mating of composer and interpreters, with Bernstein as a predestined intermediary. First-class performance and beautifully balanced reproduction.

Concerto

*For Violin and Orchestra, No. 2. Kaufman, ORD, Milhaud, Cap P 8071 (*Concertino de Printemps).*

Fine-grained, well-phrased performance by Kaufman, with the composer in authoritative command. Rather dead, studio-type recording.

Concertinos

*For Piano and Orchestra, No. 1. Jacquinot, PHI, Fistoulari, 10" MGM E 122 (*Honegger: Concertino).*

Not particularly atmospheric performance, but well recorded.

*Concertino de Printemps, for Violin and Orchestra. Kaufman, ORD, Milhaud, Cap P 8071 (*Concerto No. 2).*

Delightfully spirited performance, in the manner of the Concerto No. 2 noted above. Close-up microphoning.

Works for Orchestra

Le Boeuf sur le Toit. *MIN, Mitropoulos, 10" C ML 2032* (**Ravel: Tombeau de Couperin*).

Animated performance, but of limited reproductive fidelity.

Kentuckiana. *LOUI, Whitney, C ML 4859* (**Foss: A Parable of Death*).

A folk-derived work, well directed by Whitney and properly reproduced.

Symphony No. 1. *CBSO, Milhaud, C ML 4784* (**Sessions: Symphony No. 1*).

Absorbing matter, delivered by the composer with his own fluent command of his idiom, and very distinctly reproduced.

Works for Orchestra and Solo Instrument

Five Studies, for Piano and Orchestra. *VSY, Swoboda, W 5051* (**Sérénade; Suite Maximilien*).

An opinion of this performance (in which the later celebrated Paul Badura-Skoda is the pianist) may serve as well for the other material of the disc—*Serenade for Orchestra* (1921), a suite from the opera *Maximilian,* and *Three Rag Caprices.* None of this is self-expository music, and Swoboda's merely approximate rhythms and tonal definitions damage, rather than help, the composer's cause. In addition, there is a need for clearly defined sonorities not met in this early Vienna effort of Westminster.

MOSZKOWSKI, MORITZ (1854-1925)

Concerto for Piano and Orchestra, in E. *Kann, NET, Goehr, CH 1197.*

Some glittering generalities on the subject "piano concerto," discharged with finesse by young Kann, and colorfully reproduced.

MOZART, WOLFGANG AMADEUS (1756-1791)

Ballet Music

Les Petits Riens. *ROO, Braithwaite, MGM E 3034* (**Scarlatti: Good Humored Ladies*). *OCS, Goldschmidt, A S 33* (**Divertimento No. 2 in D*).

Much of the lilt and rhythmic verve of these pieces is conveyed by Braithwaite in an excellent reproduction. The Anthologie Sonore issue is mentioned only in warning, for the dull sound and spiritless performance ill honor such proud parentage.

Cassations

In G, K. 63, and B flat, K. 99. VSY, Sacher, Ep LC 3043.

The agreeable qualities of these boyish efforts by Mozart are a little inflated by Sacher, who imputes to them values derived from later expressions. Good sound and very artistic playing.

Concertos

For Bassoon and Orchestra

*In B flat, K. 191. Oehlberger, VSO, Rodzinski, W WL 5307 (*Concerto for Clarinet). Sharrow, NBC, Toscanini, V LM 1030 (*Symphony No. 41).*

Neither of these is in the category of such a work of old as the Oubrados or Camden, but a nominal priority goes to the well-paired items on Westminster because of superior sound. However, Oehlberger has to work hard to make his effects, and he plays an interminable cadenza that could be of interest only to other bassoonists. The Toscanini is over-mechanized, the bassoonist being permitted little latitude for personal expression. The sound has been improved in processing from 78 rpm to LP.

For Clarinet and Orchestra

*In A, K. 622. Kell, ZS, 10" D DL 7500. Lancelot, SYM, De Froment, OL 50006 (*Sinfonia Concertante, K. 297b). Cahuzac, DSTR, Wöldike, HS L 1047 (*Haydn: Symphony No. 61). Etienne, HEW, Hewitt, HS L 96 (*Quintet in A, K. 581). Wlach, VSO, Rodzinski, W WL 5307.*

The only possible objection to the Kell would be in terms of the smallish string group, and the lack of integrating leadership. It is, otherwise, highly successful. Each of the other versions has an abundance of interest, with Lancelot perhaps the most powerful and secure of the European virtuosos, Cahuzac a crafty master of his instrument with some unusual tricks of phrasing in his seventy-year-old head, and Etienne more inclined to playing *with* the supporting group than any of the others. Enthusiasts for this work could well provide shelf room for all. The best non-American recording is HS L 96, though OL 50006 is excellent in its style. The Wlach version has little more than good sound to commend it, as his inclinations in this work are pedantic.

For Flute and Orchestra

*No. 1 in G, K. 313, and No. 2 in D, K. 314. Barwahser, VSO, Pritchard, Ep LC 3033. No. 1 only. Wummer, PERP, Casals, C ML 4567 (*Concerto for Piano No. 14 in E flat).*

Barwahser doesn't have the subtlety of Wummer, nor is Pritchard such a factor of value as Casals, but the Epic is (aside from the characteristically heavy bass) a smoother acoustical product than the Columbia. Actually, No. 2 comes off better for Barwahser and Pritchard, giving this disc preference among pairings of the two.

For Flute, Harp, and Orchestra

*In C, K. 299. Wagner, Mess, TSO, Lund, Per SPLP 544 (*Concerto for Horn in D, K. 412).*

Musicianly care abounds in this performance, which is cleanly recorded in a smallish, rather dead studio.

For Horn and Orchestra

Set of Four. Brain, PHI, Karajan, An 35092.

For workmanship and congruity, these are highly desirable additions to the repertory. However, Brain's horn sound is not certain to please every taste. Nothing else currently available matches this collection in finesse or recorded quality.

*No. 1 in D, K. 412. Goermer, TSO, Lund, Per SPLP 544 (*See above).*

This issue is more notable for the fine-sounding playing of a solo violinist than for the rather labored, thick sound of the horn. Satisfactory recording.

No. 2 in E flat, K. 417, and No. 4 in E flat, K. 495. Dennis Brain, PHI, Süsskind, 10" C ML 2088.

These are the performances long honored in their 78-rpm form, and of enduring musical merit. The sound in both instances is duller than is *au fait* today, but otherwise well proportioned.

*No. 3 in E flat, K. 447. Jones, NGO, Bales, WCFM 8 (*Exsultate Jubilate, etc.). Starker, SYM, Pilzer, Per SPLP 579 (*Boccherini: Concerto in B flat).*

Mason Jones, of the Philadelphia Orchestra Joneses, is an excellent hornist, though his style is not all it might be for Mozart. The processing is passable. Of itself, Starker's playing is first-class, but the problems that make this challenging for horn are rather routine for a cellist. Good sound.

For Oboe and Orchestra

*In C, K. 314. Saillet, SAL, Paumgartner, Ren X 29 (*Concerto for Piano, No. 5).*

The text of this work is substantially the same as that of the Concerto for Flute, No. 2, bearing the same Köchel number, but transposed into D. Comparisons with any alternate version are more than odious, as Saillet's tone is singularly squealy and-not productive of much pleasure.

For Piano and Orchestra

In D, G, and E flat, K. 107. Balsam, WIN, Ackermann, CH 1164.

In these adaptations of sonatas by J. C. Bach and in the early original works (see below), Balsam is a musician of taste and discretion who gives them virtually all they ask, without undue "significance." Ackermann is an excellent director for them. The sound is brilliantly live and well balanced.

No. 1 in F, K. 37, No. 2 in B flat, K. 39. Balsam, WIN, Ackermann, CH 1119.

No. 3 in D, K. 40, No. 4 in G, K. 41. Balsam, WIN, Ackermann, CH 1163.

*No. 5 in D, K. 175. Balsam, SYM, Gimpel, Ren X 29 (*Concerto for Oboe).*

Musically, this conforms to the CH standard, but the reproduction is more confined, less live.

No. 6 in B flat, K. 238, No. 8 in C, K. 246. Balsam, SYM, Ackermann, CH 1120.

The developing resources of Mozart are beautifully conveyed in the expert work of Balsam and Ackermann. The sound is as noted above.

*No. 9 in E flat, K. 271. Novaes, PRO, Swarowsky, Vox PL 8430 (*No. 20 in D minor). Hess, PERP, Casals, C ML 4568.*[1]

Nothing in the Hess performance justifies spreading it over a full LP—rather the contrary, as Novaes is both surer of hand and more dependable of spirit. For a final fact, the Vienna orchestra and recording are superior.

*No. 11 in F, K. 413. Rivkin, VSO, Dixon, W WL 5244 (*No. 22 in E flat).*

Good straightforward musicianship is a welcome trait of this performance, but not enough of the inflection and shading is produced to make wholly satisfactory Mozart. The orchestra is reproduced better than the piano.

*No. 12 in A, K. 414. Kraus, BSO, Monteux, V LM 1783 (*No. 18 in B flat). Jensen, DSTR, Wöldike, HS 1054 (*No. 21 in C).*

Very little in the orderly but unimaginative performance of Jensen and Wöldike compares with the dash and sparkle of Monteux's leadership, the animated conversational style of Kraus's execution. Very good sound, too, from Boston.

No. 13 in C, K. 415. Balsam, SYM, Swoboda, CH 1116 (Sonata in C, K. 330).

A rather lightweight work for this composer, and not enhanced by irresistible performance. Fair recording.

*No. 14 in E flat, K. 449. Badura-Skoda, VSO, Sternberg, Oc 22 (*No. 22). Istomin, PERP, Casals, C ML 4567 (*Concerto for Flute, No. 1 in G).*

As in most of the Perpignan recordings, the recorded quality here is not distinguished. Badura-Skoda does more for the music, to my taste, and the orchestral direction of Sternberg is satisfactory.

*No. 15 in B flat, K. 450. Haebler, PRO, Hollreiser, Vox PL 8300 (*No. 18 in B flat).*

A routine performance that does not approach previous phonographic standards in this work. Clean recording.

*No. 16 in D, K. 451. Balsam, WIN, Desarzens, CH 1405 (*Variations on Je suis Lindor, K. 354).*

Balsam's manner is a little fettered and deferential for best service to this little-played but thoroughly typical work. Capable recording, not as resonant as it might be.

*No. 17 in G, K. 453. Kirkpatrick, DOO, Schneider, HS 1040 (*Con-*

[1] EDITOR'S NOTE: Where the coupled work is another Mozart concerto, the number and key alone are given, as "No. 20 in D minor."

*certo for Violin in D, K. 218). Fischer, CHAM, V LCT 6013 (*Nos. 20, 22, 24).*

Schneider's didactic leadership and Kirkpatrick's unduly cautious fingering of a Mozart-style piano put this in an "educational" category, hardly consistent with the character of the music. Good recording, though the finale is split between two sides. Fischer's effort is a good deal more sophisticated; the recording, in reprocessed guise, is passable.

*No. 18 in B flat, K. 456. Kraus, BSO, Monteux, V LM 1783 (*No. 12 in A). Henkemans, VSO, Pritchard, Ep LC 3047 (*No. 19).*

Although Kraus is not so solidly sure in rhythm and accent here as in No. 12, the combined accomplishment, with Monteux, is decidedly preferable to the alternate. In sound, too, the Boston product is more agreeable than the Viennese.

*No. 19 in F, K. 459. Kraus, VSO, Moralt, Vox PL 6890 (*No. 23 in A). Haskil, WIN, Swoboda, W WL 5054 (*No. 20 in D minor). Henkemans, VSO, Pritchard, Ep LC 3047 (*No. 18 in B flat).*

None of these compares with the inaccessible version of Schnabel and Sargent, which may, in the course of the Schnabel reissue program, finally reappear. Till then, it is a choice between the competent but far from flavorsome effort of Kraus and Moralt and the excellence of Haskil offset by the limited leadership of Swoboda. The Epic is preferable in sound, but too much afflicted by Mozart "style."

*No. 20 in D minor, K. 466. Novaes, PRO, Swarowsky, Vox PL 8430 (*No. 9 in E flat). Schnabel, PHI, Süsskind, V LHMV 1012 (*No. 24 in C minor). Fischer, LPO, Sargent, V LCT 6013* [2] *(*Nos. 17, 22, 24). Kempff, DPH, Van Kempen, 10" D DL 7515.*

Few works in the literature have been favored with more loving attention and rewarding thought than this one. Every one of the performers has something individual to say about the work, and the standard of recording is good or better even in the pre-war Fischer (one of his best performances). The relatively recent Schnabel is also excellent in sound, and thoroughly representative musically. As for the Kempff, it is one of the rare examples of his ability as a Mozartian, and extremely good. I would not quarrel with a partisan for any, but my personal preference is the Novaes, for when she is at her best—as she is here—the balance and composure of her art are peerless.

*No. 21 in C, K. 467. Casadesus, NYPH, Munch, C ML 4791 (*No. 27* *in B flat). Jensen, DSTR, Wöldike, HS L 1054 (*No. 12 in A). Demus, VSO, Horvath, W WL 5183 (*No. 26 in D).*

Lacking such a performance as the celebrated one of Schnabel (with Sargent), the efficiently musical one of Casadesus, with the Philharmonic-Symphony sounding particularly well under the direction of Munch, is warmly welcome. It is also more expressive than the detached one of Jensen, and more satisfying than the percussive one of Demus with its ornate Busoni cadenza. All are well reproduced.

*No. 22 in E flat, K. 482. Serkin, PERP, Casals, C ML 4569. Badura-Skoda, VSY, Sternberg, Oc S 22 (*No. 14 in E flat). Fischer, CHAM, Barbirolli, V LCT 6013* [2] *(*See No. 17).*

Enthusiasm is in limited supply for any of these, for the Serkin-Casals product is hardly good enough to merit the cost of a whole record, the Badura-Skoda breaks the finale between two sides, and the Fischer displays a rather dry style of performance and is not well recorded. If pedal noises (plus the price) are not unwelcome, the Serkin will probably give the most satisfaction.

*No. 23 in A, K. 488. Kraus, VSY, Moralt, Vox PL 6890 (*No. 19 in F). Curzon, LSO, Krips, L LL 918 (*No. 24 in C minor). Rubinstein, STS, Golschmann, V LM 1091 (*Falla: Nights in the Gardens of Spain). Gieseking, PHI, Karajan, C ML 4536 (Franck: Symphonic Variations).*

Were Kraus partnered here by a Monteux who could tell her when to leave well enough alone, there would be little question of her superiority. However, the inclination to rephrase every repetition of a main theme leads to fussy overplaying. Good enough sound, especially of the piano. The other versions all embody compromises of more serious sorts, with Rubinstein not so comfortable here as he was in the older version with Barbirolli, Curzon always correct but a little colorless, and Gieseking very pearly. In sound, the Curzon-Krips is outstanding.

*No. 24 in C minor, K. 491. Schnabel, PHI, Süsskind, V LHMV 1012 (*No. 20 in D minor). Curzon, LSO, Krips, L LL 918 (*No. 23). Fischer, LPO, Collingwood, V LCT 6013* [2] *(*See No. 17). Badura-Skoda, VSY, Prohaska, W WL 5097.*

The battle of the titans here is as close as possible to a draw, with Fischer blessed by better reproduction than in any other work of the four reissues credited to him, and Schnabel's clearly, cleanly defined also. Both play their own cadenzas, and the Schnabel taste in such matters is somewhat more discreet. Both newer issues are also excellent, with Krips and the London engineers organizing the fullest audibility of the wondrously rich orchestral score. However, this is only a shade of improvement on the version of Prohaska and Badura-Skoda, one of the young pianist's finest accomplishments. My personal preference would be for the Schnabel (considering the coupled performance) or—for luxurious sound— the Curzon.

*No. 25 in C major, K. 503. Fischer, PHI, Krips, V LHMV 1004 (*Bach: Concerto for Three Pianos). Roesgen-Champion, LAM, Goldschmidt, Per SPL 571 (*No. 21 in C).*

Fischer's dexterity and fluency are more than Roesgen-Champion can match, not to mention the superior resources of the English as against the French engineers. Fischer plays the finale with especial artistry after a somewhat excessive firmness in the preceding two movements.

*No. 26 in D ("Coronation"), K. 537. Landowska, CHAM, Goehr, V LCT 1029 (*Haydn: Concerto in D). Casadesus, CO, Szell, C ML 4901 (*Concerto No. 24). Demus, VSO, Horvath, W WL 5183 (*Concerto No. 21).*

For all its dullness of sound and the far-from-impelling leadership of Goehr, the Landowska performance renders more to Mozart than the blowsy, overblown one led by Szell with Casadesus as surefingered as could be and mostly very uninteresting in this performance. Landowska's finesse is sometimes a means rather than an end, but her possession of it cannot be denied. Demus is fluent and a little stilted. Having survived challenge as long as it has, Landowska's recording is likely to endure when the interests of the current competitors have been surpassed by something better.

*No. 27 in B flat, K. 595. Horszowski, PERP, Casals, C ML 4570. Badura-Skoda, VSY, Prohaska, W WL 5097 (*No. 24). Casadesus, NYPH, Barbirolli, C ML 4791 (*No. 21 in C minor).*

None of these performances measures up to the stature and possibility of the music, at least to the extent that memory attributes to the long-admired performance of Schnabel (V Set 240), which might be worth "Treasury" status. If the reader is bent on a choice anyway, he will find the musicianship—also the highest price per minute of music and the least good recording—in the Horszowski-Casals.

For Two Pianos and Orchestra

*No. 1 in E flat, K. 365. Badura-Skoda, Gianoli, VSO, Scherchen, W WL 5095 (*Concerto in F, K. 242). Vronsky, Babin, ROB, Mitropoulos, C ML 4098 (*Concerto in F, K. 242). A. and K. U. Schnabel, LSO, Boult, V LCT 1140 (*Bach: Concerto in C).*

The version of Vronsky and Babin has not improved since it was new, which means that it is swift, neat, and superficial. By contrast, the Skoda-Gianoli would be attractive without Scherchen; with him it is irresistible. The description also holds for the F major, of which Vronsky and Babin, with Rosina Lhevinne, play the original version for three pianos, and Badura-Skoda and Gianoli the later version for two. The Viennese recording is much superior to the American. The interests of the Schnabel are mostly antiquarian, for the sound is a little dim and hard to hear. Very musical, however.

For Three Pianos and Orchestra

See above.

For Violin and Orchestra

No. 1 in B flat, K. 207, No. 2 in D, K. 211. Stucki, TSO, Lund, Per 549.

Of these little-played works, the B flat is decidedly the better, well worth knowing for its slow movement alone. Stucki plays suavely and with nicely proportioned emphasis. Lund's direction is also appropriate; the recording is small in total sound, but of good quality.

No. 3 in G, K. 216, and No. 4 in D, K. 218. Grumiaux, VSY, Paumgartner, Ep LC 3060. Goldberg, PHI, Süsskind, D DL 9609.

If it is possible to be not only a specialist in Mozart, but a specialist in a particular work of Mozart, Grumiaux earns that distinction in this duplication of an experience admired "live." The purity of the sound and the closeness of its control are especially impressive in the slow movement. Fine collaborative effort by Paumgartner, and excellent sound. However, Goldberg does play No. 4 (see below) better, for those to whom that might be the decisive factor.

*No. 4 in D, K. 218. Goldberg, PHI, Süsskind, D DL 9609 (*No. 3). Heifetz, RPO, Beecham, V LM 1051 (*Bach: Concerto in D minor, for Two Violins). Szigeti, LPO, Beecham, C ML 4533 (*Prokofiev: Concerto No. 1). Gerard Poulet, ASO, G. Poulet, REM R 199–125 (*Overtures to Don Giovanni, Clemenza di Tito, etc.).*

The daringly slow tempo at which Goldberg plays his slow movement seems, initially, a disaffecting gesture, but he makes very good musical sense with it as a ground-plan for the whole movement. Similar instances of thoughtfulness make it, to me, the preferable version, though Beecham's contribution to the performances in which he participates is considerable, and the deftness of Heifetz and the incisive style of Szigeti are of themselves absorbing. The later RCA from England is, of course, a better sound than is contained on the earlier Columbia. Devotees of this work might investigate the effort of Poulet, a remarkable talent still in his teens. This is hardly a perfect product, but his instinct is as attractive as his facility is impressive. Father Gaston conducts, and the sound is quite good.

*No. 5 in A, K. 219. Heifetz, LSO, Sargent, V LM 9014 (*Beethoven: Romances). Morini, PERP, Casals, C ML 4565. Oistrakh, BSI, Golovanov, Col 154 (*Concerto No. 7).*

Though memory proclaims the superiority of the earlier Heifetz version to the present one, its qualities are still more than can be matched by either competitor. Morini's power and sensitivity are more than admirable, the appropriateness of Casals's support something more than in other works of this origin. However, the recording is without vibrance, the spreading of the single work over two sides unconscionable, Oistrakh's effort throws light on his fiddling prowess, but not much on Mozart. Penetrating reproduction.

*No. 6 in E flat, K. 268. Barchet, PRO, Reinhardt, Vox PL 7240 (*No. 4 in D).*

Despite its lack of favor, this contains some of the most gratifying music Mozart wrote for violin and orchestra. Barchet plays it with affectionate insight, but does not command the suavity of sound desirable. Clear, rather wiry recording.

*No. 7 in D, K. 271a. Stucki, TSO, Lund, Per SPLP 548 (*Rondos in C and B flat, Adagio in E flat, K. 269). Oistrakh, USSR, Kondrashin, Col 154 (*No. 5).*

Young Stucki's violin produces more Mozartian sounds than Oistrakh's, as does the modest TSO vs. the "National Philharmonic" (not too idiomatically conducted by Kiril Kondrashin). However, those who are interested in violinistic *esprit* as such, will find several steaming samovars of it here.

Concertone

*For Two Violins and Orchestra, in C, K. 190. VSY, Swoboda, W WL 5013 (*Symphony No. 23 in D).*

This delightful work (a Salzburg product of the seventeen-year-old Mozart) deserves much wider circulation than it has had. The performance, rich in sonorous values, is played with affection and sound feeling for the style.

Country Dances

Collection of Twenty (*K. 534, 600, 602, 606, 609*). *VSO, Litschauer, Van VRS, 426.*

Besides embodying the most popular works of the genre known as *Deutschetänze* (such as the ones with sleigh bells and hurdy-gurdy "effects"), this collection includes most of those phonographically available. Litschauer and men play them methodically rather than creatively, but the end result is pleasurable. Realistic recording, a little afflicted with the Viennese "hang" in the sound.

Divertimentos[1]

*No. 2 in D, K. 131. RPO, Beecham, V LHMV 1030 (*Handel: Great Elopement). LMP, Blech, L LL 586 (*Haydn: Symphony No. 49).*

Although Beecham's text omits the first of the original two minuets and adds a like movement from K. 287, the refinement and poise of the playing are more palatable than the well-ordered but mono-

[1] EDITOR'S NOTE: Because of the ambiguous nature of the works Mozart sometimes called divertimentos, sometimes serenades, sometimes cassations, their inclusion in or exclusion from a book of this scope is largely arbitrary with the author. Where they have attracted the legitimate attentions of a conductor and have become part of the symphonic literature either through his efforts or those of a predecessor, they are included as a matter of course. However, the sort that is demonstrably chamber music, into which, in Reginald Kell's phrase, a conductor comes as "a stranger in Paradise," has been omitted.

chromatic performance led by Blech. The HMV sound is, though older, superior to the London in this instance.

*In D, K. 136. SCH, Münchinger, 10" L LS 385 (*Kleine Nachtmusik).*
This could without exaggeration or affectation be called a darling work, exactly what a divertimento should be and too rarely is. Perfectly turned playing, reproduced with full, rich string bass.

*In D, K. 251. Tabuteau, PERP, Casals, C ML 4566. DOO, Schneider, Mer 10002 (*Concerto Grosso in D minor).*
Although Marcel Tabuteau is presented as the featured performer here, Casals's loose idea of balance often obscures the sound of the oboe. Moreover, the string sound is coarse, the recording of limited fidelity. Unfortunately, not much that is good can be said about the Schneider-led version.

In B flat, K. 287. Tomasow, VSO, Prohaska, Van VRS 444.
The debatable use of a larger ensemble than Mozart prescribed does not work out as well here as in K. 334. Part of the trouble is with the performance, heavier than desirable, and over-microphoned.

In D, K. 334. Boskovsky, CHAM, L LL 235. Tomasow, VSO, Prohaska, Van VRS 441.
Tomasow's work is highly creditable and Prohaska directs his ensemble with loving care, but candor compels the admission that Willi Boskovsky, concertmaster of the Vienna Philharmonic, is a prime master of such music as this, the proportions of his version with members of the Vienna Octet being much more suitable than those of the Prohaska. Rather bright reproduction in the first instance, just about perfect balance and resonance in the second.

Fantasia

*In F minor, K. 608. NEW, Autori, Bar BRS 302 (*Bartók: Dance Suite).*
This transcription by Tibor Serly puts the music into G minor, and some Stokowskyish tricks of arrangement into the music. Autori's performance is not outstanding. Good sound.

Minuets

*Collection of Twelve (K. 599, 601, 604). HEW, Hewitt, HS L 101 (*Eine Kleine Nachtmusik).*
Fragrant, unpretentious pieces, very carefully scored, especially for woodwinds, and thoroughly well played. Acceptable recording.

Overture

*In B flat, K. 311a ("Paris"). CHAM, Swarowsky, Ly 32 (*Haydn: Symphonies Nos. 54, 70).*

A rather formal piece of no special interest, indifferently performed.

Overtures (Operatic)

Apollo et Hyancinthus; La Finta Giardiniera; La Finta Semplice; Lo Sposo Deluso; Lucia Silla; Il Re Pastore; Mitridate, R'edi Ponto. NGO, Bales, WCFM 3.

In totality, these pieces make a rather agreeable suite of no notable distinction. The playing and conducting are not up to customary standards. Recording fair.

Cosi fan tutte; Don Giovanni; Magic Flute; La Clemenza di Tito. BPH, Lehmann, 10" D DL 4035.

Abduction from the Seraglio; Marriage of Figaro; Idomeneo; Impresario. The same, 10" D DL 4036.

Abduction; Impresario. LSO, Krips, 10" L LD 9033.

Magic Flute; Don Giovanni. LSO, Krips, L LD 9001.

None of these offers music-making of the sort provided in bygone performances by Beecham, Busch, Walter, Toscanini, etc. They are efficiently musical, and the London quartet is particularly well reproduced, though the care and detail formerly associated with recorded performances of Mozart overtures are not present.

Serenades

No. 4 in D, K. 203. SCA, Paumgartner, Col LPS 1033.

Despite the unlikely point of origin (Naples), this is sparkling Mozart, and very well reproduced. Altogether, worthy of Paumgartner's Salzburgian roots.

*No. 5 in D, K. 204. VSY, Swoboda, W WL 5005 (*Symphony No. 22).*

Bright, spirited performance; clear but rather thin reproduction.

*In D, K. 239. ZS, D DL 8522 (*Telemann: Suite for Flute and Strings in A minor).*

Airy, lightly expert performance by this picked group of Boston Symphony players, working with finish and style without nominal leadership. Excellent sound.

In D, K. 250 ("Haffner"). BAM, Leitner, D DL 9636.

For the most part this is energetic, orderly performance, with Dénes Zsigmondy an able solo violinist. However the microphone setting is not advantageous and resonance is lacking in the reproduction.

No. 9 in D, K. 320 ("Posthorn"). OSR, Maag, L LL 502.

Skillful performance under the direction of Maag, who would seem, on the basis of this effort, to be entitled to more prominence than has accrued to him. Fine sound.

No. 10 in B flat, K. 361. VPHW, W WL 5229. CHAM, Steinberg, Cap P 8181. BSO, Koussevitzky, V LM 1077.

Although it is the conducted versions that provide for consideration here of this superb work, the non-conducted one seems to me definitely superior. This is less a reflection on Steinberg than on Koussevitzky, for the precision of his work with the Los Angeles musicians utilized would be hard to excel. However, the woodwind tone favored on the West Coast is much leaner, less resonant than that preferred in Vienna, with not as much relevance to this music. The Boston product is fussier, the quantity of Mozartian feeling smaller than in either of the others.

*In G, K. 525 ("Eine Kleine Nachtmusik"). PRO, Klemperer, Vox PL 1690 (*Serenade, K. 239). BPH, Kleiber, Cap P 8038 (*Haydn: Symphony No. 94). SCH, Münchinger, 10" L LS 385 (*Divertimento, K. 136). VSO, Prohaska, Van VRS 435 (*Schubert: German Dances). VPH, Karajan, C ML 4370 (*Symphony No. 33). BAVR, Jochum, D DL 9513 (*Symphony No. 35).*

Anyone interested in my conception of a classic version of this work can hear it in the Klemperer performance—provided they turn the volume up full and throw in all the compensation they possess, for it is definitely limited in sound. The Kleiber has something of the same tense delicacy and tightly held control of fine nuance, but it, too, is of antique status as a recording (both are better on LP than in previous 78 form). Of the others, the opinion must be that the conductors constantly do too much with a work which was—after all—written for string quintet and no conductor at all. Münchinger's quick pace makes almost superficial music of this, but his ensemble plays beautifully, as does the less virtuoso one of Prohaska, whose fault is a weaker sense of balance than this music requires. Karajan's mannered effort is, after all, with the Vienna Philharmonic—a consideration of weight in such a work as this. I would, in the end, suggest that Jochum's puts less stamp of Jochum on this music than any conductor with a contemporary version to his name, and is very well reproduced.

Sinfonias Concertante

*In E flat, K. 297b, Anh. 9. CHAM, de Fremont, OL 50006 (*Concerto for Clarinet). PHI, Karajan, An 35098 (*Eine Kleine Nachtmusik). PRO, Reinhardt, Vox PL 7320 (*Sinfonia Concertante, K. 364).*

Both the French (Pierre Pierlot, oboe, Gilbert Coursier, horn, Jacques Lancelot, clarinet, and Paul Hongne, bassoon) and English (in the same order, Sidney Sutcliffe, Dennis Brain, Bernard Walton, and Cecil James) wind virtuosos are superior to their German counterparts, and the processing of the highly skillful performances is also better. As between the two top-grade products, a slight but appreciable sparkle in the French playing is lacking in the English. In addition, the full Philharmonia (or as much of it as is used) gives a heaviness to the tuttis which Karajan's muscular treatment does not lessen. I also am more partial to Lancelot's fine playing of the *Clarinet Concerto* as addenda than to Karajan's beautiful but showy exhibition of the Philharmonia's strings.

*In E flat, K. 364. Barylli, Doktor, VSO, Prohaska, W WL 5107. Stern, Primrose, PERP, Casals, C ML 4564. J. and L. Fuchs, ZS, D DL 9596. Barchet, Kirchner, PRO, Seegelken, Vox PL 7320 (*Sinfonia Concertante, K. 297b).*

At first glance, the combination of this work with the foregoing on a single disk (Vox) would seem a desirable bargain. However, the players are hard-pressed to encompass a work of 30–32 minutes' playing time on the single side. They accomplish it, but subtleties are sacrificed, as is proper breadth of sound. Of the others, there is the best balance of qualities in the Barylli-Doktor effort, a notable example of Mozartian mutuality, and beautifully reproduced. The Fuchses play well but a little ascetically for this work, and the combination of Stern, Primrose, and Casals produces a learned treatise on the score rather than a flowing, warmly integrated performance. It is, also, of the last three mentioned, the poorest in fidelity.

Symphonies

No. 1 in E flat (K. 16), No. 2 in B flat (K. 17), No. 5 in B flat (K. 22), No. 6 in F (K. 43). WIN, Ackermann, CH 1165.
No. 3 in E flat (K. 18), No. 13 in F (K. 112), No. 15 in G (K. 124), No. 16 in C (K. 128). NET, Ackermann, CH 1178.
No. 4 in D (K. 19), No. 10 in G (K. 84), No. 11 in D (K. 84), No. 14 in A (K. 114). WIN, Ackermann, CH 1166.
No. 7 in D (K. 45), No. 8 in D (K. 48), No. 9 in C (K. 73), No. 12 in G (K. 110). NET, Ackermann, CH 1177.

From the first of these, there is matter to engage the ear and baffle the understanding (K. 16 is the work of an eight-year-old boy). Ackermann conducts with a full sense of the challenge in the undertaking and somewhat more vigor than is heard in the succeeding issues (see below). Both orchestras perform creditably, but the Swiss engineering is a little closer, and to that extent clearer. However, the sound of the Dutch ensemble is excellent in its own way.

*No. 17 in G, K. 129. SOO, Saike, All 3055 (*No. 25 in G minor).*

The standards in this work belong exclusively to Saike, who is probably the first man to conduct it since Mozart. A little heavy-handed to my ear, but surprisingly good in sound.

No. 18 in F (K. 130), No. 19 in E flat (K. 132), No. 20 in D (K. 133), No. 21 in A (K. 134). NET, Ackermann, CH 1193.
No. 22 in C (K. 162), No. 23 in D (K. 181), No. 24 in B flat (K. 182), No. 25 in G minor (K. 183). NET, Ackermann, CH 1194.

The standard of quality in these and the foregoing works conducted by Ackermann is much the same as in the piano concertos with Balsam, which is to say, with the emphasis on taste and discretion rather than on flights of fancy. A little more vitalizing leadership than Ackermann provides would mark the slight differences among these works to better advantage. Good orchestral sound, well reproduced.

*No. 23 in D, K. 181. VSY, Swoboda, W WL 5013 (*Concertone).*

The flourishes and energy of this work profit more from the leadership of Swoboda than in the preceding sequence under Ackermann. The sound is not as good, with more accentuation than desirable at the high end.

*No. 25 in G minor, K. 183. LPO, Celibidache. L LL 88 (*No. 38 in D). DSTR, Wöldike, HS L 1055 (*No. 29 in A).*

Neither of these develops the kind of forward movement appropriate to the first movement, wherefore it might be prudent to acquire the music as part of Ackermann's more ample collection. However, if the reader is set on one or the other, the Celibidache is a bigger recording, though the Wöldike is also good.

*No. 26 in E flat, K. 184. BAM, Lehmann, 10" D DL 4045 (*No. 32 in G).*

The promise in the first movement of this work is not sustained in the other sections, but it is agreeable music nevertheless, played with good attention to detail by Lehmann. Satisfactory sound.

*No. 28 in C, K. 200. OSR, Maag, L LL 389 (*No. 34 in C).*

The semi-divertimento character of this work, with its interchanges between strings and woodwinds, is aptly projected by Maag. Good sound if the level is boosted a bit.

*No. 29 in A, K. 201. PERP, Casals, C ML 4563 (*Eine Kleine Nachtmusik). OSR, Maag, L LL 286 (*No. 36 in C). ASO, Singer, REM 199–112 (*Weber: Symphony No. 2).*

This is one work which, it seems to me, Casals has appraised perfectly, giving his fine little orchestra the kind of leadership which results in memorable music. Also, the sound has more life and body than in others of this series. The Maag is a standard Suisse Romande product, suave and expert, but a little lifeless. Excellent sound. For the price-conscious, the Singer is well-ordered Mozart, especially as paired with the Weber oddity. Quite respectably recorded.

*No. 30 in D, K. 202. VSY, Swoboda, W WL 5012 (*No. 18 in F).*

The modest charm of this work, stronger in its outside than inside movements, is effectively conveyed by Swoboda. Suitable sound.

*No. 31 in D, K. 297 ("Paris"). RPO, Beecham, C ML 4474 (*Schubert: Symphony No. 8 in B minor). LSO, Krips, L LL 542 (*No. 39 in E flat).*

As in Beecham's old "Paris," the new one has a flow of keenly controlled spirit which other interpreters hardly approximate. In any case, the distant pickup and low level of the Krips make one strain to hear details that rush to the ear in the Beecham version. Excellently realistic sound.

*No. 32 in G, K. 318. BAM, Lehmann, 10" D DL 4045 (*No. 26 in E flat). BPH, Benda, 10" Cap H 8131 (*Wolf: Italian Serenade).*

As between rarities, the Mozart-Mozart fares slightly better than Mozart-Wolf. However, there is little to choose between the performances, and the Benda is better recorded than one would expect.

*No. 33 in B flat, K. 319. VPH, Karajan, C ML 4370 (*Kleine Nachtmusik). ACG, Van Beinum, L LL 491 (*Haydn: Symphony No. 94). ASO, Heger, Rem R 199-71 (*Haydn: Symphony No. 7).*

Although the Vienna Philharmonic performance is a dubbing from 78 rpm, it dominates by virtue of its superior Mozartian feeling, the steady sense of build-up in Karajan's leadership. Also, the excess resonance is better controlled than in the 78. Van Beinum's steady but not remarkable effort is a reasonable overside acquisition in combination with the excellent "Surprise." The pickup is a little distant. Heger's orchestra does not always play in tune, but the total result, cleanly processed, is worth the bargain price.

*No. 34 in C, K. 338. LPO, Beecham, C ML 4781 (*No. 29 in A). Maag, OSR, L LL 389 (*No. 28 in C). CHO, Kubelik, Mer MG 50015 (*No. 38).*

This is one of half a dozen works by Mozart of which Beecham is a predestined and thus far unsurpassed interpreter. The 1940 recording has excellent mass and detail, but conforms to practices of the time in being studio-made, with constricting walls ever present. Those who value more luxurious sound than this will find it in the Maag, which is several levels lower on Parnassus than Beecham's, but still closer to Mozartian territory than Kubelik's. The last is good recording per se, but not suitable for Mozart.

*No. 35 in D, K. 385 ("Haffner"). LPO, Beecham, C ML 4770 (*No. 36 in C). RIAS, Fricsay, D DL 9614 (*Haydn: Symphony No. 44). NYPH, Walter, C ML 4693 (*No. 40). LPO, Van Beinum, L LL 214 (*Handel: Water Music). NBC, Toscanini, V LM 1038 (*Haydn: Symphony No. 101).*

Despite a recent freshet of recordings of this work, the Beecham remains the freshest of them in feeling and communicative power, in even accentuation throughout. To be sure, it is next to the least good in sound (the energetic but rough Toscanini has that distinction), but its other graces are many. Of the contemporary recordings, Fricsay makes the least untoward counterpull to Mozart, though his slow movement is a little brisk. Very good sound. Walter's is in his best "Now hear this" manner, which means that little squats and bends for "emphasis" mar what is otherwise a fine, upstanding account of the score. Excellent sound. Van Beinum's is in a rather showy tradition, well played but somewhat superficial. Also good sound. The versions of Reiner, Steinberg, and Karajan are, for various reasons, not as attractive as the foregoing.

*No. 36 in C, K. 425 ("Linz"). LPO, Beecham, C ML 4770 (No. 35). DSTR, Busch, V LHMV 1019 (*Haydn: Symphony No. 88). BSO, Koussevitzky, V LM 1141 (*No. 39 in E flat).*

Busch and his Danes are reproduced with a good deal more realism and accuracy of sound than Beecham and the English orchestra, but the former's tempos seem to me much too brisk from the start, wherefore a nod for Beecham, though it is not one of his outstanding performances. Studio sound, of pre-war tubbiness. Koussevitzky plays the notes pretty correctly and mostly in time, but what comes out does not strike me, either in this work or in No. 39, as in the least Mozartian. The quality of sound is alien to his thought, the swells and decrescendos far from Danubian. Fairly good sound.

*No. 37 in G, K. 444. VSY, Swoboda, W WL 5016 (*M. Haydn: Zaire music).*

As is now well known, this work is, in the main, by Michael Haydn (brother of the celebrated Joseph). However, Mozart's introduction to it is worth knowing. Swoboda conducts it cleanly, and the recording is satisfactory save for excessive emphasis on the high end.

*No. 38 in D, K. 504. CHO, Kubelik, Mer MG 50015 (*No. 34 in C). RPO, Beecham, C ML 4313 (*No. 41 in C). OSR, Ansermet, L LL 88 (*No. 25 in G minor).*

For reasons unknown to me, Beecham's remake with the Royal Philharmonic did not come out as well as the older version with the London Philharmonic, wherefore I incline toward the Kubelik-Chicago Symphony. Kubelik has a stronger feeling for this work than for the associated No. 34, and the sound is not only clear, but also reasonably resonant. The Ansermet is expert in its style, but I find the style inappropriate for the music. Neither of the economy versions (Golschmann-St. Louis, Stock-Chicago) is musically palatable.

*No. 39 in E flat, K. 543. CO, Szell, C ML 4109 (*Haydn: Symphony No. 88). VPH, Karajan, C RL 3068 (*Beethoven: Symphony No. 5). LPO, Beecham, C ML 4674 (*No. 40 in G minor). LPO, Weingartner, C ML 4776 (*Kleine Nachtmusik; Haydn: Toy Symphony). LSO, Krips, L LL 542 (*No. 31 in D).*

For some reason not easily fathomable, virtually all the estimable versions of this work appear on the Columbia label, including the Szell of previous, and continuing, long-playing favor. It combines clarity of outline with good sound to an extent not matched by any other of contemporary date, including the Krips, which lacks bite and emphasis. At the quoted price, the Karajan is decidedly advantageous, for it matches the Straussian breadth (remembered from 78's of old) in this work with reasonably good sound. Of the older versions, more interest inheres in the finely phrased performance by Weingartner than in the rather dull wartime one by Beecham. This is one of the latest Weingartner recordings, dating from 1940 and quite listenable.

*No. 40 in G minor, K. 550. NBC, Toscanini, V LM 1789 (*Haydn: Symphony No. 94). NYPH, Walter, C ML 4693 (*No. 35 in D). LPO, Beecham, C ML 4674 (*No. 39 in E flat). RSO, Leinsdorf, C RL 3070 (*Schubert: Symphony No. 8 in B minor). PSO, Reiner, 10" C ML 2008.*

In this first flight of performances (which omits others by Furtwängler, Krips, Kleiber, and Jochum, not to mention Prohaska and Dorati), each conductor has a personal view of this work which makes his an absorbing experience. With the added resonance of Carnegie Hall recording, Toscanini's concentrated, lean sound for this work exposes subtleties rarely heard in other versions. It is also remarkably well played. The special virtue of the Walter is its pulsating sound, among the best Columbia has produced. It is also less marred by little idiosyncrasies than No. 35. Beecham's conception is still the most appealing to me, but the limited appeal of the sound cannot be denied. Considering the excellence of the sound and the very good sense of the work conveyed, Leinsdorf's version is as attractive as any. Mention should be made of the fine results attained by Reiner with the Pittsburgh Orchestra of his time, though this very early LP has a shallowness of sound typical of the era in which it appeared.

*No. 41 in C, K. 551 ("Jupiter"). PSO, Steinberg, Cap P 8242 (*No. 35 in D). NBC, Toscanini, V LM 1030 (*Concerto in B flat for Bassoon and Orchestra). LSO, Krips, 10" L LS 86. VPH, Böhm, V LBC 1018 (*Beethoven: Symphony No. 5). RPO, Beecham, C ML 4313 (*No. 38 in D).*

Although the Pittsburgh Orchestra is not the NBC, and Steinberg is not Toscanini, his is better Mozart, to my taste, than the Maestro's. The palette of sound is better chosen, the violins being allowed to sing out naturally instead of being suppressed. However, I should not like to be thought wanting in appreciation for the superlative NBC performance or its generally acute (sometimes too acute) reproduction. The Krips has fine sound, but little else that is persuasive, while Böhm's sober, unadventurous performance is marred by an overhang of resonance. Good value, nevertheless. As for the Beecham, it is a disappointment, the flow of the melodic line being retarded by arbitrary pauses, the rhythmic pulse not being steady. Very good sound, however.

Works for Orchestra and Solo Instruments

For Orchestra and Piano

Rondos in D, K. 382, and A, K. 386. Seeman, BAM, Lehmann, 10" D DL 4079.
*K. 382 only. Kempff, DPH, Van Kempen, D DL 9535 (*Symphony No. 38 in D).*

As might be suspected, Kempff makes a more poetic thing of this music than Seeman—though one wonders whether the subtleties he discovers are in the music or in his own imagination. In any case, Seeman's well-phrased playing is substantially better reproduced, the work of the two conductors being about on a par. The conductor of the "Prague," incidentally, is Schmidt-Isserstedt, with the NWDRO. This is a tidy performance, reasonably well recorded with a rather distant pickup.

For Orchestra and Violin

*Rondos in C, K. 373, and B flat, K. 269; Adagio in E, K. 261. Swärdström, TSO, Lund, Per SPLP 548 (*Concerto for Violin, No. 7).*
*K. 261 and K. 373 only. Milstein, RCAO, Golschmann, V LM 1064 (*Glazounow: Concerto for Violin).*

The sweet tone and good musicianship of Swärdström are more than listenable, but Milstein commands more of the arts of sustaining the interest. As a partner to the No. 7 (played by Stucki), the two rondos and adagio are attractive value. Good sound in all instances.

MÜLLER, PAUL (1898-   )

*Sinfonia for String Orchestra. ZCM, Sacher, L LL 596 (*Burkhard: Toccata).*

A lively work, of much contrapuntal ingenuity, powerfully delivered by Sacher and his excellent ensemble. Fine sound in both balance and detail.

MUSSORGSKY, MODEST (1835-1881)

Works for Orchestra (Collection)

A Night on Bare Mountain; Prelude, Dance of the Persian Slaves, Entr'acte from Khovantschina; Overture and Gopak from The Fair at Sorochinsk; Scherzo in B flat minor; Intermezzo in B minor; Turkish March. PHI, Süsskind, MGM E 3030.

One or two versions of *A Night on Bare Mountain* noted below have more virtuosity in pace and accent than Süsskind's, but his is a thoroughly sound effort and as well reproduced as any. As all the other matter is desirable, and not otherwise available in such compact form, the disc is a worthy one.

Work for Orchestra

*A Night on Bare Mountain. OSC, Ansermet, 10" L LD 9086 (*Borodin: Steppes of Central Asia).*

Ansermet has both the work and his fine orchestra under complete command, and the recording is among London's finest. For an economy version, Malko's with the Philharmonia (see below under *Khovantschina*) is recommendable, though the sound quality hardly compares with that of the Ansermet.

Opera Excerpts (Orchestral)

Khovantschina: Prelude, Dances of the Persian Slaves, Entr'acte. PHI, Süsskind, MGM E 3030.

See entry above, under Collection.

Khovantschina: Entr'acte only. PHI, Malko, V LBC 1022.

As part of a miscellany including *Night on Bare Mountain* well delivered and various parts of Glazounow's *The Seasons* and *Raymonda* very well delivered, this finely phrased version may be highly recommended at the price. Good recording, but not outstanding.

Transcribed Works

*Pictures at an Exhibition. NBC, Toscanini, V LM 1838 (*Franck: Psyché, Part IV only). OSR, Ansermet, L LL 956 (*Ravel: La Valse). ACG, Dorati, Ep LC 3015 (*Smetana: Moldau, etc). CHO, Kubelik, Mer 50000.*

If Ansermet gives us more of Ravel, Toscanini gives us all of Mussorgsky in a vivid suggestion of what a Toscanini *Boris* might have been like. The recording is in a class with the Dvořák *New World*, ranging from fine spun detail to overwhelming climaxes. Ansermet's direction is excellent in its style, and the reproduction searches out many strands of texture not usually heard. However, the Toscanini is a more imposing totality (with the Franck a lulling anti-climax not as faithful in sound). Both other versions treat the score as a championship course for engineering competition, with the Kubelik of interest, at least, as the first in Mercury's now established series of excellent reproductions. Otherwise, for audiophiles only.

NARDINI, PIETRO (1722-1793)

*Concerto for Violin and Orchestra, in E minor. Rybar, WIN, Dahinden, W 5049 (*Viotti: Concerto No. 22).*

Rybar is a thoroughly competent violinist, but without any special sense of the style appropriate to this music. Excellent sound.

NICOLAI, CARL OTTO (1810-1849)

*The Merry Wives of Windsor: Overture. CBSO, Beecham, 10" C ML 2134 (*Von Suppé: Morning, Noon, and Night in Vienna; Strauss: Morning Papers; etc.). VPH, Furtwängler, LHMV 1020 (*Schubert: Symphony in B minor; Weber: Oberon Overture; etc.).*

One of Beecham's rare American recordings and a superb example of this musician's finesse, his feeling for a melodic phrase. Excellent ensemble, and very well reproduced. The Furtwängler performance is orchestrally immaculate, but a little prosaic in statement.

NIELSEN, CARL (1865-1931)

Concerto for Clarinet. *Cahuzac, COP, Frandsen, 10" C ML 2219. Erikson, DSTR, Wöldike, L LL 1124 (*Concerto for Flute).*

Those interested specifically in the *Clarinet Concerto* will be best off with the Columbia 10" disc, for Cahuzac is a master of this uncommon score, capable of conveying all its moodiness and drama. Good sound, also. However, there is another side to the matter, as noted below.

*Concerto for Flute. Jespersen, DSTR, Jensen, L LL 1124 (*Concerto for Clarinet).*

That a composer capable of creating this beautifully imagined, remarkably fulfilled score should have remained so little known outside his native land for nearly a quarter-century shows beyond question what a modest people the Danes are. This is perhaps the most approachable work of Nielsen I have heard, yet wholly unlike the conventional concept of a flute concerto. The scoring is full, the mood evocative, but in no *Syrinx* or flutter-tongue style. As for Gilbert Jespersen, he is a great artist on his instrument, an ideal voice for Nielsen here. This being so, Erikson's playing of the *Clarinet Concerto* comes as a welcome dividend.

*Helios (Overture). DSTR, Tuxen, 10" L LS 653 (*Schultz: Serenade for Strings).*

Tuxen's sympathy for the works of his countryman is apparent, as is the excellence of the orchestra. Good sound.

Symphony No. 1 in G minor. DSTR, Jensen, L LL 635.

A work of much dramatic power, interpreted with fine persuasiveness by Jensen. Good reproduction.

Symphony No. 3 ("Espansiva"). COP, Tuxen, L LL 100.

Perhaps the best of the Nielsen symphonies, warmly expressed and very well reproduced.

Symphony No. 4. DSTR, Grondahl, V LHMV 1006.

Like his compatriots Jensen and Tuxen, Grondahl knows his Nielsen. The good acoustical surroundings are very helpful to the total results.

Symphony No. 6 ("Sinfonia Semplice"). DNO, Jensen, Mer 10137.

Not as good sound as the predecessor works, but well performed.

OFFENBACH, JACQUES (1819-1880)

Ballet Music

*Gaité Parisienne. COL, Kurtz, C ML 4233 (*Prokofiev: March; Rimsky-Korsakov: Flight of the Bumble Bee; etc.). BPO, Fiedler, V LM 1001. PHO, Ormandy, C ML 4895 (*Chopin: Les Sylphides). ROO, Süsskind, V LBC 1065 (*Strauss: Emperor Waltz, Du and Du).*

Both Kurtz and Fiedler are old hands at this racy business, but the new version by Süsskind is hardly less skilled, while Ormandy makes a gaudy orchestral showpiece of Manuel Rosenthal's transcription (the overside *Sylphides* is not even that). If anyone cherishes the complete ballet score, Fiedler provides it. Both others use compressions, with Süsskind's as well recorded as, and substantially cheaper than, the Kurtz.

*Helen of Troy. MIN, Dorati, V LM 9033 (*Strauss: Der Rosenkavalier suite).*

As the compiler of this diverting potpourri, Dorati is eminently qualified to discourse it justly. Clear sound, a little on the boomy side.

Overtures

La Belle Hélène; Barbe-Bleu; La Grande Duchesse de Gérolstein; Le Mariage aux Lanternes; Orpheus in Hades. LPO, Martinon, L LL 350.

A hardly improvable compilation of favorite *morceaux*, brilliantly animated by Martinon and warmly reproduced.

*Orpheus in Hades. PHI, Weldon, C RL 3072 (*Mendelssohn: Fingal's Cave; Glinka: Russlan and Ludmilla; Strauss: Fledermaus overture). COL, Rodzinski, 10" C AL 2 (*Liszt: Hungarian Rhapsody No. 2).*

Columbia's self-created competition finds it balancing Rodzinski's good but hardly exceptional performance and the overside *Hungarian Rhapsody* against Weldon's brighter, better-recorded version of the same work, and four additional ones. As the price differential is but thirteen cents, I select the Weldon.

ORFF, CARL (1895-)

Works for Orchestra and Voices

Carmina Burana. BAV, Jochum, chorus, soloists, D DL 9706.

A rousing experience, with Orff's vivid material energetically served by Jochum and the associated performers: Elfride Trötschel, Hans Braun, Paul Kuen (tenor), and Karl Hoppe (baritone). The recording tends to blur a bit in climaxes, but it is large in scale, massive in effects.

Catulli Carmina. WKCH, Hollreiser, soloists, Vox PL 8640.

Whether four pianos and a large assemblage of percussion instruments constitute an "orchestra" within the scope of this volume may be questioned, but the sound output is certainly greater than that of many a Haydn symphony. Hollreiser is convincing in his exposition of the musical text, and the sound is impressively realistic and well balanced.

PAGANINI, NICCOLO (1782-1840)

*Concerto for Violin and Orchestra, No. 1 in D. Francescatti, PHO, Ormandy, C ML 4315 (*Saint-Saëns: Concerto No. 3 in B minor).*

The fine line of Francescatti's tone traces a notable series of arabesques and curves, threading Paganini's thought with a wonderfully sure hand. Excellent orchestral support and clarity of sound.

*Concerto for Violin and Orchestra, No. 2 in B minor. Menuhin, PHI, Fistoulari, V LHMV 1015 (*Vieuxtemps: Concerto No. 4 in D minor).*

This is a violinistic accomplishment very much to Menuhin's credit, up to and including the final Rondo *à la clochette*, better known as "*La Campanella.*" His tone is beautifully microphoned, and Fistoulari is an attentive collaborator.

PEIKO, NIKOLAI (1916-)

Moldavian Suite. USSR, Rachlin, *W 5132 (*Prokofiev: Winter Holiday).*

Acceptable rather than invigorating performance, the recording apparently the product of a dead, not too spacious studio.

PERGOLESI, GIOVANNI BATTISTA (1710-1736)

Concertos

For String Orchestra, Nos. 1, 3, 4, 5. WIN, Ephrikian, 10" W 4001/2.

Alert, musicianly performance, with uncommonly fine string ensemble tone. The works are all interesting and virtually unknown.

*For Flute and Orchestra, in G. Meylan, WIN, Dahinden, CH 1082 (*Haydn: Sonata in G).*

A stimulating work, spirited and individual, played with fine artistry by the soloist. Excellent sound. The performers in the second-side work are Rene Le Roy, flute, and Paul Loyonnet, piano.

Concertinos

Nos. 2, 3, 5, 6. LAM, Colombo, OL 50010.

The attribution to Pergolesi of these works is disputed, but they have substantial virtues of content and manner, whoever the composer. Thoroughly informed direction by Colombo, excellent performance and reproduction.

*No. 2. SCH, Münchinger, L LL 312 (*Respighi: Ancient Airs and Dances, Suite No. 3).*

Beautiful work by Münchinger and his men, reproduced with that blend of richness and definition which London so well commands. This is, apparently, an authentic work in F minor not included in the sequence above.

PETRASSI, GOFFREDO (1904-)

*Don Quixote (Ballet). VSO, Litschauer, Van VRS 447 (*Respighi: Ancient Airs and Dances, Suite No. 1).*

The stabbing trumpets, rolling drums, and piercing flutes make fine high-fidelity matter, but the total does not impress me musically. Excellent processing.

PFITZNER, HANS (1869-1949)

Overtures

*Das Christelflein. ORB, Rother, U RLP 7050 (*Kätchen von Heilbronn; Reger: Ballet Suite).*

A rather imaginative work, well managed by Rother, and acceptably reproduced. That judgment, however (see below), does not apply to the companion piece.

Das Kätchen von Heilbronn. BAM, Lehmann, 10" D DL 4017 (*Schumann: Manfred). VPH, Pfitzner, U RLP 7050 (*Reger: Ballet Suite).

Whatever value there is in the composer's participation is offset by the shrieky highs and wiry string tone of the reproduction. Lehmann's effort is suitable and well reproduced.

Symphonies

In C, opus 46. SAX, Böhm, U RLP 7044 (*Kleine Sinfonie, opus 44).

Like other works in this sequence, this radio tape was not successfully processed for disc use, the sound being mostly shrill and unpleasant. I could not possibly give an opinion on the performance beyond saying that it does not hold my attention.

In C sharp minor. GOH, Schmidt-Isserstedt, U RLP 7056.

A slight but not substantial improvement on the situation described above. The musical interest is hardly magnetic.

In G ("Kleine Sinfonie," opus 44). SYM, Rapf, 10" AU 1061.

A much better-sounding product than the second side of U RLP 7044 (see above), and rather pleasant to hear. Without the composer's name, it would suggest early Strauss.

PISTON, WALTER (1894-)

The Incredible Flutist. ORB, Rother, U RLP 7092 (*Copland: Appalachian Spring).

Not as good a performance as the previous one by Fiedler and the Boston Pops Orchestra. Loudly reproduced.

PLEYEL, IGNAZ (1757-1831)

Concertante Symphony No. 5 in F. EIDP, de Froment, OL 50014 (*Dittersdorf: Three Partitas).

Decidedly superior execution by the virtuosos directed by Louis de Froment, especially the hornist Gilbert Coursier. Fine balance and tone qualities.

PONCHIELLI, AMILCARE (1834-1886)

La Gioconda: Dance of the Hours. CSO, Beecham, 10" C ML 2134

(*Nicolai: Merry Wives; Strauss: Morning Papers; etc.). NBC, Toscanini, 10" V LRM 7005 (*Sibelius: Finlandia; etc.). OSC, Fistoulari, 10" L LD 9014 (*Thomas: Mignon overture).

Choice between Beecham and Toscanini rests on one's preference for the mercurial or the electrical treatment of the music. I personally incline to the Beecham (brightly reproduced), but the other contents of the Toscanini disc are highly attractive. The Fistoulari surpasses both in richness of sound and fullness of detail, but not otherwise.

POULENC, FRANCIS (1899-)

Les Biches (Ballet). LSO, Fistoulari, MGM 3098 (*Fauré: Dolly). OSC, Désormière, L LL 624 (*Scarlatti: Good Humored Ladies).

Two excellent performances, both well reproduced, though the Fistoulari is broader in emphasis and sharper in instrumental values. The second-side Scarlatti is decidedly attractive, the preferable version of this work.

Concerto Chorégraphique. Jacquinot, WES, Fistoulari, MGM 3069 (*Debussy: Fantasy).

Lively performance by pianist Jacquinot, well supported by Fistoulari.

Concerto for Organ, String Orchestra, and Timpani, in G minor. Biggs, COL, Burgin, C ML 4329 (*Franck: Prelude, Fugue and Variation, Pièce héroïque).

An imposing work, vigorously delivered under Burgin's direction, and splendidly reproduced. The variety of effects (timpani, viola, and cello) is well blended.

Concerto for Piano and Orchestra. Haas, PAS, Dervaux, per 563 (*Milhaud: Suite).

Haas is an able pianist, and the reproduction is acceptable.

PROKOFIEV, SERGE (1891-1953)

Ballet Music

Chout (Buffoon). STS, Golschmann, Cap P 8257 (*Falla: Dances from The Three-Cornered Hat).

A welcome addition to the Prokofiev literature, flashily done by Golschmann, and very well performed. Excellent sound.

*Cinderella. BSI, Stasevitch, CH 1304 (*Romeo and Juliet Suite No. 3). ROO, Braithwaite, C ML 4229 (*Gordon: Rake's Progress).*

Inasmuch as the performance by the Bolshoi orchestra is one of the best recordings I have heard from Russia (I doubt that many could distinguish it from any typical European product), the pairing with the *Romeo and Juliet* music makes it the preferable choice for the Prokofiev fancier. However there is excellent life and continuity in Braithwaite's performance, which is well reproduced.

Pas d'Acier. PHI, Markevitch, An 3518 [3] *(*Satie: Parade; Ravel: Daphnis et Chloe, Suite No. 2; Glinka: Kikimora; etc.).*

If the suitably incisive performance by Markevitch were paired with the Satie score, this would be a highly recommendable offering. However, each is on a separate disc of a three-record "package," and even if acquired in Angel's economy presentation, they would require a two-record purchase. The disadvantage is, of course, that the more standard works are all available in performances of greater subtlety than that of the generally good ones of Markevitch. Mention must be made of the superb brochure fully illustrating the title of this collection: *Homage a Diaghilev.*

*Prodigal Son. OCC, Sebastian, U LP 7139 (*Symphony No. 4).*

A utility version that serves in the absence of any other. Neither the playing nor the processing is of a particularly distinguished quality.

*Romeo and Juliet (Suite No. 3). BSI, Stasevitch, CH 1304 (*Cinderella).*

The mechanical attributes noted above are constant here, in a performance of finesse and excellent tonal qualities.

*Scythian Suite. VSY, Scherchen, W 5091 (*Lieutenant Kijé).*

One of the notably showy recordings of the day, this also embodies a sound concept of the music.

*The Stone Flower (Gypsy Fantasy only). BSI, Samosud, CE 3001 (*Glière: Concerto for Horn; etc.).*

Decidedly minor Prokofiev, rather inaccessibly placed in a miscellany. Soggy sound.

Cantata

Alexander Nevsky. Iriarte, VSO, Rossi, Van RS 451. Tourel, PHO, Ormandy, C ML 4247.

The use of a Russian text and the advantages of contemporary recording are factors of favor in the Vienna enterprise: Tourel's suitability for this music and the more personalized leadership of

Ormandy are factors of continuing interest in the Philadelphia product. All things considered, I'd incline to the former, which also has superior annotations.

Concertos

For Piano and Orchestra

*No. 1 in D flat. Richter, MOS, Kondrashin, Per SPL 599 (*Concerto No. 5; Sonata No. 5, opus 38).*

Excellent value in all instances, including the piano sonata, which is not in the scope of this survey. The present item, from the U.S.S.R., is energetically played, well reproduced.

*No. 3 in C. François, OSC, Cluytens, An 35045 (*Visions Fugitives, opus 22, Nos. 1, 3, 4, 6, 17, 18; Toccata in D minor). Mitropoulos, ROB, C ML 4389 (*Shostakovich: Piano Concerto).*

In style and sensitivity, the playing of François is considerably superior to that of his contemporaries who have recently shown an interest in this work. Particularly fine slow movement, with Cluytens in sympathetic vein, the whole very well reproduced. For those who acquire an interest in the Mitropoulos version through the Shostakovich on side two, it may be said that it can't hurt.

*No. 5 in G. Brendel, VSO, Sternberg, Per SPL 599 (*Concerto No. 1, etc.).*

A little known work of 1932, and of limited attractiveness. Brendel works diligently at it, and the reproduction of the orchestra, capably directed by Sternberg, is good.

For Violin and Orchestra

*No. 1 in D. Szigeti, LPO, Beecham, C ML 4533 (*Mozart: Concerto No. 4). Odnoposoff, RZO, Hollreiser, CH 1160 (*Stravinsky: Concerto for Piano and Winds). Oistrakh, SYM, Gauk, Per SPLP 539 (*Miaskovsky: Concerto in D minor).*

Inferior processing, including noisy surfaces, deprives Oistrakh of the honor due him for a notably fine performance. For musical pleasure, the Szigeti remains supreme, though Odnoposoff's capable but not poetic performance is much better reproduced.

*No. 2 in G minor. Francescatti, NYPH, Mitropoulos, C ML 4648 (*Bach: Concerto in E). Heifetz, BSO, Koussevitzky, 10" V LCT 6.*

The strength and security of Francescatti's performance are admirably supported by Mitropoulos in a performance of more virtue than Heifetz's certainly expert, but slightly too suave, playing. The Columbia is much better reproduced, also.

Film Music

*Lieutenant Kijé (Suite). VSO, Scherchen, W 5091 (*Scythian Suite). FNS, Désormière, Cap P 8149 (*The Love for Three Oranges suite). RPO, Kurtz, C ML 4683 (*Symphony No. 7).*

This music is not in Scherchen's evocation the lightfooted thing it is in some versions, but this is one of the more astonishing recordings of our time, and vastly enjoyable for that reason alone. Both of the others come with desirable elements in the Prokofiev literature, and are well, if not so powerfully, reproduced. The Désormière is notable for orchestral execution.

Symphonies

*No. 1 in D ("Classical"). PHI, Markevitch, An 35008 (*Dukas: L'Apprenti Sorcier; etc.) BSO, Koussevitzky, V LM 1215 (*Rachmaninoff: Isle of the Dead). BPH, Celibidache, V LBC 1009 (*Ravel: Mother Goose suite).*

Despite the other celebrated names of record in performances of this music (Toscanini, Ansermet, Ormandy, etc.), Markevitch provides the best blend of spirit, orchestral execution, and finely reproduced sound. The Koussevitzky is a gem, as ever, but a little less glowing in its colors than a dozen years ago, and the Celibidache, at the price specified, is decidedly worthy.

*No. 4. OCC, Sebastian, U LP 7139 (*Prodigal Son).*

Why this work has been so rarely performed since its creation for the fiftieth anniversary season of the Boston Symphony in 1930 is hard to understand, for it seems to be in the main path of Prokofiev's development. I use the hesitant "seems" because Sebastian's performance is not reassuring where intonation is concerned, and the dissonants may not all be written ones. The reproduction is clean, a little shallow and studioish.

No. 5. DSTR, Tuxen, L LL 672. NYPH, Rodzinski, C ML 4037. BSO, Koussevitzky, V LM 1045.

Interpretatively, there is little to choose among these—all are absorbing, none is wholly convincing. However, the advantage of techniques is with Tuxen, whose fine orchestra is better reproduced than either of the others.

No. 6 in E flat. OSR, Ansermet, L LL 527.

First-class organization of this music by Ansermet in a highly successful reproduction.

*No. 7. PHO, Ormandy, C ML 4683 (*Lieutenant Kijé suite).*

Something of a house specialty with Ormandy, tendered with care and conscience in a reproduction of brilliant power.

Opera Excerpts (Orchestral)

*The Gamblers. PHI, Schuechter, MGM E 3112 (*Kabalevsky: Colas Breugnon suite).*

Four "portraits" ("Alexis," "The General and the Grandmother," "Pauline," "Dénouement") from the opera score make a rather disjointed musical sequence, but the interesting ideas are well conveyed by Schuechter. Clear, bright sound.

*The Love for Three Oranges (Suite). LAM, Martinon, Ep LC 3042 (*Classical Symphony; Concerto No. 3). FNS, Désormière, Cap P 8149 (*Lieutenant Kijé). COP, Malko, V LBC 1022 (*Mussorgsky: Night on Bare Mountain; Glazunov: Seasons excerpts; etc.).*

Martinon's energetic performance is by much the best recorded of these, a truly rousing experience. Désormière's more fanciful conception is not as well reproduced. The Malko is a fine utility version, well worth what is asked in its category.

*The Love for Three Oranges: March only. OSR, Ansermet. 10" L LS 503 (*Debussy: L'Après-midi; Ravel: Alborado del Gracioso; etc.).*

Sheer virtuosity by Ansermet, aptly mirrored in the reproduction.

Work for Orchestra and Narrator

*Peter and the Wolf. Guinness, BPO, Fiedler, V LM 1761 (*Saint-Saëns: Carnival des Animaux). Pickles, PHI, Markevitch, V LBC 1015 (*Tchaikovsky: Nutcracker suite).*

Alec Guinness is so much the best of all the narrators who have simpered through this chore since it was invented, and Fiedler's familiarly expert direction is so well reproduced, that no other version need be considered. In the lower price group, Markevitch's good Russo-French impulses are defeated by the heavy Briticisms of W. Pickles, who raises vocal eyebrows at every comma and insists that the wolf was captured with a "lassūh."

Work for Orchestra and Voices

*Winter Holiday. USSR, Samosud, W WL 5132 (*Peiko: Moldavian Suite).*
Musical scene-painting meant for juvenile consumption, and hence somewhat limited in general interest. Good performance, listenable but not superior reproduction.

Miscellaneous

*Divertimento, opus 43. VSO, Swoboda, WL 5031 (*Sinfonietta, opus 5/48).*
Excellent reproduction of a not too perceptive performance.

*Overture on a Hebrew Theme. CHAM, Mitropoulos, D DL 8511 (*Quintet, opus 39; Swanson: Night Music).*
Lively direction by Mitropoulos of the small Philharmonic unit, and clear recording.

*Russian Overture, opus 72. BPH, Steinkopf, 10" U RLP 5005 (*Love for Three Oranges suite).*
Such music as there may be in this blary piece is obscured by poor processing of the dull-sounding recording.

*Sinfonietta, opus 5/48. VSO, Swoboda, W L 5031 (*Divertimento).*
An entertaining work first played in 1915, and revised in 1929. A creditable effort by Swoboda, well reproduced.

QUANTZ, JOHANN (1697-1773)

*Concerto No. 17. Wanausek, VPA, Adler, SPA 23 (*Frederick the Great: Concerto).*
Flexible fluting by Wanausek, and good reproduction.

RABAUD, HENRI (1873-1949)

*Marouf: Ballet Music. LAM, Fournet, Ep LC 3030 (*Delibes: Sylvia, Coppélia excerpts; Gounod: Faust ballet music).*
Those not allergic to synthetic Orientalisms will find these opera excerpts entertaining, and very professionally performed. Outstanding sound.

*Procession Nocturne. NYPH, Mitropoulos, 10" C ML 2170 (*Saint-Saëns: Danse Macabre).*
Flavorsome work by Mitropoulos, well reproduced.

RACHMANINOFF, SERGEI (1873-1943)

Concertos

For Piano and Orchestra

*No. 1 in F sharp minor. Rachmaninoff, PHO, Ormandy, V LCT 1118 (*Rhapsody on a Theme by Paganini).*

Whether or not one ranks this work with the second and third concertos (I don't), it has abundant attractions as expounded by its creator. The recording lacks the mass we expect today, but it is decidedly good otherwise.

*No. 2 in C minor. Anda, PHI, Galliera, An 35093 (*Preludes in G and G minor). Rachmaninoff, PHO, Stokowski, V LCT 1014.*

The Anda is the most musical and well-controlled of the current collection of mechanically superior reproductions, though the composer's own, dim-sounding as it is (it dates from 1929), suggests the kind of power required but not offered by the younger man. A new Horowitz or Rubinstein might be the solution.

No. 3 in D minor. Horowitz, RCAO, Reiner, V LM 1178. Lympany, NEW, Collins, L LL 617.

Horowitz is a formidable master of this score, and the current version is, in the nature of things, far more realistic than his earlier one with Coates. The only count against it is that the orchestra, admirably directed by Reiner, did not get as much valuation in the sound as it should. In this, the Lympany-Collins is perfectly accomplished, and her playing throughout is adept, if a little light. (A reissue of the composer's own version, from 1940, would be welcome.)

No. 4 in G minor. Rachmaninoff, PHO, Ormandy, V LCT 1019.

The composer's devotion to his "youngest" is understandable, and profitable also, for it gives a more graphic likeness of his performing style than any other recording now available.

Symphonies

No. 1 in D minor. DPH, Bongartz, U LP 7131.

Despite the composer's self-deprecation of this work (he suppressed the score during his lifetime), it has many characteristics of the later Rachmaninoff. The performance here is persuasive, the orchestral playing excellent, the reproduction quite decent.

No. 2 in E minor. PHO, Ormandy, C ML 4433. NYPH, Rodzinski, C RL 3049. MIN, Mitropoulos, V LM 1068.

Were the reproduction of Ormandy's excellent estimate of this situation not one of the finest ever made of the Philadelphia Orchestra, I would counsel the Rodzinski, much better in sound than in its 78-rpm version, and thoroughly just in musical concept. Mitropoulos's sympathy for this work is well known, but the sound can hardly compare with the Philadelphia, nor the price with the Columbia "Entree."

No. 3 in A minor. BSI, Golovanov, RS 7.

Were RCA to make available the composer's own powerful projection of this score (V Set 712), the outland competition would be merely academic. As it is, the opportunity is provided to hear the notes, if not much more.

Symphonic Dances. RPH, Leinsdorf, C ML 4621.

Persuasive, stylistic direction by Leinsdorf, satisfactory if not exceptional tonal qualities.

Symphonic Poem

*The Isle of the Dead. BSO, Koussevitzky, V LM 1215 (*Prokofiev: "Classical" Symphony). MIN, Mitropoulos, C ML 4196 (*Vaughan Williams: Fantasia).*

In combination with the fine playing of the Prokofiev score, this comprises one of the larger monuments to the art and industry of Koussevitzky. Its superiorities to the Mitropoulos include warmer sound, better reproduced.

Work for Orchestra and Piano

*Rhapsody on a Theme by Paganini. Rubinstein, PHI, Süsskind, V LM 1744 (*Szymanowski: Symphonie Concertante). Rachmaninoff, PHO, Stokowski, V LCT 1118 (*Concerto No. 1). Cherkassky, LSO, Menges, V LBC 1066 (*Chopin: F minor Fantasie, etc.).*

Rubinstein's feeling for this music is more akin to the composer's than any other I know, and it has intensified lately. I would not say that it is as well reproduced as it might be, for which reason attention might be directed to a possible new version. The composer's own is one of the memorable documents of our time, and of substantially good sound even now. In the latter respect, the low-priced Cherkassky is as good as any now available, and brilliantly fingered, though some of the slower sections are sentimentalized. Excellent orchestral playing under Herbert Menges.

Work for Orchestra and Voices

The Bells. SYM, Rachmilovich, RS 8.

The musical matter here is more imposing than the reproduction of it, which is dull and bombastic, lacking real fidelity. The soloists are Orietta Moscucci, soprano, Charles Anthony, tenor, and Lorenzo Malfatti, baritone.

RAKOV, NIKOLAI (1908-)

*Concerto for Violin and Orchestra. Gavrilov, ORB, Rother, U URLP 7112 (*Malipiero: Concerto for Violin).*

A work of vigor and much virtuoso detail, expounded with full competence and authority by the able Gavrilov. Powerful sound, rather close up to the microphone.

RAMEAU, JEAN PHILIPPE (1683-1764)

Six Concerts en Sextuor. HEW, Hewitt, HS 99.

The noncommittal description hardly prepares one for the dazzling variety and musical resource in these works. Four are made up of three movements in contrasted tempos, two of four movements. Through the twenty sections courses a vitalizing rhythmic pulse and deep understanding of the style communicated by Hewitt. The commentary of Henri Gheon is appropriately excellent. Clean sound, a mite thin.

RANGSTRÖM, TURE (1884-1947)

Symphony No. 1 (In Memoriam—Strindberg). STOC, Mann, L LLP 514.

A strong work, of not too apparent personal flavor, recorded with much force and dynamic definition.

RAVEL, MAURICE (1875-1937)

Concertos

*For Piano and Orchestra, in G. Blancard, OSR, Ansermet, L LL 797 (*Concerto for Left Hand).*

As much for the scintillating direction of Ansermet and the brightly sonorous recording as for the good but not exceptional piano-playing of Blancard, this pairing answers admirably the question of desirability in the Ravel piano-orchestra literature.

*Concerto for Left Hand Only. Blancard, OSR, Ansermet, L LL 797 (*Concerto in G). Casadesus, PHO, Ormandy, C ML 4075 (*Debussy: Damoiselle Élue).*

For comment on Blancard, see above. The Casadesus effort, though not as well reproduced, is a fine example of his style for those who are interested in that element, and the second side is excellent Debussy.

Works for Orchestra

*Alborado del Gracioso. OSR, Ansermet, 10" L LD 9031 (*Debussy: Prélude a l'après-midi d'un faune). ORS, Leibowitz, Vox PL 8150 (*Boléro; Pavanne; Rhapsodie Espagnole; La Valse).*

The gap between these versions is considerable, in content—which is visible—and in treatment, which is audible. Ansermet's selective combination offers two fine performances, well reproduced, Leibowitz's omnibus provides much of the Ravel orchestral literature, energetically played, but not too judiciously recorded. Generous value economically, if not on the artistic side.

*Bolero. PHO, Ormandy, 10" C AL 51 (*La Valse). OSC, Munch, L LL 466 (*Berlioz: Benvenuto Cellini; Le Corsaire). DSO, Paray, Mer 50020 (*Rimsky-Korsakov: Capriccio Espagnole).*

For the virtue of being what it is, Ormandy's *Bolero* is compactly presented with a minimum of extraneous matter. Moreover, it is, as far as listening attention to this piece can now be sustained, properly paced and very well reproduced. However, *La Valse* is done better by other hands. I cannot profess enthusiasm about either of the others.

Daphnis et Chlöe (Complete Ballet). OSR, Ansermet, L LL 693.

The history of this work, as a repertory item, is worth considering. When the first suite became available about 1920, that was favored for a time: when the more ample second suite appeared a few years later, that became a concert favortie. Now that Ansermet has brought attention to bear on the full work, and the choral interjections, it is finally possible to evaluate Ravel's total accomplishment, which is fine indeed. Granted Ansermet's kind of enlivening power, it should be the standard from now on. Excellent sound.

*Daphnis et Chloë (Suites 1 and 2). PHO, Ormandy, C ML 4316 (*Schoenberg: Verklärte Nacht).*

This seems to me a rather wary compromise between the full ballet and the popular second suite alone. Able, if not overpowering, performance.

*Daphnis et Chloë (Suite No. 2). NBC, Toscanini, V LM 1043 (*Beethoven: Leonore No. 3).*

The "last word" on this music (referred to under Beethoven overtures) is the one of Ansermet in the complete suite. However, if one relishes a virtuoso treatment of the second suite only, this is virtuosity in excelsis. Not the best sound, but a rousing likeness of Toscanini's power in this music.

*Introduction and Allegro. Berghout, ACMS, Van Beinum, 10" L LS 621 (*Debussy: Danses Sacrée et Profane).*

See under Debussy entry.

*Ma Mère l'Oye. OSR, Ansermet, L LL 388 (*Debussy: La Mer). BSO, Koussevitzky, V LM 1012 (*Boléro).*

Delicate articulation by Ansermet, beautifully reproduced. The Koussevitzky-Boston collaboration is a memorable reminder of their finest days together, if not as bright in sound as one would like.

*Menuet Antique. OSC, Fournet, Ep LC 3048 (*Rhapsodie Espagnole; Debussy: Nocturnes).*

A brief early work, arranged from the piano original by the composer. Its fragile charm is rather harshly served by the overbrilliant recording, which, like the others on the disc, bears down heavily on brass and percussion.

*Pavanne pour une Infante Défunte. OSR, Ansermet, 10" L LD 9039 (*Chabrier: España).*

This accounts splendidly for all the values involved in the Ravel, as well as those in the Chabrier.

Rhapsodie Espagnole. *OSR, Ansermet, L LL 530 (*Debussy: Nocturnes). PHI, Karajan, An 35081 (Debussy: La Mer).*

My predilection for Ansermet's Ravel is not lessened by anything in the Karajan disc. In deftness and integration, this is one of the best Ansermet efforts, the Karajan another show of sound and fury.

*Le Tombeau de Couperin. NBC, Reiner, V LM 1724 (*Debussy: Petite Suite; Mendelssohn: Midsummer Night's Dream Music). OSR, Ansermet, L LL 795 (*Valses Nobles et Sentimentales).*

Reiner's deftness and sense of proportion are beautifully appropriate to this music, and the execution is outstandingly good. The subordinate items are well played, but if Ravel enthusiasts are also interested in the *Valses Nobles et Sentimentales*, they will be best served by the Ansermet. Excellent sound in both.

*La Valse. OSC, Ansermet, L LL 956 (*Mussorgsky: Pictures at an Exhibition). DSO, Paray, Mer MG 50029 (*Franck: Psyché). PHI, Markevitch, An 35008 (*Dukas: L'Apprenti Sorcier; Falla: Three Cornered Hat; Prokofiev: Classical Symphony).*

For my taste, Paray does this ingratiating work to the greatest total effect, though I cannot endorse the lengthy Franck work as the ideal complement to it. Actually, the buyer would be well served by either the Ansermet or the Markevitch, depending on his preference in associated works, of which the latter's *Classical* is outstanding in its category, the Ansermet *Pictures* only slightly edged by the Toscanini. If one wants vigor rather than subtlety in this work, Markevitch would be the choice. Excellent sound in all.

*Valses Nobles et Sentimentales. OSR, Ansermet, L LL 795 (*Tombeau).*

An outstanding effort by Ansermet. For further comment see *Tombeau de Couperin.*

Work for Orchestra and Violin

*Tzigane. Ricci, LAM, Bigot, Vox PL 6240 (*Saint-Saëns: Concerto in B minor). Lockhart, LSO, Fistoulari, MGM 3041 (*Chausson: Poème; Honegger: Concertino for Piano; Milhaud: Concertino for Piano).*

Ricci has congruity in repertory on his side, also superior feeling for the music, though Lockhart's playing is better reproduced.

Neither is so good that it would not readily be surpassed by a newer version.

Work for Orchestra and Voice

*Shéhérazade. Tourel, COL, Bernstein, C ML 4289 (*Mussorgsky: Songs and Dances of Death*).*

Tourel is an able, if not ideal, interpreter of this music, and the playing of the background score is excellent. Good recording.

RAWSTHORNE, ALAN (1905-)

Concerto for Piano and Orchestra, No. 2. Curzon, LSO, Sargent, 10" L LPS 513.

Curzon is a vital interpreter of this work, which has more lyric impulse than is customary currently, and a decided sense of structure. Fine sound.

REESEN, EMIL (1887-)

*A Danish Rhapsody (Himmerland). DSTR, Reesen, 10" L LS 849 (*Grieg: Lyric Suite*).*

This would be of interest largely as the side coupled with the gratifying Grieg suite. It is a lively piece, folkish in character, well directed by the composer and reproduced with fine precision.

REGER, MAX (1873-1916)

*Ballet suite, opus 130. DPH, Schrader, U URLP 7050 (*Pfitzner: Overtures*).*

Rather hashed-up sound, in a work which cannot afford much degeneration of what exists. Apparently sympathetic direction by Schrader.

Böcklin Suite. GPH, Keilberth, 10" Cap L 8011.

One of the more attractive of Reger's works, reasonably well recorded, and successfully processed for LP.

On a Merry Theme by Hiller. VPA, Adler, SPA 51.

Lacking other standards of comparison, this rendition may be considered representative. It is reasonably well reproduced, a little shrilly in the brass.

Serenade, opus 95. ACG, Jochum, Cap P 8026.

A melodious, not needlessly complicated work, vigorously directed by Jochum and still of fairly accurate sound.

Variations on a Theme of Mozart. ACG, Van Beinum, D DL 9565.

Reger's pretentious decoration of Mozart's symmetrical thought lures Van Beinum into sluggish tempos and rather extravagant accentuations. Sonorous, not too well balanced recording.

REICHAL, BERNARD (1901-)

*Concertino for Piano and Orchestra. OSR, Montandon, Appia, L LL 601 (*Beck: Concerto for Viola and Orchestra).*

This contemporary Swiss composer is not so well advertised as some products of larger countries, but he has style and technique. Excellent performance, brightly reproduced.

RESPIGHI, OTTORINO (1879-1936)

Ballet Music

*La Boutique Fantasque. LSO, Ansermet, L LL 274. PHI, Irving, V LBC 1080 (*Delibes: Naïla Intermezzo; Gounod: Mors et Vita, Judex; Mendelssohn: Spinning Song, Spring Song).*

Twice as much music for a substantially smaller price makes the well-played Irving version something for the economy-minded to ponder. It is also well reproduced. However, the gloss and vivacity of the Ansermet treatment are substantially absent, as is the clarity of the reproduction. The additional pieces on the Bluebird disc are directed by Malko, dutifully.

Concerto

Concerto Gregoriano, for Violin and Orchestra. Stiehler, LRO, Borsamsky, U 7100.

Hardly dazzling execution by the soloist, and no more than routine competence in the playing of the orchestra under Borsamsky. Passable recording.

Works for Orchestra

*Ancient Airs and Dances, Suite No. 1. VSO, Litschauer, Van VRS 447 (*Petrassi: Portrait of Don Quixote).*

Beautifully phrased, well-balanced performance, admirably reproduced.

*Ancient Airs and Dances, Suite No. 2. VSO, Litschauer, Van VRS 433 (*Gli Uccelli).*

An admirable companion issue to the foregoing, especially as it carries with it the delightful transcriptions of old music known as *The Birds*. Fine, precise playing, and live, resonant recording.

*Ancient Airs and Dances, Suite No. 3. SCH, Münchinger, L LL 312 (*Pergolesi: Concertino in F minor).*

More stylized, virtuoso-sounding performance than espoused by Litschauer, but beautiful in its own way. Marvelously suave string sound.

Feste Romane. NBC, Toscanini, 10" V LM 55.

If Toscanini's projection of these and the succeeding works is not comfortably beyond challenge by other contemporary conductors, the judgments throughout this book mean nothing. The recording is not an ultimate in resonance, but it is decidedly communicative.

Fountains of Rome; Pines of Rome. NBC, Toscanini, V LM 1768. MIN, Dorati, Mer 50011.

Vividness and vitality are the twin attributes of this superb documentation of Toscanini's bred-in-the-blood recreation of these works. Moreover, the recording is of the period when the engineers were able to get virtually all of it down—"it" being his stunning sense of contrast and climax. The loud and soft noises created by Dorati are sharply conveyed in the Mercury disc, but the interests of it are mechanical, not musical.

*Trittico Botticelliano. BSO, Litschauer, Van 418 (*Locatelli: Concerto da Camera).*

Respighi's pictorial evocations (*La Primavera, L'Adorazione dei Magi,* and *La Nascita di Venere*) are reasonably served by Litschauer, though with something less than dazzling virtuosity. Very good sound.

*Gli Uccelli (The Birds). VSO, Litschauer, Van VRS 433 (*Ancient Airs and Dances, Suite No. 2).*

These "Birds" have fluttered a little more realistically, preened themselves with more musical grace, in other versions, but the sound is excellent and the orchestral values are appropriate.

REZNIČEK, EMIL VON (1860-1945)

Donna Diana: Overture. CHO, Stock, C RL 3002 (*Sibelius: Swan of Tounela; Tchaikovsky: Nutcracker; etc.*). PHI, Fistoulari, 10" MGM E 120 (*Rimsky-Korsakov: May Night; Nicolai: Merry Wives*).

The artistic value in Stock's performance is higher than in Fistoulari's, though not nearly so audible. Economy, I think, is best served by the Columbia.

RIMSKY-KORSAKOV, NIKOLAI (1844-1908)

Concerto

For Piano and Orchestra, in C sharp minor. Jacquinot, PHI, Fistoulari, MGM E 182 (*Liszt: Todtentanz*). Badura-Skoda, VSY, Swoboda, W WL 5068 (*Scriabin: Piano Concerto*).

Either of these attractive performances will suffice, depending on what the purchaser prefers in the way of a coupling. Both recordings are outstandingly good, the Westminster favoring richness in mass, the MGM clarity in detail. If there are any decisive factors, they would be the more vigorous direction of Fistoulari, the lower price of his version. (For an alternate coupling, see under *Coq d'Or: Cortège*).

Opera Excerpts (Orchestra)

Le Coq d'Or (Suite). FNS, Désormière, Cap P 8155 (*Capriccio Espagnol*). RPO, Beecham, C ML 4454 (*Franck: Chasseur Maudit*). PHI, Dobrowen, An 35010 (*Tsar Sultan*).

For me, the Désormière is outstanding for imaginative exposition, the Beecham for orchestral excellence, and the Dobrowen for sheer brilliance of sound. However, the differences among them are hardly sufficient to discourage a choice based on a second-side preference—which would be a consideration in all three.

Le Coq d'Or; Cortège only. LSO, Weldon, MGM E 3045 (*Concerto in C sharp minor; May Night; Kamarinskaya; etc.*).

Broadly sonorous performance, included in a Rimsky-Korsakov miscellany of which the largest item is the Piano Concerto.

Ivan the Terrible (Suite). LSO, Fistoulari, MGM E 3076 (*Balakirev: Tamar*).

Highly qualified direction by Fistoulari, of the Overture, Intermezzi I and II, and "Royal Hunt and Storm." Beautiful sound, especially in the anticipations of *Scheherazade*. (In some previous versions these have been identified as being from *The Maid of Pskov*, the Russian title of the opera being *Pskovityanka*.)

*May Night: Overture. PHI, Fistoulari, MGM E 3045 (*Concerto in C sharp minor; Bridal Procession from Coq d'Or; Cortège from Mlada; Kamarinskaya; Dance of the Birds and Whitsunday Festival from The Snow Maiden).*

An enjoyable item in the miscellany heretofore noted, of which the total contents are stated above. Excellent sound.

*Mlada: Cortège des Nobles. LSO, Weldon, MGM E 3045 (*See item above).*

Weldon's Rimsky is a little more downright, less incisive than Fistoulari, but nevertheless very good. Jolly good sound.

*Snegourotchka (The Snow Maiden) Suite. PHI, Fistoulari, MGM E 3017 (*Skazka).*

Much in the style of the other Rimsky-Korsakov conducted in this sequence by Fistoulari, and perhaps the best recorded of all. Included are "Introduction and Dance of the Birds," "Cortège," "Whitsunday Festival," and "Dance of the Buffoons." Thus, the sequence includes all the sections currently available in various recordings, including two extracts on MGM E 3045.

*Snegourotchka: Dance of the Buffoons only. PHO, Ormandy, C ML 4856 (*Capriccio Espagnol, Flight of the Tumblers; Tchaikovsky: Capriccio Italien).*

A more dazzling demonstration of orchestral virtuosity than the foregoing performance, splendidly reproduced.

*Tsar Sultan (Excerpts). PHI, Dobrowen, An 35010 (*Coq d'Or).*

Lively, well-balanced direction by Dobrowen, and exceptionally good sound. Included are such dazzling tonal portraits as "The Tsar's Departure and Farewell," "The Tsarina in a Barrel at Sea," and "The Three Wonders." The sequence does not include the famous item entered below.

*Tsar Sultan: Flight of the Bumble Bee. PHO, Ormandy, C ML 4856 (*Capriccio Espagnol; Tchaikovsky: Capriccio Italien; etc.).*

Expeditious work with this showpiece, powerfully droned by Ormandy's busy virtuosos. Excellent sound.

Works for Orchestra

*Antar (Symphonic Suite). OSR, Ansermet, L LL 1060 (*Glazunov:*

Stenka Razin). *LSO, Scherchen, W WL 5280* (**Grand Pâque Russe*). *DSO, Paray, Mer MG 50028* (**Grand Pâque Russe*).

It is luxury indeed to have three such excellent versions of this far from hackneyed work available, all well or excellently reproduced. Ansermet makes the most music of the opportunities presented, Scherchen the best collection of recordable effects. Paray's version is less adept in terms of advantageous microphoning, but only *vis-a-vis* such experts as Ansermet and Scherchen. The latter's, incidentally, has the disadvantage of beginning at the end of side I, thus being interrupted for a turnover. The other two are complete on one side.

Capriccio Espagnol. FNS, Désormière, Cap P 8155 (**Coq d'Or suite*). *PHO, Ormandy, C ML 4856* (**Flight of the Bumble Bee; Tchaikovsky: Capriccio Italien; etc.*). *PHI, Schuechter, 10" MGM E 138* (**Tchaikovsky: Marche Slave*).

Despite the seeming abundance of versions currently available (close on a dozen and a half), the first two sum up the virtues of the two better types, Désormière's presenting a highly sophisticated sense of the musical texture in an orchestra performance of fine *élan*, Ormandy's utilizing the opportunities provided by Rimsky to show what a fine orchestra the Philadelphia is. Both recordings are excellent, though the close-up technique for the Ormandy tends for an unnecessary clatter in the climaxes. If an economy version is desired, I would propose the 10" MGM, a fine-sounding new disc, rather than a reissue of an older one in a lower price category.

Grand Pâque Russe (*Russian Easter*). *LSO, Scherchen, W WL 5280* (**Antar*). *DSO, Paray, Mer MG 50028* (**Antar*).

A reflection of the circumstances noted above in re *Antar*, and specifically indicative that Scherchen is more adept at conducting for records, if not in the hall, than Paray.

Overture on Russian Themes, opus 28. USSR, Kovalev, A440 AC 1208 (**Taneyev: Symphony No. 1*).

An unfamiliar work, and one well worth knowing, beginning, as it does, with the Russian folk song familiar from usage by both Beethoven and Mussorgsky, and continuing with other absorbing details. In the upper bracket of Russian recording.

Scheherazade. OSC, Ansermet, L LL 6. PHI, Dobrowen, An 35009. MIN, Dorati, Mer 50009. SFS, Monteux, V LM 1002. PHO, Ormandy, C ML 4888. VSO, Quadri, W 5234. VTO, P 12-15.

Insofar as these six preferential performances are concerned, an alphabetical arrangement of merits and demerits will do as well as any other. Estimates of this work being as numerous as the conductors who perform it, the preferences of the listener will be affected by Ansermet's supple but rather world-weary attitude, Dobrowen's love for the Russian (musical) language, Dorati's passion for effects, Monteux's thorough musicality, Ormandy's dedication to the mighty mass of sound, and Quadri's diligent efforts to satisfy Westminster's engineers as to what they have on their minds. My personal preference would be for an up-to-date version of the Monteux, but lacking that, I would commend the Ormandy to the hifinatics, the Monteux to the music-lovers, and the Dobrowen to those in between. The anonymous conductor of the economy-priced Plymouth is thoroughly capable, the reproduction accurate but a little thin.

*Sinfonietta on Russian Themes. VSY, Swoboda, W WL 5008 (*Dvořák: Slavonic Rhapsody No. 2).*

Very agreeable music, especially the suggestions of Beethoven's "*Pastorale*" in the first movement, and the use, in movement two, of the identical theme used by Stravinsky in *L'Oiseau de Feu* ("*Ronde des Princesses*"). Suave performance, though not as well reproduced as later Westminster matter.

*Skazka (Orchestral Fairy Tale). PHI, Fistoulari, MGM E 3017 (*Snegourotchka suite).*

Another of Fistoulari's skillful services on behalf of Rimsky, and brilliantly reproduced. The matter is not as fresh or attractive as in most of the composer's other works.

*Symphony No. 3 in C. USSR, Gauk, Per SPL 567 (*Glière: Concerto for Harp).*

Aside from a pleasant slow movement, this early work adds little to the known character of Rimsky. The performance is lively, the pickup remote, the fidelity limited.

RIVIER, JEAN (1896-)

*Symphony No. 2 for Strings. MGS, Solomon, MGM 3104 (*Honegger: Symphony No. 2).*

A rather minor contemporary French work, done with energy and dispatch by Solomon. Good sound.

ROSSINI, GIOACCHINO (1792-1868)

Overtures[1]

*The Barber of Seville. NBC, Toscanini, V LM 1044 (*Nos. 2, 3, 6). OMM, Serafin, V LBC 1039 (*Italiani in Algeri; William Tell ballet music; etc.).*

The manner of approach is similar, but Toscanini administers it with a degree more of finesse than Serafin. Neither is an outstanding recording, though the Serafin is better than might be expected from the category of issue.

*La Cambiale di Matrimonio. RPO, Beecham, 10" C AL 11 (*Chabrier: España).*

Lively work by Beecham and orchestra, notable for some tasteful horn-playing by Dennis Brain. Excellent reproduction.

*La Cenerentola. NBC, Toscanini, V LM 1044 (*Nos. 1, 3, 6). PHI, Galliera, An 35011 (*Italiana in Algeri; also Nos. 4, 5, 6, 7).*

The Toscanini version is sparkling and decisive, the Galliera of superior quality, if not equal distinction, but decidedly better reproduced.

*La Gazza Ladra. ACG, Van Beinum, 10" L LD 9023 (*No. 4). NBC, Toscanini, V LM 1044 (*Nos. 1, 2, 6).*

The balance of sound is on the side of Van Beinum and his fine orchestra, in a splendid arrangement of tone. Toscanini's *Magpie*, like the other items on this disc, is a dashing bit of virtuosity. Sound is good, but not outstanding.

*L'Italiana in Algeri. PHI, Galliera, An 35001 (*Nos. 2, 4, 5, 6, 7).*

This is the better of two current versions, and very well reproduced. However, it is not likely to satisfy those who recall the lively give-and-take Toscanini made of it.

*La Scala di Seta. ACG, Van Beinum, 10" L LD 9023 (*No. 3). PHI, Galliera, An 35011 (*Italiana in Algeri; Nos. 2, 5, 6, 7).*

[1]EDITOR'S NOTE: *To facilitate comparison of the six or seven most-recorded Rossini overtures, they are listed below with identifying numbers which are referred to in the text.*

1 *The Barber of Seville*
2 *La Cenerentola (Cinderella)*
3 *La Gazza Ladra (The Thieving Magpie)*
4 *La Scala di Seta (The Silken Ladder)*
5 *Semiramide*
6 *Il Signor Bruschino*
7 *William Tell*

Those are who looking for an individual version of this work will find it best presented, in sumptuous Concertgebouw tonal surroundings, on the Van Beinum disc. If the other items in the Galliera disc attract, the performance of this one will be found to be of consistent quality and well reproduced.

*Semiramide. NBC, Toscanini, V LRM 7054 (*No. 7). PHO, Beecham, 10" C AL 27 (*Bizet: Carmen suite).*

As a dividend on his imperious delivery of the *William Tell* overture, the Toscanini is hardly to be caviled at; however, the Beecham has a measure of suavity and lightness not comprehended in the tigerish lunge of Toscanini. Both are splendid in sound, the Toscanini being of the best standard prior to RCA's improved recent one.

*Il Signor Bruschino. NBC, Toscanini, V LM 1044 (*Nos. 1, 2, 3). PHI, Galliera, An 35011 (*Nos. 2, 4, 5, 7). BPH, Fricsay, 10" D DL 4002 (*Nos. 4, 7).*

Allowing for less than the best sound, the Toscanini is delightfully done. Galliera is honored by the better likeness of not so good a performance, and Fricsay, for those who want the best sound in the liveliest version possible, is the hi-fi choice when it comes to bows rapping on stands.

*Tancredi. RIAS, Fricsay, 10" D 4063 (*Glinka: Russlan and Ludmilla; Verdi: Nabucco; Strauss: Ariadne auf Naxos overtures).*

Flashy playing well reproduced (save for wiry strings) in a miscellany not only of composers and styles, but also of conductors. Two others beside Fricsay participate.

*William Tell. NBC, Toscanini, V LRM 7054 (*No. 5). PHI, Galliera, An 35011 (*Italiana in Algeri; Nos. 2, 4, 5, 6).*

The happy appearance of this lustrous, impelling performance of January 1953 (not to be confused with any earlier, less vivid reproduction of a Toscanini performance) should resolve for a long time to come any question of preference in this music. It is not merely a vastly believable reproduction of a thrilling musical experience, but one which takes the "Hi Ho" silver out of this matter, restoring its original tonal gold. The Galliera is well reproduced.

Opera Excerpts (Orchestral)

*William Tell: March of the Shepherds; Dance; Passo a Sei. OASC, Serafin, V LBC 1039 (*Barber of Seville overture, etc).*

Uncommonly fine string-playing, and reproduced with real warmth of sound rather than ear-tingling "technique." Serafin's version of the item noted below is not as exceptional as Toscanini's, but it is thoroughly good nevertheless.

*William Tell: Passo a Sei. NBC, Toscanini, V LRM 7005 (*Sibelius; Finlandia; Ponchielli: Dance of the Hours; William Tell overture).*

A delightful speciality *à la Maestro*, with a rare manifestation of humor. Good, but not outstanding, reproduction. (The *William Tell* overture is not the 1953 version noted above, but an earlier one, of lesser orchestral fidelity.)

Works for Orchestra

Matinées Musicales; Soirées Musicales (arranged by Britten). ROO, Braithwaite, 10" MGM 3028.

Comment on the following item applies here also, plus a commendatory nod to MGM for putting Britten's doubly deft instrumentation of Rossini piano pieces on the same disc.

*Rossiniana (arranged by Respighi). ROO, Braithwaite, MGM E 3013 (*Cimarosa: Matrimonio di Segreto; etc.). BSOO, Steinkopf, U URLP 7030 (*Janáček: Sinfonietta).*

All the problems here are well comprehended by Braithwaite, and the sound is decidedly good. Steinkopf's performance (for anyone interested in the overside Janáček) is musicianly, the recording rather inflated, with overemphasized highs.

*Sonata (arranged by Casella). I Musici, An 35086 (*Tartini: Concerto in A for Cello; Galuppi: Concerto No. 2; etc.).*

If "sonata" connotes something academic, Rossini is just the man to perish that thought with his happy facility and melodic gift. All the values in this work and the other superb scores on the disc are wonderfully realized by the excellent young group of players calling themselves I Musici ("The Musicians"). In light, dashing passages they are superior even to the path-breaking Virtuosi di Roma and Società Corelli. Beautifully balanced reproduction.

ROUSSEL, ALBERT (1869-1937)

Ballet Music

*Bacchus et Ariane (Suite No. 2). VSO, Munch, V LM 1741 (*Honegger: Symphony No. 5).*

Agreeable work by Munch in a score rather tenuous and disjointed

without the ballet action. Accurate rather than ear-soothing sound.
*The Spider's Feast. DSO, Paray, Mer MG 50035 (*Dukas: L'Apprenti Sorcier; Fauré: Pelléas et Mélisande). LAM, Fournet, Ep LC 3058 (*Dukas: L'Apprenti Sorcier; Fauré: Pavanne; etc.).*

Paray's refinement and sense of detail are superior to Fournet's, in addition to which the recording of the Detroit ensemble is more suitable to the material. As much applies also to the Dukas.

Symphony

*No. 3 in G minor. LRO, Borsamsky, U RLP 7037 (*Bacchus et Ariane, Suite No. 2).*

I don't know this work well enough to evaluate Borsamsky's direction of it, but he doesn't make it much more than a collection of isolated effects. Rather raucous recording, with the brass overstressed. The second side, of better quality, is attributed to the Orchestra of Radio Berlin, Karl Rucht conducting.

RUBBRA, EDMUND (1896-)

*Symphony No. 5 in B flat. HO, Barbirolli, V LHMV 1001 (*Sibelius: Symphony No. 5).*

A thoughtful work by a composer who merits wider recognition than he enjoys. Barbirolli's communicative performance is very well reproduced.

RUBINSTEIN, ANTON (1829-1894)

Concerto for Piano and Orchestra, No. 4 in D minor. Levant, NYPH, Mitropoulos, C ML 4599. Wührer, SYM, Moralt, Vox PL 7780.

The recorded qualities of these performances are about equal, but Levant has a more stimulating sense of Rubinstein's kind of romanticism than Wührer. For another detail, Mitropoulos makes more of a contribution than Moralt.

SAINT-SAËNS, CAMILLE (1835-1921)

Concertos

For Piano and Orchestra

No. 2 in G minor. LPO, Lympany, Martinon, 10" L LS 408.

A competent rather than notable performance, well fingered by Lympany and suitably supported by Martinon. Good sound, though not the kind that makes London a buy-word.

*No. 3 in B flat. Pozzi, WIN, Desarzens, CH 1179 (*Carnival of Animals).*

Hardly a distinguished effort, though workmanlike on both sides. Acceptable reproduction.

*No. 4 in C minor. Casadesus, NYPH, Rodzinski, C ML 4246 (*Satie: Three Pieces in Form of a Pear).*

A new version of this work is in order, for the playing is not the best of Casadesus, and standards in sound have risen much since this was made.

*No. 5 in F major. Jacquinot, WES, Fistoulari, MGM E 3068 (*D'Indy: Symphony on a French Mountain Air).*

Miss Jacquinot has the strength and fluency this music requires, likewise the temperament. Very good reproduction of both piano and orchestra.

For Violin and Orchestra

*No. 3 in B minor. Francescatti, NYPH, Mitropoulos, C ML 4315 (*Paganini: Concerto No. 1). Menuhin, PHI, Poulet, V LHMV 1071 (*Mendelssohn: Sonata in F).*

Menuhin's sound is superior to that of most of his other recorded efforts, and there is much fine playing to his credit here. However, the Francescatti strikes me as cleaner, less strained in style, with a natural affinity for a manner foreign, in a literal sense, to Menuhin. I also think the pairing of concertos preferable to a second-side sonata, though this one is very well played, with Gerald Moore the pianist.

For Violoncello and Orchestra

*In A minor. Rose, NYPH, Mitropoulos, C ML 4425 (*Bloch: Schelomo).*

Strong, flavorsome performance by Rose, and reproduced with the same quality as that of the excellent *Schelomo* on the reverse.

Opera Excerpts (Orchestral)

*Princesse Jaune: Overture. OOC, Wolff, 10" L LD 9020 (*Massenet: Phèdre overture).*

The obscurity of this score should not discourage investigation of it, for it is a lively, well-constructed work, and decidedly well conducted by Wolff.

*Samson et Dalila: Bacchanale. OMM, Serafin, V LBC 1039 (*Rossini: Barber of Seville, Italiana in Algeri overtures, etc.).*

Serafin knows his way about this music, and the reproduction, though not in the high-fidelity tradition, is quite good.

Suite

*Algérienne. ORD, Fourestier, Vox PL 8100 (*Massenet: Les Erinnyes).*

Lively local color, concluding with a rousing *Marche Militaire Française.* Good instrumental detail in the recording.

Symphonies

*No. 2 in A minor. NET, Goehr, CH 1180 (*Concerto in A minor, for Cello).*

A not too interesting work, done with musicianship and thoroughness by the excellent orchestra. Good sound.

No. 3 in C minor. NYPH, Munch, C ML 4120.

Impassioned, remarkably convincing performance by Munch, and successfully reproduced.

Symphonic Poems

Set of Four (Le Rouet d'Omphale; Phaëton; Danse Macabre; La Jeunesse d'Hercule). OCC, Fourestier, An 35058.

For documentary purposes, this disc has its values, for the works are well played and particularly well recorded (in the Théâtre des Champs-Elysées). However, the desirable works are interpreted with more insight elsewhere, and the interest of the others is minor.

*Danse Macabre. OSR, Ansermet, 10" L LD 9028 (*Le Rouet d'Omphale). NBC, Toscanini, V LM 1118 (*Dukas: L'Apprenti Sorcier; Smetana: Moldau). DNO, Malko, V LBC 1019 (*Ippolitov-Ivanov: Caucasian Sketches, etc.).*

For once in this volume, Toscanini can be indicted for a too leisurely approach to a piece of music. He eventually finds the way to a furious climax, but the progress is not by any means so consistent or artfully contrived as it is by Ansermet. This is, however, one of the best-sounding Toscanini records. Malko's work is typically thoroughgoing, and a desirable addendum to the collection in which it appears.

Le Rouet d'Omphale. OSR, Ansermet, 10" L LD 9028 (**Danse Macabre*).

The feeling of Ansermet for this idiom is decidedly superior to anything else currently available, a statement that also applies to the more celebrated item above. Beautiful sound in the sense that it serves the purposes of the music rather than calling attention to itself.

Works for Orchestra and Solo Instruments

Carnival of the Animals. Whittemore, Lowe, BPO, Fiedler, V LM 1761 (**Prokofiev: Peter and the Wolf*). *Antonietti, Rossican, NET, Goehr, CH 1179* (**Concerto No. 3*).

As a complementary coupling to the excellent *Peter and the Wolf* with Alec Guinness, the Fiedler-directed *Carnival* would be worth shelf room even were it less good than it is. However, the Goehr treatment is extremely deft, the pianists are capable, and the reproduction is first-class. Unfortunately, its coupling cannot claim similar words. For those interested in the Ogden Nash verses delivered by Noel Coward (C ML 4355), they may be described as efficiently paraded by Kostelanetz, though the pianists are little more than accessories after the other facts.

Introduction and Rondo Capriccioso. Francescatti, PHO, Ormandy, 10" C ML 2194 (**Chausson: Poème*). *Heifetz, RCAO, Steinberg, 10" V LRM 7055* (**Sarasate: Zigeunerweisen*).

The kind of stylistic sympathy Francescatti demonstrates in the Concerto No. 3 (see above) is even more evident here, combining as it does dash with a superb singing of the melodic line. Exemplary orchestral support, and finely balanced recording. The reproduction of the Heifetz is inferior in scope and liveness, though his personal contribution is masterful in statement and control.

SAMMARTINI, GIOVANNI BATTISTA (1701-1775)

Concerto for Violin and Orchestra, No. 2 in C. Abussi, CHAM, Jenkins,

*HS L 74 (*Symphony in G; Albinoni: Concerto in D minor; Geminiani: Concerto Grosso No. 2).*

I have no other knowledge of Abussi, whose rather nasal-sounding instrument and sometimes dubious intonation are blemishes on an otherwise creditable enterprise. He has good taste, but hardly the other properties of a recording "artist." Very clear sound.

*Concerto Grosso in D minor, opus 11, No. 4. VSY, Moralt, W WL 5009 (*Pergolesi: Trio Sonata; Corelli: Concerto Grosso, opus 6, No. 9).*

A period piece of no absorbing individuality, rather heavily paced by Moralt. Good sound.

*Symphony in G. CHAM, Jenkins, HS 74 (*See under Violin Concerto above).*

Energetic, rhythmically precise performance, a little tense for the material. Exceptionally good sound.

SARASATE, PABLO DE *(1844-1908)*

*Zigeunerweisen. Heifetz, RCAO, Steinberg, 10" V LRM 7055 (*Saint-Saëns: Introduction and Rondo Capriccioso).*

The superb taste of this performance, not to mention its insuperable fluency, will long testify to the real artistry of Heifetz in reflective as well as display matter. Steinberg gives affirmative value to the orchestral score, and the recording is good in clarity and balance, but acoustically somewhat on the dead side. That factor prevents the overside from being competitive with the Francescatti, though it is magically performed by Heifetz.

SATIE, ERIK *(1866-1925)*

*Parade. HSO, Kurtz, 10" C ML 2112 (*Auric: Suite from Les Matelots).*

As noted under *Les Matelots*, a congenial task for Kurtz. Good sound.

SCARLATTI, ALESSANDRO *(1659-1725)*

*Concerto No. 6 in F. VDR, Fasano, D DL 9572 (*Tartini: Concerto in E; Vivaldi: Concerto in G; etc.).*

A little more mass of sound would seem in order here, but the sturdy patterns are well projected, with much dynamic finesse. Good reproduction.

SCARLATTI, DOMENICO (1685-1757)

*Good Humored Ladies (arranged by Tommasini). OSC, Désormière, L LL 624 (*Poulenc: Les Biches). ROO, Braithwaite, MGM 3034 (*Mozart: Les Petits Riens). VSO, Litschauer, Van 440 (*Bach-Walton: Wise Virgins).*

Désormière's crisply articulated performance is clearly the choice among these, and if the sound is a little coarse by the best current standards, it is certainly distinct. The others are listed because the second side has decided interest in each case. Both are capably done, and well recorded, but neither of the other conductors has the Frenchman's deftness.

SCHNABEL, ARTUR (1882-1951)

*Concerto for Piano and Orchestra. H. Schnabel, SYM, Adler, SPA 55 (*Songs).*

A product of 1901 which, though derivative, has much interest. A labor of love on the part of all concerned, the performance has been carefully prepared, and very decently recorded. (Helen Schnabel is the late pianist's daughter-in-law.)

SCHOENBERG, ARNOLD (1874-1951)

Concertos

*For Piano and Orchestra. Helffer, ORD, Leibowitz, Per 568 (*Piano Pieces, opus 11, 25).*

Opinions on the quality of this interpretation are hard for me to come by, as the line of musical thought eludes me. The recorded sound, especially of the piano, is sub-standard.

*For Violin and Orchestra. Krasner, NYPH, Mitropoulos, C ML 4857 (*Berg: Violin Concerto).*

Krasner does a magnificent work of clarifying this treacherously difficult design, but it remains an enigma to me. Very clean recording.

Works for Orchestra

Chamber Symphony, opus 9. PAS, Dervaux, Dia 2.

To be a wholly typical product, this should end with the hisses and catcalls apt to be provoked from a French audience. The recording is poorly processed, the basic sound apparently not well gathered in the first instance.

*Chamber Symphony No. 2 (1939). VSY, Häfner, C ML 4664 (*Survivor from Warsaw; Kol Nidre).*

Tolerably convincing performance by Häfner, and dependably reproduced. However, it is not a concept of music which appeals to me.

*Five Pieces for Orchestra. CHO, Kubelik, Mer 50026 (*Bartók: Music for Strings, Percussion, and Celesta).*

Kubelik's penetration and fine sense of orchestral definition make much of the opportunities in these pieces. They are, indeed, remarkable evocations of mood. As in the case of the Bartók, the recording is exemplary. (The Schoenberg is also available in a coupling with Hindemith's *Symphonic Metamorphosis* on Mer 50024).

Pelléas and Mélisande. FRA, Zillig, Cap P 8069.

Poorish sound and not too persuasive delivery. About the best that can be said is that it is better than no recording at all.

Work for String Orchestra

*Verklärte Nacht. PHO, Ormandy, C ML 4316 (*Ravel: Daphnis et Chloë, Suites Nos. 1 and 2). HIS, Stokowski, V LM 1739 (*Vaughan Williams: Fantasia on a Theme by Thomas Tallis).*

As a personal preference I incline to the sextet form of this music, of which a good contemporary example can be found on 10" Cap L 8118. Of these, the Ormandy is thoroughly commendable for execution and sound; the Stokowski is mentioned as a warning to the unwary—unless they are admirers of sleek sonorities tricked through echo chambers.

Work for Orchestra and Voices

Gurrelieder. NSSP, Leibowitz, soloists, HS L 100 [3]. PHO, Stokowski, soloists, V LCT 6012 [2].

The recent enterprise of Leibowitz is newer by twenty years than the Stokowski and, of course, that much improved in sound. However, it is not a work of which the younger conductor has full command, especially in projecting the total texture of the work. Richard Lewis is superb as Waldemar, Nell Tangeman reasonably good as the wood dove. The other singers are second-class, especially Ethel Semser, the Tove. The reissued Stokowski version is little more than a curio now, though vocalists Bampton and Althouse retain regard for their accomplishments. Dullish sound, especially brass and masses generally.

Gurrelieder: Song of the Wood Dove only. NYPH, Lipton, Stokowski, 10" C ML 2140.

Lipton's voice gives rich pleasure in this music, and Stokowski's conductorial art makes a picturesque vignette of the whole. Fine sound.

*Kol Nidre; A Survivor from Warsaw. VSY, Swarowsky, soloists, C ML 4664 (*Second Chamber Symphony).*

A rather ridiculous enterprise, inasmuch as the English texts are delivered, in Viennese accent, by Hans Jaray. He does his work intelligently, but it jars the ear nevertheless. Both works are well reproduced.

SCHUBERT, FRANZ (1797-1828)

Dances

*Five German Dances, Seven Trios, and Coda. VSO, Litschauer, Van VRS 435 (*Mozart: Eine Kleine Nachtmusik).*

Some of the most charming music of the young (1813) Schubert, performed with ideal sensitivity and grace by the sweet-sounding Viennese ensemble well led by Litschauer. Fine reproduction.

Incidental Music

Rosamunde (Complete). VSO, Dixon, soloists, W WL 5182.

An early recorded demonstration of Dixon's capacity as a Schubertian (there have been others more lately), and highly creditable to him. The only demur would be with the super-scholarship that has resulted in the use of the D major (*Alphonso and Estrella*) overture rather than the more familiar one in C major (*Zauberharfe*).

The response of the musicians to Dixon's direction is first-class, as is the recording. Vocal duties are well attended to by Hilde Roessel-Majdan.

*Rosamunde: Overture, Ballet Music, Entr'actes. ACG, Van Beinum, L LL 622 (*Mendelssohn: Midsummer Night's Dream music). HIS, Stokowski, V LM 1730 (*Wagner: Parsifal excerpts).*

For those who want the spirited C major overture, Van Beinum provides it in excellent order, together with the usual sequence of ballet music and entr'actes. The Stokowski boasts beautiful sound, but a little too much willfulness for Schubert.

*Rosamunde: Ballet Music, Entr'actes. VPH, Furtwängler, V LHMV 1020 (*Unfinished Symphony; Nicolai: Merry Wives of Windsor overture; Weber: Oberon overture).*

What is ear-catching here is the sound of the Vienna Philharmonic, faithfully reproduced. However Furtwängler's tempos vary between slow and slower, with repose giving way to somnolence.

Overture

*Rosamunde: Zauberharfe; C major (in Italian style). SYM, Goehr, CH F-6 (*German Dances).*

Should Concert Hall remove this from its file of "limited edition" and make it generally available, it would be well worth owning. The playing is spirited, modest but assured in its musicality, and very well reproduced. The *Rosamunde* (C major) enjoys one of the best playings since Harty's. (The term *Zauberharfe* actually identifies the D major *Alphonso and Estrella* overture used at the *première* of *Rosamunde*.)

Symphonies

*No. 1 in D. RPO, Beecham, C ML 4903 (*Symphony No. 2).*

The well-ordered pairing of the two early symphonies under Beecham's acute direction just about eliminates discussion of merits and demerits of other performances. Fine sound and highly satisfactory balance.

*No. 2 in B flat. RPO, Beecham, C ML 4903 (*Symphony No. 1). PSO, Steinberg, 10" Cap L 8161. SPO, Van Hoogstraten, Per SPLP 517 (*Symphony No. 3).*

My preference is as stated above, though Steinberg's presentation has in admirable measure the lilt and songfulness wanted in this music, and the recording is respectable in quality—if No. 2 alone is wanted. The Van Hoogstraten is mentioned only relative to the pairing with No. 3. It is a valid conception, not very well played, and rather muffled in reproduction.

*No. 3 in D. CIN, Johnson, L LP 405 (*J. C. Bach: Sinfonia in E flat). SPO, Van Hoogstraten, Per SPLP 517 (*Symphony No. 2).*

Neither of these could be termed intensely Schubertian, or, for that matter, intensely anything else. Johnson's is the better in sound, though sometimes a little echoey in Cincinnati's Music Hall. If coupling is a decisive factor, the Van Hoogstraten is preferable.

*No. 4 in C minor ("Tragic"). PSL, Dixon, W WL 5274 (*Symphony No. 5). LAM, Klemperer, Vox PL 7860 (*Mendelssohn: Symphony No. 4).*

What Dixon offers is the basis of a fine performance, but the orchestral detail is not consistently controlled. Were the sound values inverted, Klemperer's would be the preference, but not under existing circumstances. Patience would seem to be desirable.

*No. 5 in B flat. LPO, Beecham, C ML 4771 (*Haydn: Symphony No. 104). PSL, Dixon, W WL 5274 (*Symphony No. 4).*

The insuperable feeling of Beecham for this music remains as vital as it was in the past, and the sound still soothes, if it does not satisfy as it once did. Dixon is more adept with this work than with the preceding one, and the orchestra plays responsively for him. However, what Beecham offers can hardly be surpassed by something merely better-sounding.

No. 6 in C. LSO, Krips, L LL 21.

The low number in the London Long Play sequence declares the status quo that has existed with this work for half a dozen years, also identifying the recording technique as less expert than is now customary.

No. 7 (9, The Great) in C. BPH, Furtwängler, D DX 119 [2] *(*Haydn: Symphony No. 88). NYPH, Walter, C ML 4093. NBC, Toscanini, V LM 1835. ACG, Mengelberg, Cap P 8040.*

At the cost of an extra record side (plus a qualified playing of the Haydn No. 88), the Furtwängler version offers what strikes me as the best of the many performances this work has had on records in twenty years. Every turn of the great score is maneuvered with supreme confidence and control, the internal detail as clearly projected as the outward shape. Moreover, the sound is big and resonant, superior to any version comparable in artistic understanding. Mengelberg's retains its vividness of thought, its compelling impulse, though not in anything like contemporary sound. The latest of Toscanini's efforts is in many ways his best, but the absorption seems more with clarifying the intricacies of the score than with realizing the joy and warmth of the writing. In any case, Furtwängler gives us an image of writing rounder, more relaxed—in other words, more Schubertian. What Walter offers cannot be rated comparable to Furtwängler in either momentum or appeal to the ear.

*No. 8 in B minor ("Unfinished"). NBC, Toscanini, 10" V LM 54. LSO, Krips, 10" L LS 209. PSO, Steinberg, 10" Cap L 8160. PHO, Walter, 10" C ML 2010. VPH, Furtwängler, V LHMV 1029 (*Rosamunde music; Nicolai: Merry Wives of Windsor overture; Weber: Oberon overture). VSO, Prohaska, VAN 445 (*Mozart: Symphony No. 40).*

A whole new literature of "Unfinished" performances has come into existence since Walter's was considered choice circa 1949. Among these the Toscanini strikes me as the most illuminating of the musical purposes in this score, though I would not argue with anyone who deemed it somewhat tense. However, there is more to hear in it, on repeated playings, than in any of the others. The Krips has fine songful qualities if not quite the rhythmic firmness wanted, and the Steinberg is good in many ways, outstanding in none. The Walter is beautifully drawn, a little miniature in some details by the side of Toscanini, and not as notable in sound as it once appeared. Both Furtwängler and Prohaska seem to be purveying a Vienna tradition of mysterious quiets and sudden outbursts, a game at which F is more practiced than P. In pure sound, the latter is as good as any, though the variation in this respect through the group is scarcely serious enough to effect a judgment for one or another.

Symphonies Arranged from Other Works

In C (arranged by Joachim). VSO, Prohaska, Van VRS 417.

This Grand Duo (opus 140) lends itself advantageously to orchestration, whether or not it be accepted as the lost "Gastein" Symphony. Prohaska is eminently suited to interpret it persuasively, and the big, resonant recording leaves little to be desired.

In E major (arranged by Weingartner). VSO, Litschauer, Van VRS 427.

An entertaining curio that might have come to attention sooner had Weingartner not been diffident about his editorial work of 1934. Litschauer makes it sound Schubertian enough, but loose ends are not tied together as they might be. In addition, though the recording is good, wrong notes are not unheard of or unheard.

Work for Orchestra and Piano

*Wanderer Fantasie (arranged by Liszt). Johannesen, NET, Goehr, CH 1176 (*Rondo in A; Ländler).*

Johannesen is a much abler performer than his present repute would suggest, and this excellent performance is among the proofs of it. The musicianly collaboration of Goehr is enhanced by excellent sound.

Work for Orchestra and Violin

*Rondo in A. Solovieff, VSO, Swoboda, CH 1176 (*Wanderer Fantasie; Ländler).*

Whether or not coupled with the preceding, this is engaging music affectionately played and well reproduced. Solovieff gives fine flow to the music, and Swoboda's management of the "orchestral" part (originally for string quartet) is capable.

SCHULTZ, SVEND C. (1913-)

*Serenade for Strings. DSTR, Tuxen, 10" L LS 653 (*Nielsen: Helios Overture).*

Had I not been so informed by the annotation, I would not have recognized Schultz as an epigone of Nielsen, but merely as a creator descended in a line from the over-all influence of Grieg and responsive to many other tendencies of today. Very enjoyable music, beautifully performed and just about perfectly reproduced.

SCHUMAN, WILLIAM (1910-)

*Judith. LOUI, Whitney, Mer MG 10088 (*Undertow).*

Whatever the virtues of these scores (the composer is the conductor for *Undertow*) may be for their choreographic purposes, the independent listening interest is limited. Not the most skillful instrumental execution, and but moderately good recording.

*Symphony for Strings. PSO, Steinberg, Cap S 8212 (*Bloch: Concerto Grosso).*

An "actual performance" product of the Pittsburgh Contemporary Music Festival of November 1952, and, as such, highly successful. Musically, this is one of the more representative Schuman works, though I should hardly recognize a personal accent in it. Clean sound, a little thin.

Symphony No. 3. PHO, Ormandy, C ML 4413.

The ingenious plan of this work is carefully pursued by Ormandy, and impressively conveyed by the orchestra. However, the recording is oddly dry and unresonant for the elements involved—or is it the scoring?

SCHUMANN, ROBERT (1810-1856)

Concertos

*For Piano and Orchestra, in A Minor. Lipatti, PHI, Karajan, C ML 4525 (*Grieg: Concerto in A minor). Haskil, HPO, Van Otterloo, Ep LC 3020 (*Liszt: Concerto No. 1). Hess, PHI, Schwarz, V LHMV 1062. Rubinstein, RCAO, Steinberg, V LM 1050. Novaes, VSY, Klemperer, Vox PL 7110.*

As time passes and versions of this work accumulate, the sterling virtues of Lipatti's powerfully musical, warmly human feeling for it become increasingly apparent. Karajan's collaborative effort is one of his most gratifying on records, and the sound, for all its occasional dullness, is suitable in timbre and finely balanced. For those who insist on brighter ring and sharper contrasts, auditorially, the Haskil may be commended for clean statement of the music and fidelity to the sound of the orchestra (the coupling with a Uninsky Liszt is not a favorable factor). Of the versions spread over two sides, there is best sound in the Hess, which is otherwise a rather sagged likeness of her onetime eminence in this work, the most pianistic pleasure in the Rubinstein, and a lot of musicality, if not all the wanted bravura, in the Novaes.

For Violin and Orchestra, in D minor. Rybar, LAU, Desarzens, CH 1128.

The skills which have sufficed for Rybar's participation in various eighteenth-century works are a little light in substance for this more demanding score. His fine tone is a little small in size, his emotional projection limited. The balance, in a none too resonant recording, favors the violin.

*For Violincello and Orchestra, in A minor. Casals, PRA, C ML 4926 (*Bach: Adagio, etc.). Gendron, OSR, Ansermet, L LL 947 (*Tchaikovsky: Variations on a Rococo Theme). Piatigorsky, LPO, Barbirolli, V LCT 1119 (*Brahms: Sonata in E minor). Dorner, PRO, Reinhardt, Vox PL 7680 (*Concert-Allegro, opus 134; Fantasy for Violin and Orchestra, opus 131).*

It is remarkable for Casals in his seventy-eighth year to play this work with so much vitality and technical control, but what is one to say of his offenses against musical taste in phrasing, dynamics, phrase-endings, etc.? The anonymous conductor does his work very much in the style of Eugene Ormandy (Petrillo's edict permits no credit), and the sound is surprisingly good. The second side minutiae do not have much to commend them. Of the other versions, there is the best sound from London's Geneva effort, though Gendron is not a very compelling interpreter in this work, and Ansermet's influence on the result is slight. The Piatigorsky-Barbirolli collaboration was a happy one, but the sound is not what it should be. As for Dorner, he plays in first-desk-orchestra manner, which is to say competently but with no great flair, and the recording is only tolerable. The other items are described in their separate categories. I see no really satisfactory solution to this problem, unless one can filter out (mentally) from Casals's playing what is Schumann and what is not.

Overture

*Manfred. NBC, Toscanini, 10" V LM 6 (*Beethoven: Consecration of the House). VPH, Furtwängler, V LHMV 1023 (*Strauss: Death and Transfiguration; Smetana: The Moldau).*

Both in spirit and in sound, Toscanini's is a liver, more vital delivery of this moody work. Also, the coupling with the Beethoven overture provides less extraneous matter and extra charge than the Furtwängler.

Symphonies

*No. 1 in B flat. OSR, Ansermet, L LL 391. CO, Leinsdorf, C ML 4794 (*Symphony No. 4). BSO, Munch, V LM 1190.*

The advantages of mechanics are all with Ansermet, whose fine-sounding Schumann is not as surging or as spirited as Leinsdorf's. Were the latter reissued in an Encore listing, it would be worth having at the economy price. Whatever virtues there are in the Munch performance are offset by the fact that the disc plays, unfortunately, in B major.

No. 2 in C. HIS, Stokowski, V LM 1194. NYSO, Bernstein, D DL 9715.

To say that either of these would suffice were there no other is to pay high tribute to Bernstein's effort, for the Stokowski is one of his very best contributions to the literature, both as sense and as sound. However, on close examination, there is a measure of finesse in the performance under Stokowski which Bernstein's excellent ensemble is not prevailed upon to provide. Also, when the Stokowski sense of sonority is mated to as valid a conception as he conveys, it is hardly resistible.

No. 3, in E flat ("Rhenish"). NYPH, Walter, C ML 4040. MIN, Mitropoulos, V LBC 1058.

A new version of this work with proper sound values would be welcome, and on the evidence of this excellent but rather unpleasant-sounding version, Walter is the man to do it. I cannot become enthusiastic about the Mitropoulos even at Bluebird prices, for it has too many vagaries of tempo and a prevailing dullness of sound.

*No. 4 in D minor. SFS, Monteux, V LM 1714 (*Beethoven: Symphony No. 4). DSO, Paray, Mer MG 50036 (*Liszt: Les Preludes). CO, Szell, 10" C ML 2040. CHO, Stock, C RL 3026 (*Mozart: Symphony No. 38, "Prague").*

Although Monteux is not blessed with the total advantages of high-fidelity sound, he makes persuasive music in this score, and the reproduction is well managed in its style. (His Beethoven No. 4 is outstanding also.) Paray, who is, presents a reading of admirable freshness and spirit, well played by his excellent orchestra. However, his second-side *Preludes*, though capably done, must defer to the Monteux-BSO version. For top quality in this score, pick Paray; for balanced value, make it Monteux. The Szell is businesslike and efficient, acceptably reproduced. At present rates, the two Stock-directed performances have solid virtues to commend them, though anything approaching proper sound is not among them.

Work for Orchestra and Piano

Concert-Allegro, opus 134. Bohle, PRO, Reinhardt, Vox PL 7680 (**Concerto for Cello, etc.*).

No more than moderately suitable delivery of this modestly attractive work. Poorish sound.

Work for Orchestra and Violin

Fantasy, opus 131. Stucki, PRO, Reinhardt, Vox PL 7680 (**Concerto for Cello, etc.*).

Miss Stucki is the best equipped of the several instrumentalists heard on this disc, but that would hardly win her a *Concours*. The sound is slightly better than in the preceding instance.

Work for Orchestra (Arrangement)

Carnaval. ROO, Rignold, D DL 9548 (**Gounod: Faust ballet music*).
RPO, Kurtz, C ML 4367 (**Respighi-Rossini: Boutique Fantasque*).
PHI, Irving, V LBC 1025 (**Delibes: Sylvia excerpts*).

None of these conductors is equal to the heavy task of making the nondescript orchestration sound agreeable, but Rignold fares best. At the economy rate, the Robert Irving offering would seem a solution, but his choppy, angular phraseology would be dear at any price.

SCRIABIN, ALEXANDER *(1872-1915)*

Concerto for Piano and Orchestra. Badura-Skoda, VSY, Swoboda, W WL 5068 (**Rimsky-Korsakov: Concerto for Piano and Orchestra*).

A listenable piece, well fingered by Badura-Skoda, though some of the effects intended in the recording do not come off—tubby bass, muffled tympani, and rather peculiar piano tone being recurrently evident.

The Divine Poem. USSR, Golovanov, CE 3003.

Although this hardly has the properties of fidelity now possible in orchestral writing of this color and detail, it is better than one would expect from its Russian origin. Certainly Golovanov has an excellent idea of how to make it propulsive and Scriabinish, though the mind has to fill out some elements of resonance and sonority otherwise absent.

*Poem of Ecstasy. BSO, Monteux, V LM 1775 (*Liszt: Les Préludes). PPO, Rosenthal, Cap P 8188 (*Loeffler: Pagan Poem).*

An exceptional example of Monteux's capacity for tonal balance and nuance, both of which add measurably to the attractions of the work. Excellent reproduction, including the trumpet of Roger Voisin. The Rosenthal is thoroughly good, but not as masterful as the Monteux.

*Poem of Fire. NYPH, Mitropoulis, C ML 4731 (*Poem of Ecstasy).*

Not nearly so persuasive as the Monteux above, though the work, with its integral piano part well played by Hambro, is somewhat more interesting. Rather overstressed sound.

SESSIONS, ROGER (1896-)

*Symphony No. 2. NYPH, Mitropoulos, C ML 4784 (*Milhaud: Symphony No. 1).*

A rather shrilly scored, unpersuasive work to my taste. The reproduction is good.

SHOSTAKOVICH, DMITRI (1906-)

Ballet Music

*Ballet Russe. COL, Kurtz, C ML 4671 (*Tchaikovsky: Serenade Mélancolique, etc.).*

Melodic trivia, delivered with a proper absence of content by Kurtz. Very showy recording.

*Ballet Suite No. 1 (1950). USSR, Gauk, Van 6004 (*Prokofiev: Romeo and Juliet, Suite No. 2).*

Occasionally charming, more often tenuous matter, well played, but not too efficiently reproduced. The sound is clear enough, but has little resonance.

Concerto

For Piano and Orchestra, C minor, with Trumpet. Aller, Klein, CAO, Slatkin, 10" Cap L 8229.

What may without exaggeration be described as disagreeable music, well performed and acutely reproduced. The trumpet obbligato is well played by Mannie Klein, erstwhile dance-band virtuoso.

Symphonies

*No. 1 in F. USSR, Kondrashin, Van 6014. CO, Rodzinski, C ML 4881 (*Sibelius: Symphony No. 5). LRO, Pflüger, U RLP 7128 (*Symphony No. 9).*

None of these gives just what one would like to hear in this music: Rodzinski's decade-old treatment lacks appropriate resonance, the louder one from Russia is more electronics than musical sound. In addition, the performance has an odd impersonality about it, as though the performers were so many robots. As for the German, it offers the second-side No. 9 as dividend, for those who don't mind the high-fidelity screech. (The combination there is *ORB, Kleinert.*)

No. 5. STS, Golschmann, Cap P 8268. NYPH, Mitropoulos, C ML 4739.

Both conductors have strong feeling for the rhythmic energy of this work, and the engineers have been about equally successful in taking down the tonal results. If there is any difference, it would be that the Columbia is less penetratingly brassy.

No. 6. PSO, Reiner, C ML 4249.

Reiner's thoughtful performance and the fine playing of the orchestra are offset by the early LP processing, with the strident highs and not too solid bass.

No. 7 ("Leningrad"). BPH, Celibidache, U URLP 601 [2]. *BUF, Steinberg, All 3041* [2].

The Urania is an improvement in sound on the Allegro, but it is far from a sweet-sounding set, nevertheless. The bare walls of the studio in which it was played are aurally apparent, drastically so in the climaxes. In terms of this work, the merits of the conductors are about even.

*No. 9. NYPH, Kurtz, C ML 4137. ORB, Kleinert, U RLP 7128 (*Symphony No. 1).*

The American disc is a rather misbegotten matter, produced in the immediate aftermath of the first performances, when tempos had not crystallized. Kurtz's are unbearably slow for both first and second movements, the recording being no deterrent to a negative opinion. The version directed by Kleinert is better-sounding, if not more convincing interpretatively. In both respects, however, it is superior to the Symphony No. 1 which precedes it.

No. 10. NYPH, Mitropoulos, C ML 4959. LEN, Mravinsky, CH 1313.

The physical advantages enjoyed by Mitropoulos—a proper resonant frame, excellent engineering, and fine processing—make the quality of the Russian product unacceptable. The American orchestra and conductor tend to vulgarize the finale, in particular, but altogether theirs is a fuller reproduction of the sometimes absorbing content in this overlong work than the Russian version provides.

SIBELIUS, JAN (1865-)

Concerto

*For Violin and Orchestra, in D minor. Stern, RPO, Beecham, C ML 4550 (*Four Historic Scenes). Heifetz, LPO, Beecham, V LCT 1113 (*Chausson: Concerto). Wicks, SRO, Ehrling, Cap P 8175. Neveu, PHI, Süsskind, An 35129 (*Suk: Four Pieces).*

The Heifetz-Beecham collaboration was hardly a superable one, and I suspect that it will be listened to years hence when the louder, more searing, and withal vigorously played later work of Stern and Beecham has given way to something else. Obviously the latter has advantages not enjoyed by the other, but a deeper pleasure in the music abides in the older version nevertheless. Wicks, incidentally, does her work well, and the recording is efficient. However, the spread on two sides of an LP is uneconomical. The reissue of Neveu's expressive performance is a service to the memory of this unfortunate artist (killed in a plane crash), but the recording is poorish.

Incidental Music

*Kuolema: Valse Triste. HIS, Stokowski, 10" V LRM 7024 (*Berceuse; Swan of Tuonela; Debussy: L'Aprés-midi d'un faune). VSO, Litschauer, Van VRS 430 (*Rakastava; Grieg: Norwegian Dances).*

Aside from a minor vulgarity or two, Stokowski produces this little musical drama with high artifice and tonal distinction. The Litschauer lacks the vulgarisms, also the artifice and tonal distinction.

The Tempest: Berceuse. HIS, Stokowski, 10" V LRM 7024.

A longtime favorite of Stokowski, done with finesse and remarkable washes of sound. For other contents of the disc, see above.

Symphonies

No. 1 in E minor. RPO, Beecham, C ML 4653. HIS, Stokowski, V LM 1125. LSO, Collins, L LL 574.

Each of these has ponderable virtues, but the preferable combination of them seems to me to be in the Beecham. All are well reproduced.

No. 2 in D. LSO, Collins, L LL 822. PHO, Ormandy, C ML 4131. BSO, Koussevitzky, V LM 1172.

The Koussevitzky unfortunately belongs to no such era of sound as the superbly reproduced version by Collins, or even as the early-LP Ormandy. It has many virtues of execution, but they are rather on the blurred and indistinct side now.

*No. 3 in C. SRO, Ehrling, Mer MG 10125 (*Symphony No. 7).*

Ehrling belongs to the genus conscientious-rather-than-compelling conductor, but his uncontested examination of this music is capably accomplished. Clear sound.

*No. 4 in A minor. PHI, Karajan, An 35082 (*Tapiola). LSO, Collins, L LL 1059 (*Pohjöla's Daughter).*

The exceptional qualities of the Philharmonia players and Karajan's discerning view of this score are combined with sound of highly discriminating texture. Excellent in all ways. For those who prefer another coupling, the Collins No. 4 is very well played and beautifully reproduced, if not with the virtuoso overtones of the Karajan.

*No. 5 in E flat. PHI, Karajan, An 35002 (*Finlandia). SRO, Ehrling, Mer MG 10142 (*Symphony No. 6). DSTR, Jensen, L LL 634 (*Karelia Suite).*

For those who want the unequivocally "best" performance among these, the Karajan is undoubtedly superior for the excellence of the players, the sound musicianship of the conductor, and the big, bright reproduction. However, those who prefer a coupling with either the Symphony No. 6 or the Karelia Suite will find each a very acceptable No. 5, the Jensen notably well recorded.

*No. 6 in D minor. SRO, Ehrling, Mer MG 10142 (*Symphony No. 5).*
See comment above.

*No. 7 in C, SRO, Ehrling, Mer 10125 (*Symphony No. 3). HO, Barbirolli, V LHMV 1011 (*Rubbra: Symphony No. 5). NYPH, Beecham, C ML 4086 (*Wagner: Siegfried Idyll).*

There is little question that Ehrling's recording will have the most interest for the Sibelius community, combined as it is with the third symphony. However, there are durable virtue, and reasonably good sound in the Barbirolli. The most personal performance of all is in the Beecham, though the sound is indistinct and attenuated by present standards.

Miscellaneous

*Finlandia. NBC, Toscanini, 10" V LRM 7005 (*Ponchielli: Dance of the Hours; Rossini: Passo a Sei). PHI, Karajan, An 35002 (*Symphony No. 5). PHO, Ormandy, 10" C AL 9 (*Swan of Tuonela).*

Given such proclamative, blood-stirring music as this, Toscanini can hardly fail to provide all the heat to inflame it fully. The sound is not as good as that on the Angel disc, but it is quite vivid nevertheless, especially in the hymnal climax. The attractions of the Philadelphia are illusory, for the version dates from an unsatisfying period of LP processing.

*Four Historic Scenes. RPO, Beecham, C ML 4550 (*Concerto for Violin).*

Beecham's enthusiasm for these works (*Festivo, The Chase, Love Song*, and *At the Drawbridge*) and an uncommonly fine recorded sound contribute to more interest in the result than would seem inherent in the music itself.

Four Legends (Lemminkäinen Suite). PHO, Ormandy, C ML 4672. SRO, Ehrling, Cap P 8226.

The matter of moment here is the superb sound of the Philadelphia Orchestra in one of its very best reproductions to date. Definition and detail, timbre and nuance are wonderfully conveyed in performances of breadth and plasticity. Ehrling does his work conscientiously, but he has no such compelling allies as the great orchestra and its ear-filling reproduction.

*Four Legends: Swan of Tuonela only. PHO, Ormandy, 10" C AL 9 (*Finlandia). HIS, Stokowski, V LRM 7024 (*Valse Triste; Berceuse; etc.).*

This is as near a dead heat as anything I have come upon in this survey: two performances of striking interpretative art, both superbly reproduced. Stokowski's underlines the dramatic emphasis in the writing, Ormandy's the finely subtle musical values. (It should be noted that this is decidedly better reproduction than the overside *Finlandia:* an excerpt, in fact, from the complete *Lemminkäinen Suite* commended above.)

*Karelia Suite. DSTR, Jensen, L LL 634 (*Symphony No. 5).*

If my taste is a criterion, this is something for the confirmed Sibelian, rather than for one who can take his music or leave it. Good-sounding, rather dull-spirited performance by Jensen.

*Pohjöla's Daughter. BSO, Koussevitzky, V LCT 1152 (*Copland: Lincoln Portrait; Fauré: Pelléas et Mélisande; Stravinsky: Capriccio). LSO, Collins, L LL 1059 (*Symphony No. 4).*

A performance of classic definition, and still of absorbing fidelity to the sound of the orchestra as molded by Koussevitzky, is in this miscellany more relevant to conductor than composer. Collins does his work very well, and the sound is characteristically fine.

*Rakastava. VSO, Litschauer, Van VRS 430 (*Valse Triste; Grieg: Norwegian Dances, opus 35).*

Litschauer's sympathy for this music is hardly pervasive. Good sound, however.

*En. Saga. ACG, Van Beinum, L LL 737 (*Tapiola).*

Two fine accomplishments for Van Beinum, and a decidedly creditable one for the London technicians.

*Tapiola. PHI, Karajan, An 35082 (*Symphony No. 4). ACG, Van Beinum, L LL 737 (*En Saga).*

Inasmuch as Karajan's fine performance of the Fourth Symphony is the best now available, the *Tapiola* will go to many automatically. However, I also prefer it, in vividness and orchestral detail, to the very good one by Van Beinum. Excellent sound.

SIEGMEISTER, ELIE (1909-)

*Ozark Set. MIN, Mitropoulos, 10" C ML 2123 (*Lalo: Roi d'Ys overture).*

The hillbilly idiom in not quite Chabrieresque ennoblement, but listenable for all that. However, the recording is no credit to Columbia, dating from one of its poorer periods.

SMETANA, BEDRICH (1824–1884)

Opera Excerpts (Orchestral)

The Bartered Bride: Overture, Dance of the Comedians, Furiant, Polka. LAP, Wallenstein, 10" D DL 4014.

Lively performances by Wallenstein and his able orchestra, though the sound is not all it might be.

*Libussa: Overture. ORB, Rother, U URLP 7094 (*Dvořák: The Jacobin; Carnaval overture).*

Unconvincing performance of a work rather more "classical" in style than most of those by Smetana to which we are accustomed. Not much resonance in the sharp-edged recording.

Dances

*Bohemian Dances. CHAM, Byrns, Cap P 8174 (*Suk: Serenade for Strings).*

Reasonably representative work by Byrns and ensemble, though the reproduction suffers from a rather confining studio.

Symphonic Poems

*Hakon Jarl. Sym 1 (*Richard III).*

Possibly the worst longplaying record I have ever heard: poorly processed from 78's, and miserably pressed. Not enough of the music is audible to evaluate the work of the anonymous conductor.

Ma Vlast (My Fatherland), Complete Cycle (Vyšehrad, Vltava, Sárka, From Bohemia's Meadows and Forests, Tábor, Blanik). CHO, Kubelik, Mer OL 2-100 [2].

An enduring evidence of Kubelik's career in Chicago, and a decidedly creditable one, as indication both of his abilities as an orchestral technician and of the depth of his sympathy for this music. I don't know of a better performance of the *Moldau* (see below), and the others are set forth with equal clarity and persuasion. Highly realistic orchestral sound, without false emphasis on any choir.

*Ma Vlast: The Moldau (Vltava) only. NYPH, Szell, C ML 4785 (*From Bohemia's Woods and Fields; Dvořák: Five Slavonic Dances). NYPH, Walter, 10" C ML 2075 (*Brahms: Academic Festival overture). NBC,*

*Toscanini, V LM 1118 (*Dukas: L'Apprenti Sorcier; Saint-Saëns: Danse Macabre). VPH, Furtwängler, V LHMV 1023 (*Strauss: Death and Transfiguration; Schumann: Manfred).*

Although the best available performance is not included in the accounting above, a glance at the preceding item will disclose why. It will also prove that eminence is not everything in music, that there are some works a Kubelik will understand better and direct more persuasively than a Toscanini. For those who don't want the total cycle, however, the Szell will be the preferable alternative. It is not done with the lilt and facility of Kubelik's naturalistic interpretation, but it has much motive power and is particularly well reproduced—a statement that applies to the companion piece as well. Of the others, the Toscanini is over-driven and under-relaxed, the Furtwängler rather too portentous and heavily accented, the Walter of many excellent traits, but no longer satisfying as sound.

Richard III. Sym 1.

See entry under *Hakon Jarl.*

*Wallenstein's Camp. VSY, Swoboda, W WL 5011 (*Suk: Fantasy). CPH, Kubelik, Mer MG 10013 (*Moldau; From Bohemia's Woods).*

Inasmuch as the imported Kubelik is a close contender for honors mentioned under *Hakon Jarl*, the music-lover is fortunate to have so desirable an alternative as the sonorously played, well reproduced version suitably directed by Swoboda.

Work for Orchestra (Arrangements)

Aus meinem leben (arranged by Szell), CO, Szell, 10" C ML 2095.

A worthy enterprise on Szell's part, and mostly well carried out. However, the rather tubby sound of the recording diminishes the pleasure in the result.

SPOHR, LUDWIG *(1784-1859)*

Concertos

*For Violin and Orchestra, No. 7 in E. Schulz, ORB, Heger, U URLP 7049 (*Concerto No. 8).*

Suave violin-playing by Schulz and a reasonable standard of artistry throughout under Heger's able direction. Better sound than in the generality of these ORB tapes.

*For Violin and Orchestra, No. 8 in A ("Gesangscene"). Stiehler, LGO, Schmitz, U URLP 7049 (*Concerto No. 7).*

The grade of performance here is about as above: thoroughly competent, but not marked by any flights of interpretative eloquence. Good sound.

Overtures

*Faust; Jessonda. ORB, Goerlich, U URLP 7028 (*Gluck: Alceste, Iphigenia in Aulis overtures).*

The Beethovenish patterns are set forth with definition and clarity by conductor Goerlich, who is otherwise unknown to me. Quite decent recording.

Symphony

No. 3 in C minor. ORF, Schlemm, 10" U URLP 5008.

Were this work played and recorded with the insight and mechanical resources commonly lavished on Beethoven, the results might be more impressive. However, it is all very routine, and not very persuasive.

SPONTINI, GASPARO (1774-1851)

*La Vestale: Overture. LSO, Previtali, V LBC 1039 (*Rossini: Italiana in Algeri overture; Saint-Saëns: Samson bacchanale, etc.).*

Carefully shaped, well-played performance, and soundly reproduced. However, it is rather awkwardly placed on this disc, between two other works.

STAMITZ, KARL (1746-1801)

*Concerto for Viola and Orchestra, in D major (arranged by Beck). Wigand, PRO, Reinhardt, Vox PL 7540 (*Telemann: Concerto in G).*

Aside from some tortuous execution by the viola soloist, this is honest, purposeful music-making, and successfully reproduced. The work itself is absorbing for its anticipations of the characteristics we associate with Mozart.

Sinfonia Concertante in F. VSY, Swoboda, W WL 5017.

A thoroughly engaging work, with the solo parts (flute, oboe, clarinet, two horns, violin, and cello) brightly played against the background provided by Swoboda. Clear recording, not as resonant as Westminster later achieved.

STRAUSS, EDUARD *(1835-1916)*

*Clear Track. PHO, Ormandy, C ML 4589 (*See J. Strauss, Jr.: One Night in Venice overture).*

A noisy little opus, to which Ormandy gives his all. Giant sound.

STRAUSS, JOHANN *(1825-1899)*

Marches

*Egyptian. VPH, Krauss, L LL 484 (*P14, P18, W10; Josef Strauss: Jokey and other polkas). PHO, Ormandy, C ML 4686 (*See Queen's Lace Handkerchief above).*

It would absurd to predicate purchase of the collections involved for this brief *morceau*, but Krauss's is so superior, in its tasteful delicacy, to Ormandy's Poli Circuit manner as to be a lesson in interpretative understanding.

*Persian. VSO, Paulik, Van VRS 443 (*P7, P3, W6, W10, W14; Josef Strauss: Village Swallows, etc.).*

A not too distinctive work, played with rather offhand lack of care. Good sound.

Opera Excerpts (Orchestral)

*Die Fledermaus: Overture. VPH, Krauss, 10" L LD 9008 (*Gypsy Baron). VSY, Moralt, Ep LC 3022 (*Gypsy Baron, W1, W15; Josef Strauss: Acquarellen; Von Suppé: Poet and Peasant).*

No more fitting introduction to a Strauss survey could be contrived than Krauss's spirited, highly polished performance of this classic overture. The sound on the 10" disc listed above is fuller, more brilliant than that on L LL 454. In this regard it is still short of the superbly resonant Epic, on which Moralt performs stylishly but without Krauss's finesse.

*The Gypsy Baron: Overture. VPH, Krauss, 10" L LD 9008 (*See above). VSY, Moralt, Ep LC 3022 (*See above).*

The comments above are equally applicable here.

*One Night in Venice: Overture. PHO, Ormandy, C ML 4589 (*W1, W6, W16, Perpetual Motion; Josef Strauss: Feuerfest; Eduard Strauss: Bahn Frei).*

A very engaging piece, played with spirit by Ormandy and brilliantly reproduced. The collection as a whole is first-class.

*The Queen's Lace Handkerchief: Overture. PHO, Ormandy, C ML 4686 (*Waldmeister, Fledermaus overtures, P1, P8, P9, P14, P17, P19, Egyptian March; J. Strauss, Sr.: Radetzky March).*

A performance of verve and superb orchestral execution, reproduced in Columbia's best manner.

*Waldmeister: Overture. PHO, Ormandy, C ML 4686 (*See above).*

Only in a literature of Johann Strauss's abundance could such a work as this be virtually unknown. The performance and recording are first-class.

Perpetuum Mobile (Musikalischer Scherz)

*Opus 257. VPH, Krauss, L LL 683 (*P3, P15, P16, W7; Josef Strauss: Village Swallows, etc.). BPH, Fricsay, D DL 9507 (*W16, P11, P4, P14). LSO, Krips, 10" L LPS 212 (*P1, P13, P19, W13, W16).*

It is hardly possible to play this minor masterpiece in any but the light, darting manner attested to in all the performances above, though Messrs. Ormandy and Steinberg attempt ingenious if unsuccessful variations in their versions. The listener will be safe with any noted above, choice depending on combined items, though Krauss has the edge by more than a bit. Krips uses a "version" by Aubrey Winter, concluding, as does Krauss, with the traditional "and so on."

Polkas (Collections)

EDITOR'S NOTE: To simplify reference to the much-duplicated waltzes and polkas, they are listed herein by the following key.

POLKAS		*WALTZES*	
Annen	P1	Acceleration	W1
Auf der Jag'd	P3	Adele	W2
Bitte Schön	P4	Artist's Life	W3
Brautschau	P5	*Bei uns z'Haus*	W4
Champagne	P6	*Du und Du*	W5
Dot on the I	P7	Emperor Waltz	W6
Explosion	P8	Morning Papers	W7
Fledermaus	P9	On the Beautiful Blue Danube	W8
Furioso	P10		

POLKAS		*WALTZES*	
High Spirits	P11	Roses from the South	W9
Im Krapfenwald'l	P12	Tales from the Vienna Woods	W10
Piefke und Pufke	P13	Thousand and One Nights	W11
Pizzicatto	P14	Treasure Waltz	W12
Ritter Pasman	P15	Vienna Blood	W13
Stadt und Land	P16	Voices of Spring	W14
Thunder and Lightning	P17	Where the Lemon Trees Bloom	W15
Train Polka	P18		
Tritsch-Tratsch	P19		
Um Sturmschnitt	P20	Wine, Women, and Song	W16

*Annen; Champagne; Thunder and Lightning; Tritsch-Tratsch. PSO, Steinberg, Cap P 8222 (*Perpetuum Mobile, W1, W2, W6).*

Auf der Jag'd; Im Krapfenwald'l; Pizzicato; Train; Stadt und Land. VPH, Krauss, 10" L LD 9044.

Bitte Schön; High Spirits; Pizzicato; Tritsch-Tratsch; Annen. BPH, RIAS, Fricsay, WSO, Leitner, 10" D DL 4043.

*Brautschau; Fledermaus; Furioso; Im Krapfenwald'l; Ritter Pasman; Um Sturmschritt. BPO, Fiedler, V LM 1226 (*Waldteufel: España, etc.).*

*Dot on the I; Auf der Jag'd. VSO, Paulik, Van VRS 443 (*See Marches, Persian).*

*Explosion; Annen; Pizzicato; Tritsch-Tratsch; Thunder and Lightning. PHO, Ormandy, C ML 4686 (*See Queen's Lace Handkerchief overture).*

*Piefke und Pufke; Annen; Tritsch-Tratsch. LSO, Krips, 10" L LPS 212 (*See Perpetuum Mobile).*

Among them, these seven discs contain all the twenty or so Strauss polkas now available. Moreover, close to half the total—and much of the best playing—may be found on the three 10" discs directed by Krauss, Krips, and Fricsay-Leitner. Of the others, the Fiedler presents some additional repertory played with his typical zest if not the ideal "cushioned" impact of the Vienna style (also interesting Waldteufel); while Steinberg's generous collection, including a bangy *Thunder and Lightning* and the only *Adele* waltz, if almost exhausting in its unremitting energy, is well reproduced. Krauss's *Pizzicato* is a lecture on the anatomy of this gay but by no means trifling work, and Krips's *Piefke und Pufke* is worth knowing, his *Tritsch-Tratsch* one of the best.

Quadrilles

*Festival. CBSO, Barlow, C RL 3020 (*P6, P8, Motoren Walzer, etc.).*

Whatever the interests of this repertory, it is offset by the feebleness of the pre-war recording, no bargain even at the bargain price.

*Fledermaus. WSO, Leitner, D DL 9507 (*W16, P4, P11, P14, Perpetuum Mobile).*

An entertaining reprise of favorite bits from the operetta, mostly *not* in the original rhythmic form. Much of the other material is contained on 10" D DL 4043. Excellent sound.

Waltzes

*Acceleration. NEW, Krips, 10" L LD 9016 (*W9). BPH, Kleiber, Cap P 8061 (*W11, W8, W9, W14). VSY, Salmhofer, Ep LC 3022 (*See Fledermaus overture).*

Kleiber's pre-war delight is, unfortunately, quite faded in sound, but there need be no regret, for Krips's flavorsome performance is a reasonable replacement, of very good sound. For those who want the fullness of high fidelity, Salmhofer provides it.

*Adele. PSO, Steinberg, Cap P 8222 (*See Annen Polka).*

This charming tribute to Strauss's wife (No. 3, and final) is the attractive element of Steinberg's collection. His brass-band manner in this repertory could be tempered considerably. Clear sound, but not much tonal glamour.

*Artist's Life. VPH, Krauss, L LL 454 (*W14, overtures to Fledermaus, Gypsy Baron). VPH, Karajan, 10" C AL 28 (*W6).*

Esteem for Karajan's efforts is offset by shrillish processing to LP, and consequent aural irritation. In any case, Krauss's masterful work would be hard to surpass. Good sound.

*Bei uns z'Haus. VPH, Krauss, L LL 970 (*W8, P1; Josef Strauss: Music of the Spheres, etc.).*

Krauss's affectionate treatment of this unfamiliar work is typical of the fine series of "New Year" concerts of which this is the third, and, by reason of his recent death, the last to be directed by him. Strauss enthusiasts should need but the numbers LL 484 and 683 for action. Johann, Sr., and Josef are also liberally represented in each sequence. Extra good sound.

*Du und Du. MPH, Rieger, Mer MG 10024 (*W8, W13, W14). SYM, Seidler-Winkler, V LBC 1065 (*W6; Offenbach: Gaité Parisienne).*

A low ebb for this excerpt from *Fledermaus*, for both performances are dull and decidedly poor reproductions.

*Emperor. SYM, Krips, 10" L LD 9015 (*W8). PHO, Ormandy, C ML*

*4589 (*See One Night in Venice overture). BAM, Leitner, 10" D DL 4062 (*W7).*

Krips conveys the most music with the least extraneous noise, though Ormandy is not far behind in a performance especially well reproduced. Leitner also manages well, despite shrillish strings.

*Morning Papers. RPO, Beecham, 10" C ML 2134 (*Nicolai: Merry Wives; Von Suppé: Morning, Noon, and Night in Vienna; Ponchielli: Dance of the Hours). RIAS, Fricsay, 10" D DL 4062 (*W6). VPH, Krauss, 10" L LD 9030 (*W10).*

The overturn of the repertory has deprived Beecham of honors due him as an accredited Straussophile, but this recent effort shows him as responsive as ever to the style, as practiced as ever in conveying it. Both of the other performances are excellent and equally well recorded.

*On the Beautiful Blue Danube. VPH, Szell, V LBC 1008 (*W9, W7, W14, etc.). SYM, Krips, 10" L LD 9015 (*W6). VPH, Krauss, L LL 970 (*Bei uns z'Haus). VSY, Moralt, Ep LC 3004 (*W10, W13, W14).*

According to my personal view, Szell's is still the best *Blue Danube* known to me, though I don't expect others to indulge the weakish recording for that reason. However, at the price, the collection is a very attractive one. For those who want well-oiled springs to carry them over this course, Krips provides it with even more style than in his earlier London version, and in richly resonant reproduction. My esteem for the Krauss goes up with each hearing, and it is now practically at a parity with the Szell and Krips. In this New Year concert for 1954 it blooms most attractively. Moralt's effort with the Vienna Symphony is very good, the sound particularly good. There is no American version even close to these.

*Roses from the South. NEW, Krips, 10" L LD 9016 (*W1). VPH, Krauss, Cap P 8061 (*W8, W14, W1, W11). VPH, Böhm, V LCB 1008 (*See Blue Danube). RIAS, Fricsay, 10" D DL 4062 (*W16).*

As other able conductors have suggested in the past, the singing sound for Strauss reposes in the conductor rather than the orchestra, as Krips demonstrates in this suave and highly satisfactory English enterprise. Krauss's lovely sense of line comes through in his pre-war performance, but too many details are lacking for satisfaction (note that he shares the disc with Kleiber). Böhm's sound performance is part of the collection with Szell's *On the Beautiful Blue Danube*, but not otherwise irresistible. Fricsay performs well in the Berlin manner—which is to say, with a harder shell of sound than is favored in Vienna—and the reproduction is excellent.

*Tales from the Vienna Woods. VPH, Krauss, 10" L LD 9030 (*W7). Also L LP 484 (*P14, P18, P12; Josef Strauss: Jokey, etc.). VSY, Moralt, Ep LC 3004 (*W8, W13, W14). BAM, Leitner, 10" D DL 4041 (*W14).*

Whether acquired as partnered by *Morning Papers*, or in the more extensive "New Year" concert on L LP 484, Krauss's *Tales* could hardly be told better. As a sample of the ever increasing quest for authenticity in recordings, it is worth noting that this version, as well as the others cited, honors the original by employing a zither soloist. Moralt's effort is commendable, the sound especially good. I am no passionate partisan for the hard, shallow sound of the Bamberg ensemble, but the overside *Voices of Spring* with Wilma Lipp, soprano, is outstanding.

*Thousand and One Nights. BBC, Weingartner, C ML 4777 (*W8, W14, W16).*

It is a gratifying surprise to discover that this restoration from the Weingartner catalogue preserves a considerable likeness to the original sound. As a performance it was, and is, a joy.

*Treasure (Schatz). PSO, Reiner, C ML 4116 (*W9, W13; Brahms: Eight Hungarian Dances).*

As in the associated works, Reiner shows in this borrowing from *Gypsy Baron* that he is a master of the Strauss style, as he is of many others. What was formerly considered good recording is now rather pale and shrill, but this is a *Treasure* to treasure.

*Vienna Blood. LSO, Krips, 10" L LD 9013 (*W16). BPH, Fricsay, 10" D DL 4009 (*W8). VSY, Moralt, Ep LC 3004 (*W8, W10, W14).*

Each of these has its special splendors, the Krips performance striking an especially happy note for the London engineers. Otherwise, the characteristics are as previously noted.

*Voices of Spring. BPH, Fricsay, Lipp, 10" D DL 4041 (*W10). VPH, Krauss, L LP 454 (*W3, overtures to Fledermaus, Gypsy Baron). VSY, Moralt, Ep LC 3004 (*W8, W10, W13). SYM, Weingartner, C ML 4777 (*See W11).*

Lipp is more conscientious about her musical P's and Q's than most sopranos who flirt with these inviting patterns, the results being a diverting equivalent of the Straussian original. However, I find the orchestra minus voice a more restful way of following the composer's thoughts, especially as conveyed by Krauss and Moralt. The Weingartner is poorly reproduced.

*Where the Lemon Trees Bloom. VSY, Salmhofer, Ep 3022 (*See Fledermaus overture).*

Whether Salmhofer does more than give the downbeat is questionable, but the players manage well with or without urging, which is mostly absent. First-class sound.

*Wine, Women, and Song. LSO, Krips, 10" L LD 9013 (*W13).*

There being no Krauss, Krips is quite without challenge in this music, especially as the recording shares the decidedly sonorous properties of *Vienna Blood.*

Miscellaneous

Graduation Ball (arranged by Dorati). NEW, Fistoulari, L LL 883. DAL, Dorati, V LM 1061.

Fistoulari does better by Dorati's arrangement than the creator of it, aided no little by the London engineers and hospitable Kingsway Hall. However, neither is a stylist in this music to compare with those heretofore mentioned.

STRAUSS, JOHANN, SR. (1804-1849)

*Radetzky March. VPH, Krauss L LL 970 (*See Johann Strauss, Jr.: Bei uns z'Haus). PHO, Ormandy, C ML 4686 (*See Johann Strauss, Jr.: Queen's Lace Handkerchief overture).*

This is considerably more than the exercise for cymbal and bass drum which Ormandy makes of it, as Krauss aptly illustrates. His sound is not as big, but much better.

STRAUSS, JOSEF (1827-1870)

Polkas

Feuerfest; Jokey; Moulinet; Ohne Sorgen; Die Libelle. VPH, Krauss, 10" L LD 9045.

This handy compilation extracts the relevant matter from the "New Year" concerts for 1953 and 1954, sounding as superlatively well as they do on LL's 484 and 683.

*Auf Ferienreisen; Plappermaülchen. VPH, Krauss, L LL 970 (*See J. Strauss, Jr.: Bei uns z'Haus).*

In the tradition, creatively and re-creatively.

Waltzes

*Acquarellen. VSY, Salmhofer, Ep LC 3022 (*See J. Strauss, Jr.: Fledermaus overture).*

A stunning work, to which Salmhofer gives appreciably more personal accent than to the other matter assigned to him on this disc. Extra-fine sound.

*Delerien. BAVR, Schroder, Mer MH 10022 (*Acquarellen; Music of the Spheres; etc.).*

A good performance may be buried here, but the hash of sound is something to avoid.

*Music of the Spheres. VPH, Krauss, L LL 970 (*See J. Strauss, Jr.: Bei uns z'Haus). VPH, Böhm, V LBC 1008 (*See J. Strauss, Jr.: On the Beautiful Blue Danube).*

One of the grandest waltzes written by anyone, given red-carpet treatment by Krauss. Fine sound. The Böhm is almost as good musically, and very listenable tonally.

My Life Is Full of Joy; Village Swallows. VPH, Krauss, 10" L LD 9029.

As in the instance of the polkas cited above, this disc is derived from the "New Year" concert series. Better performances are scarcely imaginable, the sound being a salve to the ears.

Village Swallows. See above.

STRAUSS, RICHARD (1864-1949)

Ballet Music

Josephslegende. MSO, Eichhorn, U 602 [2] (**Der Rosenkavalier*).

A throw-in with the Kempe-directed performance of *Der Rosenkavalier*, where it is an acceptable bounty. Hardly worth an investment for its own sake, however.

Schlagobers. FRO, Kloss, Ly 41.

Lightness is hardly a house specialty with this organization and its conductor. Fair auditory values.

Burleske

*In D minor. Jacquinot, PHI, Fistoulari, MGM E 3004 (*Dohnányi: Variations on a Nursery Theme).*

This is the best of three current versions, none wholly satisfactory. Mme Jacquinot, at least, is fluent and accurate, the recording bright and clear.

Concertos

*For Horn, No. 1 in E flat. Brain, PHI, Galliera, C ML 4775 (*Concerto for Oboe).*

There is little to choose between this performance by Brain and one by Lohan on Urania (7108), but the happy combination with Leon Goossens's splendid playing of the late oboe concerto (1945) adds to the attraction of the disc for Straussians. Excellent English sound in both, if not all-out high fidelity.

*For Oboe. Goossens, PHI, Galliera, C ML 4775 (*Concerto for Horn).*
*Ertel, ORB, Rother, U 7032 (*Concerto for Violin).*

Both oboists are capable—though I am partial to Goossens's tone—which leaves a determination to other factors. Borries is a decidedly good violinist, and his version of the violin concerto is the only one available. Both sides are well reproduced.

*For Violin. Borries, ORB, Rother, U 7032 (*Concerto for Oboe).*

See entry under Concerto for Oboe above.

Concertino

*For Bassoon and Clarinet. LACS, Byrns, Cap P 8115 (*Honegger: Concerto da Camera).*

Both works are delectable examples of woodwind writing by masters of the genre, and the playing of the Los Angeles Chamber Symphony is thoroughly good. Gerald Caylor is the clarinetist, Don Christlieb the bassoonist.

Divertimento

*After Couperin. BRS, Rother, U 7042 (*Taillefer).*

The combination offering of the lively divertimento and the early choral work is an engaging one, but I would not recommend the orchestral work on its own, for the recording leaves more than a little to be desired.

Incidental Music

Le Bourgeois Gentilhomme. VPH, Krauss, L LL 684. PSO, Reiner, C ML 2062.

As the first of the Krauss-Strauss discs to occur in this sequence, this may be noted as a typical instance of the conductor's superior understanding of the composer's idiom, the probability that any given interpretation will be superior to all save someone else's *tour de force*. Moreover, London's recording in Vienna has been among its consistently creditable accomplishments. In justice to Reiner, it may be said that his direction of the *Bourgeois Gentilhomme* music is such a *tour de force*, though the recording of the Pittsburgh Symphony is thinner than current standards recognize as good, and the record itself is scheduled for withdrawal.

Opera Excerpts (Orchestral)

*Ariadne auf Naxos: Overture. WSO, Leitner, 10" D DL 4063 (*Glinka: Russlan and Ludmilla overture; Rossini: Tancredi overture; Verdi: Nabucco overture).*

Fair enough woodwind-playing in this tricky material, but hardly the integration wanted in the total. Good sound, but hardly sufficient to justify the other items in the miscellany.

*Der Rosenkavalier (Suite). HO, Barbirolli, V LBC 1017 (*Grieg: Peer Gynt, Suites 1 and 2).*

Of the several alternatives, this is the most attractive in sum, combining a vigorous playing of the Strauss excerpts with a very acceptable one of the Grieg. Also, the recording is spacious, the price advantageous.

*Der Rosenkavalier: Waltzes. PHO, Ormandy, 10" C AL 46 (*Till Eulenspiegel). NYSO, Smallens, 10" D DL 4032 (*Dance of the Seven Veils).*

For a luxury version of these waltzes, the Philadelphia playing can hardly be surpassed, though Ormandy almost, but not quite, overproduces some of his effects. However, the overside *Till* is inferior to several others. Both sides are among the best-sounding Columbia has made in Philadelphia. At the lower price, the Smallens effort is decidedly attractive, especially for the *Salome* excerpt, for which he has a decided flair.

*Salome: Dance of the Seven Veils. CHO, Reiner, V LM 1806 (*Also Sprach Zarathustra). NYSO, Smallens, 10" D DL 4032 (*Der Rosenkavalier: Waltzes).*

Those who accept my recommendation in *Zarathustras* will find this as an eminently suitable encore, directed by Reiner with enormous control of the orchestra and powerfully reproduced. The virtues of the Smallens treatment are by no means slight, and in the economic category indicated give fair enough value.

Songs with Orchestra

*Four Last Songs. Della Casa, VPH, Böhm, 10" L LD 9072. Schwarzkopf, PHI, Ackermann, An 35084 (*Final scene from Capriccio).*

Both performers have a sure understanding of the material, each has a fine voice well used, and the recording allows little latitude for preference. However, Della Casa's introspective manner appeals to me more than the beautiful tracery of line by Schwarzkopf. Moreover, the London issue may be obtained without extraneous matter, but the Angel is pressed only with the closing scene from *Capriccio*. Those who are interested may be assured that it is admirably performed.

Symphonies

In F. VPA, Haffner, SPA 17.

This product of 1883–4 is an interesting contribution to the developing Strauss literature, though the performance is hardly insinuating and the recording leaves much to be desired. Oddly, there are few reminiscences of predecessors to be heard and little indication of the personality that showed itself in *Burleske* the next year.

For Winds. MGMO, Solomon, MGO 3097.

Though Strauss clearly labeled this work of 1944–5 a "sonatina," his friends are persuaded he really meant "symphony"—or so they say. It is, in substance, a work on the order of Mozart's E flat serenade for winds (K. 375), with five clarinets rather than two in the total of sixteen players. Excellent spirit in the playing, transparent recording.

Tone Poems

*Also Sprach Zarathustra. CHO, Reiner, V LM 1806 (*Salome: Dance of the Seven Veils). VPH, Krauss, L LL 232.*

Though it was barely months ago that the Krauss version seemed unsurpassable, Victor has accomplished that formidable end by bringing out of Chicago's Orchestra Hall a tape of surpassing breadth and clarity on which Reiner has inscribed the performance of his life. It has almost as much warmth of statement as the Krauss and much more dynamic force. With the *Dance* as dividend, it is fine value indeed.

Aus Italien. VPH, Krauss, L LL 969.

Sumptuous-sounding Strauss, with a high standard prevailing in all respects—performance, leadership, and engineering.

*Death and Transfiguration. NYPH, Walter, C ML 4650 (*Don Juan). RCAO, Reiner, V LM 1180 (Till Eulenspiegel). ACG, Mengelberg, Cap P 8100 (*Till Eulenspiegel).*

Thanks to a highly charged contact between conductor and orchestra, this is an eloquent statement by Walter of a work he has lived with long and profitably. As much applies to the *Don Juan*, even though it is not my preference (see below). The Reiner version is in every way admirable, though not on such a level of personal expression. Good recording, not as powerful as the Walter. The Mengelberg is remarkably vivid in the projection of his personal views of Strauss, though the recording is pale by today's standard.

*Don Juan. NBC, Toscanini, V LM 1157 (*Wagner: Siegfried's Rhine Journey). NYPH, Walter, C ML 4650 (*Death and Transfiguration). PHI, Krauss, L LL 233 (*Till Eulenspiegel). ACG, Mengelberg, 10" Mer 15000 (*Tchaikovsky: 1812 Overture).*

Of itself, the Toscanini version of *Don Juan* is the most compelling I have heard, in both action and repose. In combination with the "Rhine Journey," it stands as one of the notable recordings of his literature. The recording, if not as resonant as the Krauss, is thoroughly good. Those who prefer Strauss back to back will be well off with either the Walter or the Krauss, depending on their preference in couplings. This Mengelberg is much like the *Death and Transfiguration* noted above: actually a tremendous *Don Juan* hobbled by inferior reproduction.

Don Quixote. BAV, Strauss, D DL 9539. Fournier, VPH, Krauss, L LL 855. Piatigorsky, BSO, Munch, V LM 1781.

Most of the music in this score is conveyed by the version under the direction of the composer, especially as this is the best-reproduced of the self-directed ones currently available. The cellist and violist, though of no name-appeal in this country, are both excellent. However, if the listener places a primary importance on sound, he will be happier with the Fournier-Krauss than with the Piatigorsky-Munch, for the former preserves a proper relationship of solo instruments with orchestra, the latter tends too much to a concerto-like prominence of the cello. In a long-range view, the Strauss version would be my preference till the 1953 broadcast by Toscanini becomes available.

Ein Heldenleben. PHO, Ormandy, C ML 4887. CHO, Reiner, V LM 1807. VPH, Krauss, L LL 659. ACG, Mengelberg, Cap P 8013. BAV, Strauss, D DL 9602.

Where performances of the exceptional quality of these by Ormandy and Reiner are concerned, a preference must be largely a matter of personal disposition—slightly colored by the fact that, for a score of this magnitude, the Philadelphia at its best is richer, more transparent, than any orchestra known to me. In reproduction, the Reiner is of the order of his *Zarathustra*, the performance not quite so glowing; the Ormandy is as good as anything Columbia has ever done in Philadelphia, which is—superb. Moreover, it is a performance that holds the attention from first to last, with every instrumental detail beautifully managed. The Krauss is, of course, much fuller in sound than the others cited primarily for historical interest, though Mengelberg's direction of the great work dedicated to his orchestra is, so far as can be heard, impressive.

*Macbeth. VSY, Swoboda, W 5004 (*Martinu: Concerto Grosso).*

Inasmuch as this is the only performance of this work I have ever heard, reservations may be entertained as to its total justice. However, it conveys a persuasive idea of the kind of music Strauss was writing at this early point in his career, and if the recording is not so good as Westminster subsequently achieved, it is quite acceptable.

Symphonia Domestica. VPH, Krauss, L LL 483. VPH, Strauss, Vox PL 7220.

Krauss has as much to say on this subject as any recent conductor, and London's recording plus the virtuosity of the Vienna Philharmonic make it possible for him to say it with maximum eloquence. If there is ever a competitive effort from either Ormandy or Mitropoulos, it would be worth sampling. The composer's self-directed version (preserved from a concert of 1944) has incontestable atmosphere and sufficient fidelity to make it a valuable documentation.

*Till Eulenspiegel. RCAO, Reiner, V LM 1180 (*Death and Transfiguration). VPH, Krauss, L LL 233 (*Don Juan).*

As between two such qualified Straussians as Reiner and Krauss, the distinctions of treatment would be necessarily narrow. However, it strikes me that Reiner has a little sharper perception of the wit in this music, and delivers it with more sparkle than Krauss. Decidedly good sound in either instance.

Work for String Orchestra

*Metamorphosen. ORD, Horenstein, An 35101 (*Stravinsky: Symphony of Psalms).*

What Horenstein offers is neither the first (that was contained in a 78-rpm version by Karajan) nor last word on this subject, but an intermediate one that will repay close attention. The intricacies of the work are well worth pondering, and the fine-sounding performance facilitates that considerably. A score is also advised.

STRAVINSKY, IGOR (1882-)

Ballet Music

*Apollon Musagète. RCAS, Stravinsky, V LM 1096 (*Concerto Grosso in D).*

This is hardly a model of sound, save as what should be avoided; but despite its dryness and lack of vibrance, the performance has such vitality as to interest nevertheless.

*Le Baiser de la Fée (Divertimento). RCAO, Stravinsky, V LM 1075 (*Danses Concertantes). OSR, Ansermet, L LLP 390 (*Martin: Petite Symphonie Concertante).*

Stravinsky, who is to be involved in many competitions with Ansermet for preference in the ensuing survey, wins this one by default. For one thing, the spare, jerky patterns are well rendered in his dry, precise reading, and the recording is reasonably good. For the other, however, Ansermet is hardly in brilliant form here, and the recording leaves more than a little to be desired.

*Circus Polka. NYPH, Stravinsky, C ML 4398 (*Feu d'artifice; Ode; Norwegian Moods; etc.). OSR, Ansermet, 10" L LS 503 (*Ravel: Alborada del Gracioso; Debussy: L'Après-midi d'un faune; etc.).*

As it isn't probable that anyone would search out this elephantine gambol for its own sake, it may be related in this wise to the other contents of the collections in which it appears: the Stravinsky is all-Stravinsky and broadly reproduced, the Ansermet is diluted somewhat with French dressing, but well served by the recorders.

*Danses Concertantes. RCAO, Stravinsky, V LM 1075 (*Le Baiser de la Fée).*

Well-paced performance, better reproduced than the companion piece, and that much more satisfactory therefore.

*L'Histoire du Soldat. BSO, Bernstein, V LM 1078 (*Octet for Wind Instruments).*

A virtuoso accomplishment for the Boston Symphony personnel involved (Victor Polatschek, clarinet; Raymond Allard, bassoon; Jacob Raichman, trombone; Roger Voisin, trumpet; Charles Smith, percussion; Richard Burgin, violin; and Georges Moleux; bass), as well as conductor Bernstein. Fine sound values.

*Jeu des Cartes. BPH, Stravinsky, Mer 10014 (*Dumbarton Oaks).*

Of the forms in which Stravinsky's pre-war (and hence hardly dazzling) recording is available, this would seem preferable. However, any qualified new recording would be preferable.

*Les Noces. CHAM, Rossi, Van 452 (*Histoire du Soldat). NYCO, Hillis, Vox PL 8630 (*Mass: Pater Noster; Ave Maria).*

Neither of these is as compelling, musically, as the new dim-sounding C Set 204 directed by the composer, but the Hillis would have to be much better than it is to offset the use of an English text against Rossi's preference for the Russian. Both are well reproduced.

*L'Oiseau de Feu (Suite). HIS, Stokowski, 10" V LM 44. OSR, Ansermet, 10" L LPS 300. PHO, Ormandy, C ML 4700 (*Mussorgsky-Ravel: Pictures). MIN, Dorati, Mer MG 50004 (*Borodin: Symphony No. 2). NYPH, Stravinsky, C ML 4046.*

At the risk of seeming unaware of proper thinking in re Stravinsky, I direct attention to the latest of Stokowski's versions (No. 4 at least) as the best he has done, and one of the most veristic recordings anyone has done. It strikes me that he handles some bridge passages better than Ansermet, and everything else as well. Both the Dorati and the Ormandy are superior recordings in their ways, but neither has the thrust or impact of the other two. All these use the text of the 1919 edition. Stravinsky prefers his recent "augmented" version, which has one more section of the score included. However the good recording of approximately 1946 no longer impresses.

*Petrouchka. OSR, Ansermet, L LL 130. NYPH, Stravinsky, C ML 4047 (*Scènes de Ballet).*

Nothing has happened in half a dozen years to alter a preference then expressed for the perceptive, wonderfully articulated performance directed by Ansermet. The LP transfer has enhanced the virtues of Stravinsky's direction of his own music, which stands as one of his most persuasive efforts of the sort. However, he offers only four sections of the score, and though the sound is good, it cannot be rated ffrr.

Pulcinella (Complete). CO, Stravinsky, soloists, C ML 4830.

The abundance of greatest Stravinsky has limited the circulation of the lesser but highly characteristic works, such as this. It is delightfully produced under the conductor's direction, and well if not remarkably reproduced (balance is not all it should be, and echo occasionally intrudes). The soloists (Mary Simmons, soprano, Glenn Schnittke, tenor, and Phillip MacGregor, bass) are more talented than experienced, but on the whole satisfactory.

Le Sacre du Printemps. BSO, Monteux, V LM 1149. PHI, Markevitch, V LHMV 1. PSO, Steinberg, Cap P 8254. OSR, Ansermet, L LL 303. MIN, Dorati, Mer 50030. NYPH, Stravinsky, C ML 4092. WWS, CMD CAL-100.

It would take more self-assurance than I possess to pontificate on the fine distinctions among these fine performances, and point to one as "superfine." I personally prefer to hear the music as Monteux conveys it, especially in partnership with the Boston

Symphony and this acute pickup of it. However, the recently issued Markevitch has almost persuaded me otherwise. Steinberg's possesses some salient merits of instrumental detail not to be heard elsewhere, and the Ansermet is fine-sounding, informed by his own kind of musical approach. For the Dorati I have regard primarily for the engineers who took down his dictation with microscopic precision, but the message doesn't seem to me suitable to the subject. Stravinsky's sounds better than one would suspect it would, and that is even more pronounced in the instance of the Camden "World Wide," which is actually the Stokowski-Philadelphia of V Set 74, amazingly restored in its LP bargain form.

*Scènes de Ballet. NYPH, Stravinsky, C ML 4047 (*Petrouchka).*

A reminder of Stravinsky's contribution to the Billy Rose revue *The Seven Lively Arts*, and decidedly pleasant, if not altogether restful. The transfer to LP from C Set X 245 is very successful.

Concertos

*For Piano and Orchestra, 1923–24. S. Stravinsky, RCAO, I. Stravinsky, 10" V LM 7010 (*Scherzo à la Russe; Russian Church Choruses). Mewton-Wood, RES, Goehr, CH 1160 (*Prokofiev: Concerto No. 1 for Violin).*

Other things being equal, it would seem that a performance by the two Stravinskys would have clear priority. However, this is another of the dull reproductions that Stravinsky was accorded by RCA, and hence the much brighter, more resonant alternate is recommended. The late Mewton-Wood is a better pianist than young Stravinsky, and Goehr contributes properly to the total. (R. Odnoposoff is the violinist for the overside Prokofiev, with H. Hollreiser conducting the Radio Zurich Orchestra.)

*Dumbarton Oaks. DOO, Stravinsky, Mer 10014 (*Jeu des Cartes).*

A Long Play reissue of the performance formerly on Keynote (DM 1), and a much better reproduction than the overside ballet music.

*Ebony. WHO, Stravinsky, C ML 4398 (*Feu d'artifice; Ode; Circus Polka; etc.).*

One of the most engaging elements in this grab bag of Stravinsky, reflecting high credit on the jazz-band players who participate, and on the engineering thereof. In the wake of *The Rake's Progress*, in which the rhythmic patterns of Movement I were conspicuous, the musical sense of the whole is clarified.

Concerto Grosso

*In D major ("Basle"). RCAO, Stravinsky, V LM 1096 (*Apollon Musagète).*

Highly persuasive performance by Stravinsky of a work which grows in appeal with acquaintance, especially the lyric slow movement. However, the total pleasure is diminished by the scrappy sound of the strings in the dry, unresonant reproduction.

Works for Orchestra

*Feu d'artifice. NYPH, Stravinsky, C ML 4398 (*See item above).*

One of the best performances this work has had on records, and very well reproduced.

*Norwegian Moods. NYPH, Stravinsky, C ML 4398 (*See Ebony Concerto).*

Minor Stravinsky, suitably performed.

*Ode. NYPH, Stravinsky, C ML 4398 (*See Ebony Concerto).*

A tribute to the late Mme Natalie Koussevitzky, and appropriately eulogistic. Good reproduction.

*Scherzo à la Russe. RCAO, Stravinsky, 10" V LM 7010 (*Concerto, 1923-24).*

Small but lively exercise, created for Paul Whiteman. Good reproduction.

Suites pour Petit Orchestre (Nos. 1 and 2). LOS, Scherman, 10" D DL 7529.

Not all the points are made with equal effectiveness, but the playing is clean, the reproduction clear, though a little lacking in resonance.

*Symphony in Three Movements. NYPH, Stravinsky, C ML 4129 (*Symphony of Psalms).*

A recent (1950) winner of a Grand Prix awarded by French record pundits, the continuing excellence of the reproduction confirms the soundness of that judgment. Fine performance, too.

Work for Orchestra and Piano

*Capriccio. RIAS, Haas, Fricsay, D DL 9515 (*Ravel: Concerto in G). BSO, Sanroma, Koussevitzky, V LCT 1152 (*See Sibelius: Pohjóla's Daughter).*

Not as bright or vivacious a sound as one would expect from a contemporary recording, but a musicianly performance. Recommendation: patience. The reissued Sanroma-Koussevitzky has a degree of interpretative force not duplicated in the newer playing, but the instrumentation is not well served by the thinnish, though remarkably clear, sound.

Works for Orchestra and Voices

Oedipus Rex. CRO, Stravinsky, soloists, C ML 4644.

An impressive effort under the composer's direction, with Jean Cocteau as narrator. The soloists have been carefully selected, but the qualifications of Peter Pears for the music of Oedipus are much less conspicuous than those of Heinz Rehfuss for Creon and a Messenger, or those of Martha Mödl for Jocasta. The others are Otto von Rohr (Tiresias) and Helmut Krebs (Shepherd). Very clean, resonant reproduction.

*Symphony of Psalms. CBSO, Stravinsky, C ML 4129 (*Symphony in Three Movements). ORD, Horenstein, An 35101 (*Strauss: Metamorphosen).*

The sound values in Horenstein's performance are clearly superior to those in the Stravinsky, but this is a work, certainly, in which manner is more important than matter: hence, a continuing preference for the Stravinsky. The orchestra and voices lack some of the richness present in the Horenstein, but the sense and purpose of the music are much better conveyed by the composer's interpretation. Likewise, the second side is a more congruent element than on the Angel offering.

SUK, JOSEPH (1874-1935)

*Fantasy for Violin and Orchestra. Rybar, VSO, Swoboda, W WL 5011 (*Smetana: Wallenstein's Camp).*

A rather meandering work, tolerably played by Rybar, but not reproduced with anything like the fullness or definition expected today.

*Serenade for Strings. BCO, Byrns, Cap P 8174 (*Smetana: Bohemian Dances).*

Fair enough performance, not too well reproduced.

SUPPÉ, FRANZ VON *(1819-1895)*

Overtures (Collections)

Light Cavalry; Morning, Noon, and Night in Vienna; Pique Dame; Poet and Peasant. LPO, Solti, L LL 352.

Solti's vigor and the virtuoso assistance of London's engineering staff make this one of the choice discs in this total survey. There may be, here or there (see below), an individual performance that is superior, but this is a grand continuity of effects. (Note that the first two are available as a pair on 10" *L LL 9005*, the others on 9006.)

Overtures

*Beautiful Galatea. BASO, Graunke, 10" D DL 4021 (*Jolly Robbers).*

Neither of these is a model of reproduced sound, but the zest for the material is there, as is a warm melodic feeling.

*Morning, Noon, and Night in Vienna. RPO, Beecham, 10" C ML 2134 (*Strauss, J.: Morning Papers; Nicolai: Merry Wives overture, etc.).*

Beecham's style in this work is more rarified, less earthy than Solti's and perfectly realized. The recording is excellent. However, for Suppé *qua* Suppé, Solti is not easily excelled, and his sound is remarkable.

SWANSON, HOWARD *(1909-)*

*A Short Symphony. VSO, Litschauer, 434 (*Kupferman: Little Symphony).*

Excellent-sounding reproduction of a not very sympathetic interpretation.

SZYMANOWSKI, KAROL *(1883-1937)*

Concerto for Violin and Orchestra, No. 1. Uminska, PHI, Fitelberg, 10" D DL 7516.

A work that should be better known, warmly played by Uminska and well reproduced.

Symphonie Concertante for Piano and Orchestra. Rubinstein, LAP, Wallenstein, V LM 1744 (**Rachmaninoff: Rhapsody on a Theme of Paganini*).

A labor of love by Rubinstein on behalf of his countryman, ably seconded by Wallenstein. The reproduction is satisfactory.

TANEYEV, SERGEI IVANOVICH (1856-1915)

Symphony No. 1 in C minor. USSR, Gauk, A440 AC 1208 (**Rimsky-Korsakov: Overture on Russian Themes*).

A vigorous work, full of songful themes and dramatic contrasts, affectionately treated by Gauk. The recording is sharp and rather penetrating, as though electronically enhanced.

TANSMAN, ALEXANDRE (1897-)

Triptych for String Orchestra. ZS, D DL 9625. (**Vaughan Williams: Concerto Accademico*).

First-class effort in every way, with the virtuoso group from the Boston Symphony brilliantly reproduced.

TARTINI, GIUSEPPE (1692-1770)

Concertos

For Violoncello and Orchestra

In A major. Altobelli, I Musici, An 35086 (**Rossini: Sonata; Galuppi: Concerto No. 2; etc.*).

This magnificent work has a familiar contour, but I cannot say whether I know it from a public performance or from a transcription in another guise. In any case, the cellist plays it with sonorous tone and the ensemble is of the sturdy solidity associated with these players. Beautiful sound.

For Violin and Orchestra

In D minor. Rybar, WIN, Dahinden, W WL 5118 (**Sonatas in E and E *minor*). *Szigeti, COL, Szell, C ML 4891* (**Bach: Concerto in G minor; Handel: Sonata in D; etc.*).

Generally speaking, the Columbia is tonally a smoother product than the Westminster, but this does not include the sound of Szigeti's violin—wiry and rough. His artistry counts for much, of course, but the basic stuff of music is sound, which here is unpleasant.

In E. Ferro, VDR, Fasano, D DL 9572 (**A. Scarlatti: Concerto No. 6; Vivaldi: Concerto in G; etc.*).

Delightfully poised, musicianly performance in a real chamber-music style. As in the other matter of this disc, the recording is good.

In G minor. Rostal, WIN, Goehr, CH 1174 (**Bach: Sonata in E minor, etc.*).

Rostal is a strong-fingered violinist with a sweeping tone and fine musical perceptions. Goehr works well with him, and the total sound is beautifully reproduced.

Works for Orchestra

Symphony Pastorale. CHAM, Schrader, 10" U LP 5007 (**Telemann: Don Quixote*).

An unusually attractive disc combining the celebrated early program music of Telemann with a fragrantly melodic work that deserves a history of performance it lacks. Well-studied performance, cleanly reproduced.

Sinfonia in A. LBE, Haas, 10" D DL 4081 (**Cherubini: Pater Noster; Lully: Marche; Philidor: Marches*).

A trilly work (suggestive of the celebrated sonata by the same composer) with a notable slow movement. Fine performance, excellent reproduction.

TAYLOR, DEEMS (1885-)

Through the Looking Glass. ERO, Hanson, Mer MG 40008.

A long overdue enterprise for LP. Hanson is a devoted, if not too imaginative, interpreter, and the recording is first-class.

TCHAIKOVSKY, PETER ILYICH (1840-1893)

Ballet Music

The Nutcracker (*Complete*). *MIN, Dorati, Mer OL 2-101* [2].

Either those who have lost their taste for the familiar excerpts, or those whose taste has been whetted for more, will find this total sequence a new and pleasurable experience. Dorati has an excellent sense of the style, his orchestra plays precisely, and the recording is one of Mercury's best.

The Nutcracker (*Suites 1 and 2*). *OSC, Fistoulari, L LL 441.*

As a midway compromise between the Suite No. 1 made by Tchaikovsky (plus additional elements to comprise a Suite No. 2) and the total ballet noted above, this has its point. Both sections are well played and sonorously reproduced. However, there are several better performances of the familiar Suite No. 1.

The Nutcracker (*Suite*). *HIS, Stokowski, 10" V LM 46. PHI, Markevitch, V LBC 1015* (**Prokofiev: Peter and the Wolf*). *FNS, Désormière, 10" Cap L 8141*). *NBC, Toscanini, V LRY 9000* (**Rossini: William Tell overture; Waldteufel: Skaters waltz*).

The abundance of other versions provides nothing to contravene a lasting preference for the superb Stokowski performance and its highly attractive reproduction. This is orchestral art of a high order, beautifully preserved. Of the others, there is the most dollar value in the excellent-sounding Markevitch, though the voice of W. Pickles is a blight on the overside *Peter* (q.v.). Désormière does his work well, though not with so much high gloss as Stokowski, and the reproduction is good though not *as* good. Toscanini's rather over-stressed version is included in a sequence with the **old** *William Tell* and the not too graceful *Skaters.*

The Nutcracker (*Suite No. 2*). *BPO, Fiedler, V LM 1029* (**Khatchaturian: Masquerade suite*).

A compilation by Fiedler himself, including "Winter Scene," "Waltz of the Snow Flakes," a pas de deux, "Chocolate," and "Waltz Finale." Bright playing, well reproduced.

Sleeping Beauty (*Complete*). *OSC, Fistoulari, L LL 636/7* [2].

For my taste, this is the preferable way to hear this music, especially if one is reasonably familiar with the action—in which case a dimension of visual recollection is added to the aural enjoyment. I would not call Fistoulari the ideal conductor (his name, after all, is not Lambert) for this score, but it is a well-controlled and non-offending effort he offers. The sound is decidedly good.

*Sleeping Beauty (Excerpts, also Aurora's Wedding). ROO, Lambert, C ML 4136 (Gounod: Faust ballet music). SWO, Lambert, V LBC 1007 (*Romeo and Juliet). HIS, Stokowski, V LM 1774.*

Although far from contemporary in recorded quality, the two Lambert sequences are valuable for the evidence they convey of his superior qualities as a conductor of ballet, especially Tchaikovsky ballet. (It will be noticed that the V LBC disc attributes this performance to Malko, and, in an inversion of credits, the overside *Romeo* to Lambert.) Stokowski's is so far the best *Aurora's Wedding* (Act III of the original ballet) as to discourage mention of an alternate. Superb sound as well as majestic performance.

Swan Lake (Complete). LSO, Fistoulari, L LL 565/6 [2].

As in the instance of *Sleeping Beauty*, the total ballet is another kind of experience than a mere sequence of excerpts. However, I would not be dogmatic about it in this instance, for there are more *longueurs* in *Swan Lake* than in *Sleeping Beauty*. Fistoulari is competent enough, the sound excellent.

*Swan Lake (Excerpts). PHI, Irving, V LBC 1064. PHI, Karajan, An 35006 (*Sleeping Beauty). STS, Golschmann, V LM 1003. FNS, Désormière, Cap P 8142.*

Even were it not substantially cheaper than the other offerings, Irving's vigorously paced, superbly reproduced performance would be hard to resist. At the price, it is one of the choice "buys" now current, especially as the first-desk men of the Philharmonia outdo themselves. The last observation also applies to the same orchestra's work under Karajan, though his virtuoso delivery is not as idiomatic as Irving's and, of course, the number of items is much smaller. This leaves little more than honorable-mention status for Golschmann and Désormière, both of whom do expert service for Tchaikovsky, without sharing the special advantages offered by Irving's version.

Concertos

For Piano and Orchestra

No. 1 in B flat minor. Rubinstein, MIN, Mitropoulos, V LM 1028. Uninsky, HPO, Van Otterloo, Ep LC 3010. Cherkassky, BPH, Ludwig,

D DL 9605. Ciccolini, OSC, Cluytens, V LBC 1020. Petri, LPO, Goehr, C RL 3018. Horowitz, NBC, Toscanini, V LCT 1012.

Despite the host of challengers, old and new, none has quite duplicated Rubinstein's master hand with this work, though both the recording and the orchestral direction are inferior to several others mentioned above. For those who prefer a contemporary sound, Uninsky's has that and a considerable amount of pianistic prowess to commend it, also good co-operation from Van Otterloo. The Cherkassky is an interesting experiment in revaluation of this much-abused work, tending to slower tempos than customary, a modicum of display, and fine, broad sound. Sometimes the thinking is almost visible, but the results are well worth hearing. Neither of the economy versions is really that, for Ciccolini's is merely flashy though well reproduced, the Petri rocklike in steadiness but deplorably quavery in sound. The Horowitz-Toscanini curio sounds somewhat better than it used to, but doesn't make much more artistic sense.

*No. 2 in G. Mewton-Wood, WIN, Goehr, CH 1125. Moïséiwitsch, LIV, Weldon, V LCT 1127 (*Rachmaninoff: Concerto No. 1).*

The ring and bite of sound in the Concert Hall issue is not matched by that of the Victor, but the qualities of performance are not far apart. In addition, the second-side Rachmaninoff is practically contemporary in sound, and charmingly played by Moïséiwitsch. The conductor here is Sargent.

*No. 3 in E flat. Mewton-Wood, WIN, Goehr, CH 1126 (*Concert Fantasia).*

The qualities of musicianship and technical command noted in other performances by Mewton-Wood are evident here also. The appeal of the single-movement work is not overpowering, but the recording is well managed. Much of the playing time on the disc is given over to the three-movement Fantasia, a work of melodic charm and solid workmanship.

For Violin and Orchestra

In D. Milstein, BSO, Munch, V LM 1760. Stern, PHO, Hilsberg, C ML 4232. Heifetz, PHI, Süsskind, V LM 1111. Oistrakh, SAX, Konwitschny, D DL 9755. Milstein, CHO, Stock, C RL 3032. Morini, CHO, Defauw, V LBC 1061.

Previous indecision about a choice version of this work has been resolved recently with the appearance of the new Milstein, a superb example of his ever increasing stature as an interpreter. Violinistically, it is pure and vibrant, with remarkably plastic phrasing. Munch does his portion well, and the recording is very good if not of the quality of some late Boston releases. Stern and Heifetz are almost on a par with Milstein in disposing smoothly and fluently of the technical problems, but each has traits of style that leave the ear a little offended: Stern a tendency to the showy, Heifetz his almost baffling composure. Of the others, Oistrakh's is in many ways outstanding, and, in the later Dresden guise, very satisfactory in sound. My only complaint would be that he is too often primarily playing the violin rather than Tchaikovsky. Morini's is the best of the economy versions, though her swooping and sliding are more than the occasion requires.

Incidental Music

The Snow Maiden. USSR, Gauk, soloists, CH 1301.

At first hearing, this music might well be regarded as part of an opera, considering its choral elements, tenor and mezzo-soprano solos, etc. What is even more absorbing is that the work dates from 1873, for all its suggestions of Mussorgsky's *Boris* (which was not produced till some time later). The performance is typically good, the reproduction among the best to come along from the Soviet Union.

Opera Excerpts (Orchestral)

*Eugen Onègin: Waltz and Polonaise. NYSO, Smallens, 10" D DL 4033 (*Andante Cantabile). Waltz only. RCAO, Reiner, 10" V LM 103 (*Waltz of the Flowers; Waltz from Sleeping Beauty; etc.).*

Both records fulfill the purposes indicated, the Reiner with more finesse and orchestral precision. The sound in both instances is good.

*Pique Dame. NYPH, Kostelanetz, C ML 4904 (*Gershwin-Bennett: Porgy and Bess).*

I am not partial to the montage treatment of operatic excerpts—still less to Kostelanetz's usurpation of the operatic literature for non-vocal profit—but it has been carried out here with reasonable taste. The playing and processing are good. (The sequence traces the main points of the drama in eleven excerpts linked together.)

*The Slippers. PHI, Fistoulari, MGM E 3026 (*Mozartiana).*

Characteristically rhythmic and melodic excerpts from a work also known as *Les Caprices d'Oxane,* which preceded *Eugen Onegin* by five years. Among the items well directed by Fistoulari are "Minuet," "Russian Dance," and "Cossack Dance." Bright sound.

Symphonies

No. 1 in G minor. VPA, Häffner, SPA 11.

The impression here is of hard work for all concerned, including the listener. Loud sounds, but not resonant or rounded enough to be enjoyable. The performance is vigorous, anyway.

*No. 1: Andante only. COL, Kurtz, C ML 4671 (*Serenade Mèlancolique; Shostakovich: Ballet Russe).*

The sound here is far superior to that in the disc above, the playing likewise. *Swan Lake* type Tchaikovsky, well projected by Kurtz.

*No. 2 in C minor ("Little Russian"). RPO, Beecham, C ML 4872 (*Waltz of the Flowers).*

A proper companion for Beecham's version of No. 3, should RCA ever reinstate its V Set 1279 to service on LP. Finely perceptive direction by Beecham, in recording of sweep and sonority.

No. 3 in D ("Polish"). VSO, Swoboda, CH 1139.

Nothing here diminishes a desire for the restoration of the Beecham noted above, which could hardly sound less satisfactory and would certainly have a livelier feeling for the music.

No. 4 in F minor. CHO, Kubelik, Mer 50003. VPH, Furtwängler, V LHMV 1005. PHI, Malko, V LBC 1052. HPO, Van Otterloo, Ep LC 3029.

This is barely more than a fourth of the versions currently available, but none of the others is more carefully prepared than the Furtwängler, more soundly recorded than the Kubelik, better worth the price than the Malko, or more suggestive of the excellence of the Philips engineers than those itemized. Aside from being a wonderful example of orchestral cultivation, powerfully reproduced, the Furtwängler is a little ponderous, which inclines me to the meticulous Kubelik and its finely realistic reproduction. Only the last element, personality, keeps Malko from qualifying in the upper bracket, for his men play well for him and the sound is excellent. As for the Dutch product, one can only regret that the conscientious Van Otterloo rather than the forceful Van Kempen is in charge. Tremendous climaxes, nevertheless.

No. 5 in E minor. ACG, Van Kempen, Ep LC 3013. HIS, Stokowski, V LM 1780. BSO, Koussevitzky, V LM 1047. BPH, Mengelberg, Cap P 8053. PHI, Kletzki, C RL 3036.

Van Kempen's direction of the great orchestra and its overpowering reproduction seem to me so superior to other contemporary versions as to eliminate discussion. His absorption of the Mengelberg manner in this music is graphically revealed by a comparison with the rather thin-sounding Capitol version, in which the great man caricatures his own style by exaggerations and underscorings. Stokowski's presentation has plenty of fine sound, but some oddities of accentuation that suggest electrical enhancement, as well as a good many mannered musical details. Of all available versions, Koussevitzky's still makes the most of the slow movement in a richness of sound implied rather than stated in the processing of the old 78. Other aspects of it do not stand up as well. The Kletzki is the best of the economy versions, not at all bad in sound, though a shade reckless in its energy.

No. 6 in B minor ("Pathétique"). PHO, Ormandy, C ML 4544. ACG, Ven Kempen, Ep LC 3003. NBC, Toscanini, V LM 1036. CHO, Kubelik, Mer 50006. PHI, Malko, V LBC 1002.

Whatever RCA's reasons are for withholding from LP circulation the legendary performance of Furtwängler with the Berlin Philharmonic (V Set 553), the effect of that interdiction is to make one dissatisfied with current versions, no matter how well reproduced. The Ormandy is certainly a sumptous-sounding disc, as is the Van Kempen, but neither seems to stir this music into the same kind of engulfing emotional torrent that Furtwängler achieved. Toscanini achieves his purpose more successfully, perhaps, than any other interpreter, but the end result is not choice Tchaikovsky. I cannot muster more than moderate enthusiasm for the Kubelik, though it matches his version of No. 4 as a recording, while the Malko, for all its good craft, strikes me as under-rehearsed for the scope of the undertaking.

Manfred. NBC, Toscanini, V LM 1037. USSR, Gauk, CH 1308.

Neither of these is a wholly successful exposition of this complicated, perhaps excessively scored, work: that would require a high fidelity to which neither conform. Gauk disdains the cut of 157 measures (some twenty-two pages of the miniature score) which Toscanini endorses, but the interpretative total is not enhanced thereby.

Works for Orchestra and Piano

*Concert-Fantasia, opus 56. Mewton-Wood, WIN, Goehr, CH 1126 (*Concerto No. 3).*

See entry under Concerto No. 3.

Miscellaneous (Collection)

Capriccio Italien; Overture 1812; Romeo and Juliet. ACG, Van Kempen, Ep LC 3008.

As will be noted in several subsequent instances, the Philips engineers who originate these Epic discs have been uncommonly successful with Tchaikovsky in the Concertgebouw. Van Kempen is a very keen man with this repertory, and the total of the value proffered is high fa, as well as high fi.

Miscellaneous

*Capriccio Italien. COL, Beecham, C ML 4287 (Bizet: *Carmen suite). PHI, Galliera, An 35047 (*Liszt: Les Préludes). PHO, Ormandy, C ML 4856 (*Rimsky-Korsakov: Capriccio Espagnol). DNO, Malko, V LBC 1014 (*Overture 1812).*

The Beecham is quite different in style from any contemporary presentation of this score: more cognizant of the orchestral texture per se, and full of subtleties and nuances. It does not have the high-fidelity effects of the Ormandy (in which the intention, obviously, is to make an impression rather than music) or the Van Kempen noted above, but it is an absorbing experience for all that. The Galliera has no special virtues to commend it. Malko does his usual competent work in a recording of considerable brilliance. However, the Epic (see above), with its extra item, is almost as attractive for the price-conscious.

*Francesca da Rimini. NYPH, Stokowski, C ML 4381 (*Romeo and*

Juliet). *PHI, Dobrowen, V LBC 1010* (**Brahms: Variations on a Theme by Haydn*).

For reasons beyond my speculative ken, this work has escaped its due share of high-fidelity exposition. The Stokowski is nearly half a decade old, not normally a period of great penalty, but rather costly in terms of LP. Dobrowen's well-conceived performance is not more than tolerably reproduced. Thus, a reluctant assent to the Stokowski, despite its interpretative lapses.

Hamlet, opus 67a. LPO, Boult, L LL 582 (**Overture 1812*).

Straightforward, authoritative direction by Boult, with ample "passion." The recording is spectacularly good.

Marche Slave. LSO, Scherchen, W 5282 (**Overture 1812; Romeo and Juliet*). *PHO, Ormandy, 10" C AL 24* (**Overture 1812*). *NYSO, Smallens, 10" D DL 4031* (**Overture 1812*).

As may be expected, Scherchen's *Marche Slave* is a searching résumé of the sounds, musical and otherwise, contained in these pages. The result is a sonorous hash of cymbal crashes, bass drum blasts, etc., with an occasional snatch of music from the violins. However, as recorded sound goes, it is superior to either of the others. Ormandy does his usual efficient work, and the Smallens is good value at the stated price.

Mozartiana. PHI, Fistoulari, MGM 3026 (**The Slippers suite*).

Not a notably delicate effort by Fistoulari, so that the end product is much more arranger than arranged. Good sound.

Overture Solenelle "1812." ACG, Van Kempen, Ep LC 3008 (**Romeo; Capriccio Italien*). *LPO, Boult, L LL 582* (**Hamlet*). *LSO, Scherchen, W 5282* (**Romeo; Marche Slave*). *PHO, Ormandy, 10" C AL 24* (**Marche Slave*). *NYSO, Smallens, 10" D DL 4031* (**Marche Slave*).

As the listing indicates, the *1812* is predominantly an "overside" phenomenon, to be acquired with or without volition in association with some other work of Tchaikovsky. The performance in the Van Kempen collection is excellent, and very well reproduced; but the Boult—utilizing a full side, and thus spreading the sonorities to the utmost—is as good interpretatively and massively reproduced. As much may be said for the Scherchen, but it has no such "leader" as Boult's *Hamlet*. Of the versions coupling *1812's* and *Marche Slaves*, the Smallens appeals to me for economy reasons.

Romeo and Juliet Overture Fantasia. ACG, Van Kempen, Ep LC 3008 (**Capriccio Italien; Overture 1812*). *LSO, Scherchen, W WL 5282* (**Marche Slave; Overture 1812*). *NBC, Toscanini, V LM 1019* (**Ber-*

*lioz: Romeo and Juliet excerpts). PHI, Malko, V LBC 1007 (*Sleeping Beauty excerpts).*

As a blend of stunning sound, superb orchestral execution, and interpretative finesse, Van Kempen's performance has few equals in this survey. I dare say that this disc will reveal more and more as the reproductive elements improve. I am also impressed with the Scherchen, though not to the point of similar enthusiasm. As for the Toscanini, what he does for the music is not sufficient to offset what the lack of proper sound does to the total of Tchaikovsky's intention. Masterful, to be sure, but not well favored in this area. The Malko hardly seems an economy in comparison with the Van Kempen.

*Serenade for Strings. ACG, Mengelberg, Cap P 8060 (*Dvořák: Serenade). PHO, Ormandy, C ML 4121 (*Theme and Variations, Suite No. 3). BSO, Koussevitzky, V LM 1056. PHI, Dobrowen, V LBC 1021 (*Glinka: Valse-Fantasie).*

Considering that none of these was recorded directly for LP, the prognosis would be that something more suitable in sound will be forthcoming fairly soon. The Mengelberg retains its appeal for felicity of statement and grace of style, though the sound is smudgy. Ormandy's men hardly sound themselves in the early LP treatment, while the Koussevitzky is not good enough to be accepted as the total matter of a 12" LP. Dobrowen's conducting is serviceable here, the sound not exciting.

Souvenir de Florence. VSO, Swoboda, W WL 5083.

A creation originally for string sextet, and not too responsive to its present usage, at least so far as Swoboda can affirm. Decidedly blurry sound, not at all in the label's later tradition.

Suites Nos. 1, 2, 3. WIN, Goehr, CH 1121, 1122, 1144.

Goehr has a warmly companionable feeling for these works, which should be better-known than they are. The recording ranges from good to excellent, with Nos. 2 and 3 a marked improvement on the duller-sounding No. 1.

*Suite No. 3: Theme and Variations only. PHI, Malko, V LBC 1024 (*Borodin: Symphony No. 2). NYPH, Barbirolli, C ML 4121 (*Serenade for Strings).*

The age of the Barbirolli-Philharmonic being self-apparent (fifteen years at least), the cheaper and much better-sounding Malko is obviously preferable.

TELEMANN, GEORG PHILIP (1681-1767)

Concertos

For Flute, Oboe d'Amore, Viola d'Amore, and Strings

*In E. CHAM, 10" D DL 7537 (*Vivaldi: Concerto in D).*

Six strings, plus cembalo, make up the ripieno against which the oboe d'amore, flute, and viola d'amore perform their solo parts. The consequence is more of a chamber work than of a concerto in any contemporary sense. The ensemble is a little dull in sound, but clearly recorded.

For Viola and Strings

*In G. Wigand, PRO, Reinhardt, Vox PL 7540 (*Stamitz: Concerto in D).*

A work of Handelian suggestions, well and musically performed by soloists and ensemble. The studioish recording is acceptable.

*In G. Kirchner, SCH, Münchinger, 10" L LS 686 (*Gabrieli: Two Canzone).*

A brisk, active work which would well become the name of Handel both as to solo writing and as to treatment of the ensemble. Kirchner is a deft, solid-sounding violist, the reproduction satisfactory.

Overture

*In D. Scheck-Wenzinger, CHAM, U URLP 7031 (*Haydn: Concerto for Flute).*

Not the most gracious-sounding record in the catalogue, in part because of the ensemble of viols whose resinous sound is not one to which we are accustomed. Spirited performance, reasonably reproduced.

Suite

*Don Quichotte. Schrader, CHAM, 10" U URLP 5007 (*Tartini: Symphony Pastorale).*

Invention and ingenuity abound in this work, which is attentively performed under Schrader's thoughtful direction. However, the processing deteriorates as the work progresses, with a final section wavery in pitch.

Work for Orchestra and Solo Instrument

*Suite in A minor, Flute and Strings. Pappoutsakis, ZS, D DL 8522 (*Mozart: Serenata Notturno, K.239).*

About the most interesting of the Telemann works known to me, with a beautiful performance of the flute part by Pappoutsakis of the Boston Symphony. Fine sound.

THOMAS, AMBROISE (1811-1896)

*Mignon: Overture. NBC, Toscanini, 10" V LRM 7013 (*Bizet: Carmen suite). OSC, Fistoulari, 10" L LD 9014 (*Ponchielli: Dance of the Hours).*

Although the French orchestra plays this music beautifully and the sound is lush, the personal distinction Toscanini gives to its phrases is of a special sort. Moreover, this is thoroughly good Carnegie Hall sound.

THOMPSON, RANDALL (1899-)

*Testament of Freedom. ERO, Hanson, choir, Mer MG 40000 (*Hanson: Songs from Drum Taps).*

Stunning reproduction of a rather impressive score, very well presented by Hanson. David Meyers is the solo baritone. Some of the choral masses outdo anything of the sort on discs.

THOMSON, VIRGIL (1896-)

Concerto

*For Cello and Orchestra. Silva, JSO, Janssen, C ML 4468 (*Mother of Us All suite).*

The entertainment values of this performance are not enhanced by the too often approximate playing of Silva, whose intonation is unreliable. Reasonably good recording.

Film Music

Louisiana Story (*Suite*). *PHO, Ormandy, 10" C ML 2087* (**Five Portraits*).

Sonorous, beautifully phrased playing of the "Pastoral," "Chorale," "Passacaglia," and "Fugue" in a somewhat expanded orchestral text.

Louisiana Story: Acadian Songs and Dances. LOS, Scherman, D DL 9616 (**Copland: The Red Pony*).

Thomson's setting of the attractive material is both deft and tasteful, the realization of it in Scherman's performance successful. Warm sound, well microphoned.

The Plow That Broke the Plains (*Suite*). *LOS, Scherman, 10" D DL 7527* (**Copland: Our Town*).

Not quite as communicative a performance as the previous one by Stokowski (V Set 1116), though orderly enough and well reproduced.

Opera Excerpts (Orchestral)

The Mother of Us All (*Suite*). *JSO, Janssen, C ML 4468* (**Concerto for Cello*).

Lacking the text and voices that made the original as diverting as it was, this suite makes thin listening as presented with orchestra alone. The sound is better than in the companion side.

Works for Orchestra

Five Portraits. PHO, Thomson, 10" C ML 2087 (**Louisiana Story*).

Substantially the same performance as was circulated in C Set X255, though the sound is a bit more ample in the new form.

Three Pictures. PHO, Thomson, C ML 4919 (**Five Songs from William Blake*).

I have a good opinion of the Blake settings sung by Mack Harrell, which do not really belong in this compilation, but not of the orchestral pieces, which do. The titles are *The Seine at Night*, *Wheat Field at Noon*, *Sea Piece with Birds*, and they all strike me as derivative and insubstantial. The fine players give of their best, but there is not much to listen to in the consequences. Very good sound.

TRAVIS, ROY ELIHU (1922-)

*Symphonic Allegro. NYPH, Mitropoulos, 10" C AL 16 (*Couperin-Milhaud: Overture and Allegro from La Sultane).*

All the notes seem to be here, but the consequence does not strike me as music. Fair enough recording.

TURINA, JOAQUIN (1882-1949)

Danzas Fantasticas; La Procesión del Rocio; La Oracion del Torero; Canto a Sevilla. SYM, Freitas Branco, W WL 5320.

Neither of the duplicated works is given the advantages heard in the performances below by Argenta and Jorda, but the collection as a whole has merit, especially for the vocal excerpts of the *Canto a Sevilla*, sung expressively by Lola Rodríguez de Aragón, if not always with the desired vocal control. Fairly good sound, though not in the category of Westminster's Vienna or London reproduction.

*Danzas Fantásticas. OSC, Argenta, L LL 921 (*Albéniz: Iberia). PHI, Schuechter, MGM E 3018 (*Granados: Tres Danzas Españolas).*

A compelling example of the difference between a very good and an outstanding performance, with Argenta's sensitive management of phrase and timbre beautifully served by the engineers. With the overside *Iberia* it ranks as one of the most enjoyable of recent issues.

*La Procesión del Rocio. OSC, Jorda, 10" L LD 9042 (*Albéniz: El Puerto; Triana).*

Sinuous, well-phrased performance under the vigorous direction of Jorda. Typically spacious London reproduction.

*Rapsodia Sinfónica. PHI, Lympany, Süsskind, V LHMV 1025 (*Mendelssohn: Concerto No. 1, Rondo Brilliant).*

A melodious work of much coloristic detail, very well played by Lympany, and uncommonly well reproduced.

VALENTINI, GIOVANNI (17th century)

*Concerto for Oboe and Orchestra, in C. Prestini, ICO, Jenkins, HS L 77 (*Giordani: Piano Concerto; Brunetti: Symphony in C minor).*
A lightfooted work, well valued in the performance of oboist Prestini and conductor Jenkins. Good sound.

VARÈSE, EDGAR (1885-)

Integrales; Density 21.5; Ionisation; Octandre. NYWE, Waldman, EMS 401.
The very good engineering work supervised by Robert E. Blake is the principal distinction of this collection of noises, definite and indefinite. "Times Square on Election Night" would be a better title than any of those offered. Rene Le Roy is flute soloist in *Density 21.5*, and is, of course, excellent.

VAUGHAN WILLIAMS, RALPH (1872-)

Concertos

*For Oboe and Strings, 1944-45. Miller, SCO, Saidenberg, Mer 10003 (*Cimarosa: Concerto for Oboe).*
The durable values in this collaboration remain as sizable as at the time of issue, half a dozen years ago. SSS (still satisfactory sound).

*For Violin and Orchestra, in D minor (Concerto Accademico). Fuchs, ZS, D DL 9625 (*Tansman: Triptych).*
Artistry and musicianship abound in this excellent performance, which, with its admirable companion piece, makes for an attractive pairing of twentieth-century works. Fine sound.

For Two Pianos and Orchestra, 1926-30. Whittemore, Lowe, ROB, Golschmann, 10" V LM 135.
Not the most gratifying aspect of Vaughan Williams, especially as the utilization of the two pianos was an afterthought of 1946 and the sonorous texture is somewhat thick. However, the performance is energetic, the reproduction successful.

Symphonies

No. 1 ("Sea Symphony"). LPO, Boult, soloists, L LL 972/3 [2].
London's monumental cycle of the Vaughan Williams symphonic sequence is a notable tribute to the application and devotion of all concerned, from the composer himself, who sat in on most of the sessions, through Boult and the orchestra, to the soloists and engineers. In this instance, they produce a singular effect of eloquent expression in the work based on Walt Whitman—"they" being, in addition to the performers named, Isobel Baillie, soprano, John Cameron, baritone, and the London Philharmonic Choir.

No. 2 ("A London Symphony"). LPO, Boult, L LL 569.
Boult does not seem to make quite as much effect in this work as in the preceding score with chorus, but it is beautifully played and richly reproduced.

No. 3 ("Pastoral"). LPO, Boult, L LP 721.
Margaret Ritchie's participation as soprano soloist is an element of value in a performance of much mood and atmosphere, also excellent tonal properties.

No. 4 in F minor. LPO, Boult, L LL 974.
Boult's performance is certainly superior in sound to the BBC composer-conducted one circulated here as V Set 440, and has some underscorings of his own which contribute to the total effect. Impressive reproduction done, as all in this series, in the resonant area of Kingsway Hall.

No. 5 in D. LPO, Boult, L LL 975.
Vaughan Williams's evolution from the early programmatic symphonies to the later more absolute ones (based, though this is, on matter in Bunyan's *Pilgrim's Progress*) results here in a tonal texture of remarkable subtlety and sequence. Boult responds with a fluent, nobly proportioned performance that is tonally one of the best in the series.

*No. 6 in F minor. LPO, Boult, L LL 976. NYPH, Stokowski, C ML 4214 (*Messiaen: L'Ascension).*
Stokowski's driving energy, his absorption in the problem of this score when it was new, give a special kind of atmosphere to his performance. However, both in sound and as a settled conception of the music it contains, Boult's wears better. The London disc contains a little speech by the composer to the men of the orchestra (also "the lady harpist").

Works for Orchestra and Voices

Five Tudor Portraits. PSO, Steinberg, Cap P 8218.

This vein of Vaughan Williams's writing—roistering, jouncy, voluble—is something new to us, but not to Steinberg, who solves its problems convincingly. An actual performance "take," it comes to the ear with full concert character and few intrusive noises. Clean, not too resonant sound.

Miscellaneous

*English Folk Song Suite (arranged by Jacobs). SYM, Boult, W WL 5270 (*Norfolk Rhapsody; Fantasia on Greensleeves; Fantasia on a Theme of Thomas Tallis). COL, Barlow, C RL 3023 (*Beethoven: Contra Tänzen).*

As the listing indicates, this is a compendium of virtually all of the shorter Vaughan Williams works. They are played with compelling sympathy and finesse under Boult's knowing direction. First-class sound. The Barlow is mentioned because other good discs in this series might tempt attention. This is not one of them.

*Fantasia on Greensleeves. SYM, Boult, W WL 5270 (*See under English Folk Song Suite). NEW, Collins, L LL 583 (*Fantasia on a Theme by Tallis; Elgar: Serenade, Introduction and Allegro).*

Collins's fine performance may be reproduced with a shade more warmth of sound than Boult's, but there is otherwise little to choose between them.

*Fantasia on a Theme of Thomas Tallis. NEW, Collins, L LL 583 (*See under Greensleeves). SYM, Boult, W WL 5270. HIS, Stokowski, V LM 1739 (*Schoenberg: Verklärte Nacht).*

Neither of the English conductors "produces" this work with the "meestical" quality beloved of the Englishman turned American, but the hushes and antiphonal effects end by defeating the purpose of the music. My preference for the Collins is in part owing to the exemplary processing, though the Boult is a worthy element of the sequence in which it appears and Westminster's sound is as good, if finer-grained, than London's.

*Flos Campi. Tursi, CHAM, Hull, chorus, CH 1151 (*Johnson: Letter to the World).*

This does not quite measure up to the previous standard of Primrose, Boult, etc., but it is well considered and musical, expertly reproduced.

*Old King Cole. SYM, Boult, W WL 5228 (*The Wasps).*

Lively work by Boult in the score of 1923. Very good sound.

Sinfonia Antartica. LPO, Boult, L LP 977.

An expansion of the music written by Vaughan Williams for the film *Scott of the Antarctic* in 1947, this is something between a tone poem and a formal symphony. In any case, its coloristic devices and sizable orchestral effects add several dimensions to our appreciation of the composer. Wonderfully detailed reproduction. The verbal "superscriptions" are spoken by Sir John Gielgud.

*The Wasps. SYM, Boult, W WL 5228 (*Old King Cole). LPO, Boult, L LL 972/3 (*Sea Symphony).*

Whether acquired individually with *Old King Cole*, or with the multi-side version of the "Sea Symphony," Boult will be the attentive, wholly qualified conductor. Little to choose in sound values.

VERDI, GIUSEPPE (1813-1901)

Overtures, Preludes

*Aïda. PHI, Galliera, An 35012 (*Forza del Destino; Nabucco; Traviata).*

The *Aïda* prelude is well shaded by Galliera and beautifully played by the Philharmonia strings. The others, however, are not of much more than conventional quality. Very good recording.

*La Forza del Destino. PHI, Galliera, An 35012 (*See Aïda). LPO, Solti, L LP 200 (*Bartered Bride; Hansel and Gretel dream pantomime; etc.). BAM, Leitner, 10" D DL 4016 (*Traviata preludes).*

The Galliera is about as good as any of the others, and is the best reproduced. None approach the quality of the Toscanini, not presently available on LP.

*Nabucco. RIAS, Fricsay, 10" D DL 4063 (*Rossini: Tancredi; Glinka: Russlan and Ludmilla; R. Strauss: Ariadne auf Naxos). PHI, Galliera, An 35012 (*See Aïda).*

Fricsay develops rather more dramatic impetus than does Galliera, and his orchestra is reproduced with uncommon brilliance. However, the performance is part of a particularly pointless miscellany, and the Galliera may on this account be preferred.

*La Traviata. PHI, Galliera, An 35012 (*See Aïda). BAM, Leitner, 10" D DL 4016 (*Forza del Destino).*

The suavity in the string sound of the Galliera-led ensemble is preferable to the alternative. Neither is outstanding.

*I Vespri Siciliani. RIAS, Fricsay, 10" D DL 4046 (*Boïeldieu: Caliph of Bagdad; Adam: If I Were King). PHI, Galliera, An 35012 (*See Aïda).*

The comment for *Nabucco* is equally applicable here, with the added observation that it is even a more mixed dish. The two Verdi overtures would be preferable paired.

VIEUXTEMPS, HENRI (1820-1881)

*Concerto for Violin and Orchestra, No. 4 in D minor. Menuhin, PHI, Süsskind, V LHMV 1015 (*Paganini: Concerto No. 2).*

Sometimes rough but always vigorous performance by Menuhin. The intonation threatens frequently to go off, but rarely does. The collaboration with Süsskind is an especially happy one, the orchestral playing excellent. Fine "open" recording.

*Concerto for Violin and Orchestra, No. 5 in A minor. Heifetz, LSO, Sargent, V LM 1121 (*Walton: Violin Concerto).*

Dazzling execution by Heifetz in just the right style and with an abundance of suave, well-formed tone. Good accompaniment by Sargent. The recording has much to commend it, but the volume level is low, and has to be brought up more than is customary.

VILLA-LOBOS, HEITOR (1884-   )

*Bachianas Brasileiras No. 1. JSO, Janssen, Cap P 8147 (*Chôros No. 4, Chôros No. 7). BFO, Marx, V LCT 1143 (*Nonetto; Serèsta No. 8, other songs).*

Both performances are well based on sound understanding of the content and on excellent cellists (eight in each instance) to carry out the plan. The Victor recording of 1940 is astonishingly good still, though the Capitol has plenty of bite and definition. (The song recital by Elsie Houston on the overside of the Victor disc will make this an automatic part of many collections.)

*Bachianas Brasileiras No. 2. Toccata and Aria only. JSO, Janssen, Cap L 8043 (*Chôros No. 10).*

Janssen directs the toccata-like "Little Train of the Caipira" with plenty of humor, and the aria with appropriate repose. However, the recording is not more than passable.

*Bachianas Brasileiras No. 5. Aria and Dansa. Albanese, CHAM, Stokowski, 10" V LM 142 (*Tchaikovsky: Letter Scene from Eugen Onégin). Aria only. Sayão, CHAM, Villa-Lobos, 10" C AL 3 (*Verdi: Ah fors'è lui from La Traviata). Curtin, CHAM, Paige, Cook 1062 (*Stravinsky: Concerto in D; Brandenburg Concerto No. 3; etc.).*

Stokowski adds the dansa to Albanese's singing of the aria, and there is little question that the cellos have more distinctness of sound than in the version directed by Villa-Lobos. However, the justly celebrated accomplishment of Sayão is not otherwise matched in either vocal quality or artistry of expression. Curtin's tense voice is rather over-produced for this material, and phrase ends tend to get away from her. (The dansa is included.)

*Chôros Nos. 4 and 7. JSO, Janssen, Cap P 8147 (*Bachianas Brasileiras No. 1).*

The wanted technical skill on wind instruments is in good supply here, and Janssen leads the players effectively. No. 7 is much better recorded than No. 4, which suffers from a lack of resonance.

*Chôros No. 10. JSO, Janssen, chorus, 10" Cap L 8043 (*Bachianas Brasileiras No. 2).*

The ability of Janssen to get the sense out of a Villa-Lobos score must be firmly established by now: however, this is a singularly dull and unattractive-sounding record.

Concerto for Piano and Orchestra, No. 1. Ballon, OSR, Ansermet, L LL 77.

For a rarity, here is a London record that must be condemned for poor sound and shoddy workmanship. Or perhaps the lack of music befitting Villa-Lobos's name makes one more conscious of quavery piano tone, dim orchestra, and noisy surfaces.

*Nonetto. CHAM, Ross, V LCT 1143 (*Bachianas Brasileiras No. 1; Songs).*

Successful restoration of a performance admired since its first appearance in 1940. Acceptable sound.

*Origin of the Amazon River. LOUI, Whitney, C ML 4615 (*Dello Joio: Triumph of St. Joan Symphony).*

One of the best recordings made by Columbia in this country, brilliantly colorful and resonant. The work has some impressive climaxes, but not quite the continuity expected.

*Serestas Nos. 1-9. Tourel, COL, Villa-Lobos, C ML 4357 (*Rach-*

*maninoff: Songs). No. 8 only. Houston, V LCT 1143 (*Bachianas Brasileiras No. 1, etc.).*

Apt performance by Tourel, who understands the style thoroughly. Good reproduction. Houston's inimitable performance of the "Ox-Cart Driver's Song" makes one wish there were more material by her. Her vocal timbre and the accompanying piano are very well reproduced.

*Uirapuru. NYPH, Kurtz, C ML 4255 (*Chopin: Les Sylphides).*

Villa-Lobos's fanciful bird in his imaginary forest sings persuasively in this appropriate performance. Good sound.

VIOTTI, GIOVANNI BATTISTA (1753-1824)

*Concerto for Violin and Orchestra, No. 22 in A minor. Rybar, WIN, Dahinden, W 5049 (*Nardini: Concerto in E minor).*

About the best performance by Rybar on record: suave, sensitive, assured. Dahinden provides fine support, and the recording is exemplary. The music, incidentally, is about Viotti's most distinguished.

*Concerto for Violin, Piano and Orchestra, in A major. Bussotti, Abussi, ICO, Jenkins, HS 78 (*Brunetti: Symphony No. 22).*

More of a historical curio than a present pleasure, well ministered to save for the rather acidulous violin-playing of Abussi.

VIVALDI, ANTONIO[1] (1680?-1743)

Concerti Grossi

Opus 3, L'Estro Armonico ("Harmonic Whim"): Nos. 1-12. Barchet, PRO, Reinhardt, Vox PL 7423 [3].

It was from this set of twelve imposing works that Bach made

[1]Editor's Note:-
Vivaldi organized only a small portion of his vast output in a system of opus numbers, and the several later systematizers have yet to enjoy universal recognition. Hence, it has been decided here to present first those bearing Vivaldi's opus numbers, and to arrange the others with whatever identifying symbols are available.

most of his transcriptions of Vivaldi, some of which have now been transcribed back to their original instrumentation, but utilizing Bach's realization. Here they are performed with great clarity and thrust by the Stuttgart ensemble, reproduced with fine balance and fidelity, to a result that it is not easy to imagine being improved upon.

*Opus 3: No. 3 in G major. Amfiteatrof, VDR, Fasano, D DL 9572 (*A. Scarlatti: Concerto No. 6 in F; Tartini: Concerto in E; etc.).*

Fasano has used the organ transcription of Bach as a basis for this arrangement. It is rather roughly played by the cellist, and the reproduction is dull.

*Opus 3: No. 9 in D. Fournier, CHAM, AS 31 (*The same as arranged by Bach: Concerto in C for Two Harpsichords).*

Closely integrated work by the ensemble and soloist, very well reproduced. It is, perhaps, most interesting in the inverse relationship with Bach: but the point is well made.

*Opus 3: No. 10 in B minor (Bach-Tamburini). RIO, Salerno, La Rosa Parodi, Cet 50023 (*No. 11 in D minor).*

A rather pointless arrangement, for piano, of Bach's arrangement for harpsichords. The performance is aimless and without style, the recording outmoded.

*Opus 3: No. 11 in D minor. CHAM, La Rosa Parodi, Cet 50023 (*Vivaldi-Bach: Concerto No. 10 for Harpsichords arranged by Tamburini for piano).*

The "classic" Vivaldi in D minor, known in the past from editions of Franko and Siloti (also as arranged by Bach for organ), does not receive its due from the Italian players. Deadish studio reproduction of a rather unvital performance.

Concertos

For Flute and Orchestra

*Opus 10: Nos. 1-6. Rampal, Lacroix, CHAM, Vox PL 7150. Nos. 1, 4, 5. Renzi, Groen, CHAM, CH 56 (*Concerto in B flat for Bassoon).*

Neither of these is close to a high-fidelity recording, with the favor, therefore, inclining to the comprehensive treatment of Rampal et al. He is a more agile flutist, also, then Renzi, and the little group behind him performs well. Per se, the Concert Hall sound is a little fuller, less dry.

For Viola d'Amore and Orchestra

Opus 25: in A minor, P. 37 (arranged by Casella); D minor, P. 288.[1] *Sabatini, LCO, Bernard. 10" L LS 256.*

With or without the material provided by Vivaldi, the art of Sabatini, soloist on the viola d'amore (he is one of the celebrated members of the Virtuosi di Roma), would be a cherishable thing. With it, the pleasures are manifold. Excellent sound also.

*Opus 25: in D minor, P.288. Sabatini, VDR, Fasano, D DL 9679 (*Concerto in E flat, etc.).*

Although not actually identified as such, this is the same work as the foregoing, included with three other works of Vivaldi. Sabatini is again the excellent soloist, but the tonal properties of the recording are not nearly so good as those in the London.

For Violin and Orchestra

Opus 4, La Stravaganza (Extravaganzas): Nos. 1-12. Barchet, PRO, Reinhardt, Vox DL 103 [3].

An encompassing enterprise on the order of *L'Estro Armonico*, carried out with equal care and efficiency by much the same personnel. Excellent sound, very thoughtfully balanced. The accompanying brochure by Joseph Braunstein is one of the best provided in any of these recordings. As for the title of the series, no sure explanation is available—save as an attention-catching device on Vivaldi's part.

Opus 8: Nos. 1-4, Le Quattro Stagioni (The Four Seasons). Barchet, SCH, Münchinger, L LL 386.

Both in interpretative art and in the mechanics of reproduction, this is decidedly the best version of this music to come along to date. Whatever the name given to them, or who their conductor is, the Stuttgart musicians are redoubtable experts in the lore of Vivaldi. Rather brighter sound than in the Vox.

Opus 8: Nos. 5-12, Il Cimento dell'Armonia e Dell' Invenzione (The Conflict between Harmony and Invention). Kaufman, SYM, Dahinden, CH 1064 [2].

As in his previous brush with *The Four Seasons*, Kaufman is inclined to a tone rather oleaginous for Vivaldi. However, his vigor

[1]As prefix for numbers herein cited, P refers to the catalogue of Marc Pincherle.

and musicianship are matters of no small merit, not to mention his unflagging accuracy of pitch and sound sense of ensemble. The titles of these works are hardly material, for the sound is the familiar virile one of Vivaldi. Very good reproduction.

Opus 9, La Cetra (The Lyre). ONA, Kaufman, CH 1134 [2].

Some of the finest service by Kaufman on behalf of Vivaldi, in a series of works stressing the lyric aspects of that composer's art. As *chef d'orchestre* as well as solo violinist, Kaufman has plenty with which to occupy himself. Excellent sound, a little on the thin side, attesting to the French taste in such matters.

*Opus 12: No. 1 in G minor. Rybar, VSY, Moralt, W WL 5006 (*Concerto in E flat).*

As edited by Nachez, this is one of the better-known Vivaldi concertos for violin. No such intermediation is acknowledged here. Rybar's tone is slightly nasal, but the fullness and blend of the recording are admirable, as is the musical sense conveyed.

*Opus 33: No. 1 in E flat. Rybar, VSY, Moralt, W L 5006 (*Concerto in G minor). Minetti, LSSO, Valdinoci, Col CLPS 1015 (*Concerto in A minor for Bassoon).*

The opus number here seems to be assigned by the Vivaldian authority Antonio Fanna, who has systematized the vast output of Vivaldi into sixteen categories. In that sequence it bears the designation F. VIII, No. 7. In any case, it is strikingly beautiful work, well played by both instrumentalists, but much better reproduced in the Westminster edition.

Sonata

For Violoncello and Continuo

*Opus 14: No. 5 in E minor (arranged for orchestra by D'Indy). Fournier, SCH, Münchinger, L LL 687 (*Boccherini: Concerto in B flat; Couperin: Pièces en Concert). Amfitheatrof, VDR, Fasano, Cet 50045 (*Vivaldi: Concerto in A minor for Two Violins, etc.).*

Nothing in the London edition points to this source, but the texts are, obviously, similarly derived. Fournier commands a more sonorous tone and it is much better reproduced than Amfitheatrof's. However, the latter is a worthy part of the collection in which it appears.

Works Without Opus Numbers

Concertos

For Strings

*In A major, P.235. VDR, Fasano, Cet 50045 (*Concertos in A minor, D major, etc.).*

Not as good sound as in the later recordings by the same ensemble. Fine artistry, however.

*In D minor. I Musici, An 35087 (*Concerto in D minor for Viola d'Amore; Concerto in D for Violin; Concerto in A for Strings and Cembalo).*

A total lack of any relevant material in the "annotation" and the late appearance of this disc prevent adequate identification of the works involved. However, every work is a joy, and the performances, especially Bruno Giuranna's playing of the viola d'amore, are as rewarding as those cheered under Rossini and Tartini. Just about ideal sound.

For Orchestra

*In A major. VDR, Fasano, D DL 9575 (*Concerto in G minor, etc.).*

A grave and beautiful work, perfectly performed by the small ensemble. Clear, rather thin recording. The work is identified as No. 12 in Volume VI of the Renzo Giordani Collection in Turin.

*In B flat. VDR, Fasano, D DL 9679 (*Concertos in D minor, C major, etc.).*

See comment under foregoing. No identification is available.

*In E minor, P.127. OSDP, Bruck, Pol RLP 1006 (*Concertos in F, B flat, etc.).*

Rough-toned, not too accurate playing. The reproduction is clear but unresonant. The work is identified as Vol. IV, P.167, in the Mauro Foà Collection.

In F major, P.279. OSP, Bruck, Pol RLP 1006.

See foregoing. This is No. 9, Vol. VI, of the Renzo Giordano collection.

*In G ("alla rustica"), P.143. VDR, Fasano, D DL 9575 (*Concertos in A, G minor, etc.).*

An uncommonly energetic work, very well performed, rather dryly reproduced (No. 14 of Volume III in the Renzo Giordano collection).

*In G minor, P. 407. VDR, Fasano, D DL 9575 (*See above).*

A disc mate of the foregoing, and of similar characteristics (No. 1 of Volume V in the RG collection).

For Bassoon and Orchestra

*In A minor, F. VIII, No. 7. Muccetti, LSSO, Valdinoci, Col LPS 1015 (*Concerto in E flat).*

An ingenious, carefully written work for the odd solo instrument, expertly played. The processing, though not perfect, is better than in the violin concerto on the overside.

*In B flat ("La Notte"), P. 401. Garfield, CHAM, CH 56 (*Concertos for Flute and Strings).*

The bassoonist is competent enough, but the playing of the assisting ensemble can only be described as miserable, almost a travesty on how a recording should sound. Inexpert recording.

*In D minor. Helaerts, OSR, Ansermet, 10" L LS 591 (*Marcello: Concerto for Oboe and Orchestra in C minor).*

A real gem among Vivaldi's considerable musical jewelry, polished to perfection by the excellent soloist and Ansermet. Fine sound, especially in the low range of the bassoon. (Identification is lacking, save that it is a Malipiero transcription.)

For Oboe and Orchestra

*In D minor. Zanfini, VDR, Fasano, D DL 9679 (*Concerto in B flat, etc.).*

Delicate, finely controlled articulation by the oboist. Sound if unspectacular recording.

For Viola d'Amore and Orchestra

*In D minor ("Sordini"). Seiler, CHAM, 10" D DL 7537 (*Telemann: Concerto in E).*

A work of great beauty and expressiveness, especially the F major *Largo*. In addition to a string quintet, the solo instrument is offset by a lute and cembalo, resulting in a texture of special aural appeal. Excellent performance, beautifully reproduced.

*In D minor. Sabatini, VDR, Fasano, D DL 9575 (*Concerto in G, "alla rustica," etc.).*

Whether or not D minor was Vivaldi's favorite key, this addition to the collection is a substantial one. Sabatini's art is in excellent order, and though the recording is far from high fidelity, it passes. The attribution is No. 312, Volume II, of the Mauro Foà collection, Turin.

*In D, P. 166. Sabatini, VDR, Fasano, Cet 50045 (*Concerto in E minor for Violoncello, etc.).*

Fine art, rather muddy reproduction.

For Violin and Orchestra

*In B flat, P. 405. Magaziner, OSP, Bruck, Pol PRLP 1006 (*Concerto in E minor, etc.).*

Sub-standard intonation and lax direction diminish by much the inherent interest of the material. Not good recording, either.

In C, P. 88. Magaziner, OSP, Bruck, Pol PRLP 1006.

The same sad story as the foregoing.

*In C. Pelliccia, VDR, Fasano, D DL 9679 (*Concerto in D minor for Viola d'Amore and Orchestra, etc.).*

Finespun violin-playing, thoroughly in style and adequately reproduced. (No identification is provided.) The prominent cello roles are also well filled.

*In E major ("Il Riposo"), p. 248. Gramegna, VDR, Fasano, Cet 50022 (*Overture to L'Olimpiade, etc.).*

Somewhat subdued music-making, though finely turned out. The ornamented finale is especially well played. Fair recording.

For Two Violins and Orchestra

*In A minor, P. 28. Malanotte, Scaglia, VDR, Fasano, Cet 50045 (*Concerto in E minor for Cello, etc.).*

Excellent teamwork by the two soloists in a work which might well have been the model for Bach's famous double concerto. Clear sound, also thin. The Casella edition is used.

For Violoncello and Orchestra

In E minor. See under Sonata, opus 14.

Overture

*L'Olimpiade. RIO, Rossi, Cet 50022 (*Vivaldi: Concerto in E for Violin; Boccherini: Quintet in C; etc.).*

Typical example of the classic Italian overture, with a slow section between two fast ones. The performance of the Mortari arrangement is good, the sound dead.

WAGNER, RICHARD (1813-1883)

EDITOR'S NOTE: *To facilitate comparison of the many duplications and combinations of Wagner's familiar works, they are listed below with identifying symbols as utilized in the text.*

OPERA EXCERPTS

The Flying Dutchman	Overture	1
Das Liebesverbot	Overture	2
Lohengrin	Prelude	3
	Prelude, Act III	3 A
Die Meistersinger	Prelude	4
	Prelude, Act III	4 A
	Dance of the Apprentices	4 B
	Procession of the Guilds	4 C
Parsifal	Prelude	5
	Transformation Scene	5 A
	Good Friday Music	5 B
Rienzi	Overture	6
Der Ring des Nibelungen		
Das Rheingold	Prelude	7
	Entrance of the Gods	7 A
Die Walküre	Prelude	8
	Ride of the Valkyrics	8 A
	Wotan's Farewell	8 B
	Magic Fire Music	8 C
Siegfried	Prelude	9
	Waldweben	9 A
	Prelude, Act III	9 B
	Interlude, Act III	9 C
Götterdämmerung	Prelude	10
	Siegfried's Rhine Journey	10 A
	Funeral March	10 B
	Finale	10 C
Tannhäuser	Overture	11
	Overture, Paris Version	11 A
	Bacchanale only	11 B
	Entrance of the Guests	11 C
	Prelude, Act III	11 D
Tristan und Isolde	Prelude	12
	Liebesnacht	12 A
	Prelude, Act III	12 B
	Liebestod	12 C

ORCHESTRAL WORKS

Eine Faust-Ouvertüre	13
Siegfried Idyll	14

Opera Excerpts (Orchestral)

*Die Feen: Overture. MSO, Konwitschny, U RLP 7069 (*No. 2).*

Well-disciplined playing of the interesting early effort. Good sound. The associated *Liebesverbot* receives about the same treatment, but is not as well reproduced.

*The Flying Dutchman: Overture. RPO, Beecham, C ML 4962 (*Nos. 4A, 4B, 4C, 5B, 10A, 10B). VPH, Knappertsbusch, 10" L LD 9064 (*No. 8A). DNO, Malko, LBC 1048 (*Beethoven: Leonore No. 3, Egmont; Wagner: No. 4; etc.). MSO, Konwitschny, U RLP 7069 (*Nos. 2, 6, Overture to Die Feen).*

Either the Beecham or the Knappertsbusch performance will satisfy, for both are in a truly stormy mood, superbly played by the orchestras and spaciously reproduced. (As is apparent, the Beecham collection is fairly extensive, and the level throughout is high.) The Malko is workmanlike, but does not sound as well as either of the foregoing. Those who are attracted to the Konwitschny disc for *Die Feen* and *Das Liebesverbot* will find this performance steady, well controlled, not unduly dramatic, acceptable in sound.

*Das Liebesverbot: Overture. MSO, Konwitschny, U RLP 7069 (*Nos. 1, 6, etc.).*

Lively treatment of the overture to Wagner's early effort based on *Measure for Measure*. How this composer came to be the philosopher-poet of *Die Meistersinger* is well worth pondering. Big, broad reproduction.

*Lohengrin: Prelude. NBC, Toscanini, 10" V LRM 7029 (*Nos. 3A, 4A, 9A). PSO, Reiner, C ML 4054 (*Nos. 3A, 4, 8A, 9A).*

The excellencies of Toscanini are a little more than Reiner matches, though his performance is very good. The former benefits from brighter, more resonant sound, though it is hardly epical high fidelity.

*Lohengrin: Prelude to Act III. NBC, Toscanini, 10" V LRM 7029 (*Nos. 3, 4A, 9A). PHO, Ormandy, C ML 4865 (*Nos. 11A, 8A, 8C, 4A, 4B, 4C).*

For power and jubilation, the Toscanini version retains its legendary prominence. However, the Ormandy-Philadelphia is decidedly more ear-filling, if tone quality is of the essence.

*Die Meistersinger: Prelude. VPH, Knappertsbusch, 10" L LD 9026 (*No. 4A). NBC, Toscanini, V LM 6020 [2] (*Nos. 3, 3A, 4, 4A, 5,*

*5B, 10, 10A, 10B, 12, 12C, and Siegfried Idyll). PSO, Reiner, C ML 4054 (*See: Lohengrin Prelude). PHI, Dobrowen, V LBC 1048 (*See: Flying Dutchman). VPH, Furtwängler, V LHMV 1049 (*Nos. 4B, 8A, 10A, 10B, 14).*

The Toscanini is, without question, to me the firmest in pace, the biggest in climax, if not the best-sounding, of the group presently available. Unfortunately, its circulation now is limited to a two-disc set containing mostly material previously available in other couplings. (The exceptions are new versions of the *Tristan: Prelude and Liebestod*, the *Funeral Music* from *Götterdämmerung*, and the *Siegfried Idyll*.) Otherwise, Knappertsbusch's normal inclination to slow tempos is replaced here by an unexpected briskness. Reiner's crisp performance is poorly reproduced, as is Dobrowen's without being crisp. (The Furtwängler, for those who might be interested in the other contents of the disc, is broad in stride and well phrased, though not as well reproduced as the Knappertsbusch or as dynamic as the Toscanini.)

*Die Meistersinger: Prelude to Act III. VPH, Knappertsbusch, 10" L LD 9026 (*No. 4). NBC, Toscanini, 10" V LRM 7029 (Nos. 3, 3A, 9A). PHO, Ormandy, 10" C AL 43 (Nos. 4B, 4C, 3A, 8A, 8C).*

Common sense would dictate a preference for the Knappertsbusch pairing with the overture, and a fine-sounding record it is. However, the appeal of Toscanini's thoughtful performance is hard to resist. Those who do resist, on behalf of a sequence embracing the subsequent items (see below), will find Ormandy's tempos satisfying, his magnificent orchestra warmly reproduced. (This is a ten-inch form of ML 4865, minus the *Tannhäuser* overture and bacchanale.)

*Die Meistersinger: Dance of the Apprentices; Procession of the Guilds. PHO, Ormandy, 10" C AL 43 (*Nos. 4A, etc., as above). Dance only, VPH, Furtwängler, V LHMV 1049 (*Nos. 4, 8A, 10A, 10B, 14).*

Ormandy's performances of these excerpts have more to do with the Philadelphia orchestra than they have with Nuremberg, but the sound is certainly full. Furtwängler's *Lehrbuben* must be named Fafner and Fasolt, to judge from his pace. It is also part of a miscellany in which the Siegfried funeral music precedes and the "Ride of the Valkyrico" follows. Excellent sound, poor programming.

*Parsifal: Prelude; Good Friday Music. NBC, Toscanini, 10" V LM 15. Prelude only. VPH, Knappertsbusch, L LP 451 (*Nos. 5A, 6).*

Only personal preference could elect a choice between two such fine re-creations, the Knappertsbusch a little more spacious and flowing than the Toscanini, but the latter of its own noble musicality. Both are well recorded, with the London sound warmer and richer.

*Parsifal: Transformation Scene. VPH, Knappertsbusch, L LL 451 (*Nos. 5, 6).*

Of the same quality as the foregoing.

*Parsifal: Good Friday Music. RPO, Beecham, C ML 4962 (*See: Flying Dutchman). NBC, Toscanini, 10" V LM 15 (*No. 5). LPO, Krauss, L LP 14 (*Nos. 12, 12C). MSO, Konwitschny, U RLP 7069 (*See: Die Feen).*

Those to whom Beecham's powers in this music are unknown will find it a thoroughly rewarding experience, full of pastoral feeling and coloristic detail very well reproduced. Toscanini's rarefied concept of the music makes a wonderful partner for his *Prelude*, though the sound is not so good as the Columbia. Krauss's is also highly respectable, though with less orchestral distinction. The Konwitschny, mentioned for those interested in the subjoined *Ring* excerpts, is clean and capable, though not informed with much poetic feeling.

*Rienzi: Overture. VPH, Knappertsbusch, L LP 451 (*Nos. 5, 5A). NYPH, Stokowski, 10" C ML (*Nos. 8B, 8C). MSO, Konwitschny, U RLP 7069 (*See overture to Die Feen).*

The felicity of the Knappertsbusch treatment is its softening of garish excesses in the scoring, a refining hand on its melodic exaggerations. Splendidly played and reproduced. However, if one wants the full impact of what is in the score, Stokowski provides it, in a dazzling tonal show. This Konwitschny is like the others: thoroughly professional, vigorous, and no trifling with subtleties. Big recording.

DER RING DES NIBELUNGEN (Das Rheingold, Die Walküre, Siegfried, Götterdämmerung)

Collection of Excerpts. Das Rheingold: Entrance of the Gods; Die Walküre: Nos. 8A, 8C; Siegfried: 9C; Götterdämmerung: 10A, 10B, 10C. MSO, Konwitschny, U RLP 603 [2] (*Nos. 5, 5B, 14*).

Although all of the *Ring* excerpts could have been included on a single disc, they are spread over single faces of two LP's, with other matter on the reverses. The workmanship of Konwitschny is, as previously noted, competent enough, the sound well rendered. However, no single performance excels other versions when they exist.

*Die Walküre: Ride of the Valkyries; Magic Fire Music. PHO, Ormandy, 10" C AL 43 (*Nos. 3A, 4A, 4B, 4C). Ride only. VPH, Knappertsbusch, 10" L LD 9064. VPH, Furtwängler, V LHMV 1949 (*See Dance of the Apprentices).*

Each of these seems the aural assault of all time as it is in progress, and the final impression is flattering to all. However, reflection directs the most respect to Knappertsbusch, a recording of weight as well as power. The Columbia is also excellent in this respect (particularly in the Fire Music), the HMV less good.

*Die Walküre: Wotan's Farewell. NYPH, Stokowski, 10" C ML 2153 (*No. 6).*

A longtime favorite of Stokowski's, here offered in one of his best versions. Highly successful sound.

*Siegfried: Waldweben. NBC, Toscanini, 10" V LRM 7029 (*Nos. 3, 3A, 4A).*

Inasmuch as one virtually never hears this music played in the theater with such flavorsome imagination and orchestral distinction, one need look no further for a recorded version. It is one of the better NBC reproductions.

*Siegfried: Interlude, Act III. MSO, Konwitschny, U RLP 603 [2] (*See Entrance of the Gods).*

The musical accompaniment for Siegfried's progress through the flames, up to his discovery of the sleeping Brünnhilde. Good, blary recording.

*Götterdämmerung: Rhine Journey; Funeral Music; Finale. MSO, Konwitschny, U RLP 603 [2] (*See under Rheingold).*

No separate comment is required here. The duplicated items do not compare with those mentioned below.

*Götterdämmerung: Rhine Journey, Funeral Music. NBC, Toscanini, V LM 6020 [2] (*See: Meistersinger Prelude). VPH, Furtwängler, V LHMV 1049 (*See: Meistersinger Prelude). RPO, Beecham, C ML 4962 (*See: Flying Dutchman). NYPH, Stokowski, C ML 4273 (*Tschaikovsky: Romeo and Juliet). OSC, Weingartner, C ML 4680 (*Nos. 11D, 12B, 14). Rhine Journey only. NBC, Toscanini, V LM 1157 (*Strauss: Don Juan).*

Even though it means duplication of material otherwise at hand, few dyed-in-Toscanini's-Wagner music-lovers would willingly forgo these performances, especially as the *Funeral Music* includes—according to his admirable custom—the foregoing "Apostrophe of Siegfried to Brünnhilde" in orchestral form. It is also highly charged reproduction, if not the ultimate in decibels. The same performance of the *Rhine Journey* is separately available as noted, though the *Funeral Music* unfortunately is not. Those who do not care to invest in the two-disc Toscanini issue will find Furtwängler's eloquent without being hysterical and dramatically impressive without theatrical overtones. The Beecham is a better recording, and full of flavor, though not the fervor to make the skin creep. Oddly, too, the *Rhine Journey*—a jubilant affair—comes *after* the *Funeral Music* in this issue. The Stokowski is montaged from *Rhine Journey* to *Funeral Music* by one of his favorite bridges, as if five seconds of silence would be unwelcome. Good sound, though. The probity of the Weingartner performances remains, sadly served in this instance by French-style studio recording of the mid-thirties.

*Tannhäuser: Overture and Bacchanale (Paris Version). HIS, Stokowski, V LM 1066 (*Wesendonck Songs). VPH, Knappertsbusch, L LL 800 (*Nos. 1, 8A). PHO, Ormandy, C ML 4865 (*Nos. 3, 4A, 4B, 4C, 8A, 8C). PHI, Kletzki, An 35059 (*Nos. 12, 12C). Overture only. WSO, Leitner, 10" D DL 4061 (*No. 13).*

The qualities admired in the Stokowski version in its first form as V 530—dramatic suitability and musical understanding—are still much in its favor, though what was then regarded as "luminous fidelity" is outdone in the versions of Knappertsbusch and Ormandy. The latter is a particular example of fine sound, but the music hardly comes to life as it does with Stokowski (the voices of the "sirens" are, for once, an editorial change which is an improvement). Leitner's orchestra is rather smaller than the others, but it does its work in good style.

*Tannhäuser: Introduction to Act III. OSC, Weingartner, C ML 4680 (*Nos. 10A, 10B, 12B, 14).*

Weingartner's feeling for this little-played work is apparent, though the recording is hardly of contemporary quality. At that, it is decidedly fuller than that of the *Götterdämmerung* excerpts previously noted.

Tristan und Isolde: Prelude and Liebestod. NBC, Toscanini, V LM

6020 [2] (**See: Meistersinger Prelude*). *LPO, Krauss, L LP 14* (**No. 5B*). *PHI, Kletzki, An 35059. WSO, Leitner, 10" D DL 4038.*

As noted under the *Götterdämmerung Funeral Music*, few will want to be without the ultimate version of this music now audible, though their passion lead them to the duplication of items previously acquired in other couplings. However, these playings of the *Tristan* music have the Toscanini thumbprint on every measure, the way of building a climax, retarding where others rush, vibrating a chord till all its sonority is spent. Krauss's performances have excellent justice and deliberation, if not the ardor of Toscanini, and appreciably inferior reproduction (very early LP). The unpredictable Kletzki does well with this music, but in terms of the musical lowlands, rather than the heights of Toscanini. At the price asked, the Leitner version is good musical value, surprisingly adept in sound.

Tristan und Isolde: Prelude; Liebesnacht; Liebestod. HIS, Stokowski, V LM 1174. PHO, Ormandy, C ML 4742 (**Immolation Scene*).

Stokowski's version of this pastiche covers both sides of his disc, and thus contains more of the score than Ormandy's, which allots side II to the Immolation Scene from *Götterdämmerung* with Harshaw. Stokowski's, as well as being longer, is louder and lustier.

Tristan und Isolde: Introduction to Act III. OSC, Weingartner, C ML 4680 (**Nos. 10A, 10B, 11D, 14*).

Better sound than might be expected, to go persuasively with a performance of fine mood and detail.

Works for Orchestra

Eine Faust-Ouvertüre. NBC, Toscanini, 10" V LRM 7023 (**Beethoven: Leonore No. 3*). *MPH, Rieger, D DL 4061* (**No. 11*).

For those who find the Toscanini treatment of this work rather overdriven, it should be said that Rieger and his men are honored with surprisingly fine sound. The LP (Carnegie Hall in origin) is an improvement on the 78, very vivid evidence of Toscanini's sense of orchestral values.

Siegfried Idyll. VPH, Furtwängler, V LHMV 1049 (**Nos. 10A, 10B, 8A, 4, 4A*). *SCH, Münchinger, L LL 525* (**Haydn: Symphony No. 45*). *NBC, Toscanini, V LM 6020* [2] (**See: Meistersinger Prelude*). *NBC, Toscanini, V LCT 1116* (**Immolation Scene*). *MSO, Konwitschny, U*

RLP 603 [2]. *LPO, Weingartner, C ML 4680* (**Nos. 10A, 10B, 11D, 12B*).

For a full measure of contemporary sound in a performance of authority and insight, the Furtwängler is an almost inescapable choice. However, those who prefer the original version for sixteen instruments will find it poetically conveyed by Münchinger and men, also admirably reproduced. The recent Toscanini issue, in the two-disc set, is the least attractive to me of all the offerings in that collection, certainly no incentive for investing in other things if all one wants is the choice version of the *Siegfried Idyll* now available. The same rather too allegro, not too warming concept can be observed more advantageously as side two of the historic recording with Traubel of the *Immolation Scene.* The newer version *is* very much better in sound. Konwitschny finishes as he began, with good esteem for his competence, but not much personal viewpoint on this score. Weingartner of course does convey one, in affectionate terms, though the outlines are dim, the details blurred in this pre-war product.

Work for Orchestra and Voice

Wesendonck Songs. Farrell, HIS, Stokowski, V LM 1066 (**No. 11A*).

The soaring ease of Farrell's voice and the masterful direction of Stokowski are only occasionally blemished by her less than full command of the texts, and the total is decidedly fine. Excellent sound, if a little too much room tone.

WALDTEUFEL, EMILE (1837-1915)

Waltzes

Estudiantina; Très Jolie; España. BPO, Fiedler, V LM 1226 (**Strauss Polkas*).

Estudiantina; Pomona; The Skaters. PHI, Lambert, C RL 3054 (**Von Suppé: Morning, Noon, and Night in Vienna; Nicolai: Merry Wives, etc.*).

Between them, these two discs contain the three best-known works of Waldteufel, one duplication, and one oddity worth knowing. On performance (and the disparity of the second side material) I'd recommend both: but if it is a choice of one, the Fiedler is slightly better recorded. Otherwise, the Lambert is quite as good.

WALTON, SIR WILLIAM (1902-)

Concerto

*For Viola and Orchestra. Primrose, RPO, Sargent, C ML 4905 (*Hindemith: Der Schwanendreher).*

Probably the best recorded performance this work has yet had, completing an accomplishment of exceptional credit for Primrose. Sargent also does his work well, and the reproduction is outstandingly good.

*For Violin. Heifetz, PHI, Walton, V LM 1121 (*Vieuxtemps: Concerto No. 5).*

Although the previous version with Goossens and the Cincinnati Orchestra was full of virtue, the new one with the composer conducting is even better. Heifetz's performance, intent, sharp-faceted, is beautifully reproduced.

Marches

*Crown Imperial; Orb and Sceptre. PHI, Walton, 10" An 30000 (*Portsmouth Point Overture; Bach-Walton: Sheep May Safely Graze).*

Big, boomy reproductions, energetically directed performances.

Overture

*Portsmouth Point. PHI, Walton, 10" An 30000 (*See above).*

Walton does well by himself here, and the sound is excellent.

Symphony

(1934). PHI, Walton, V LHMV 1041.

One of Walton's most consequential works, performed with zest and purpose by the fine orchestra. Good sound, a little shrill.

Works for Orchestra and Narrator

*Façade. Sitwell, CHAM, Prausnitz, 10" C ML 2047. Orchestral Suite. PHI, Lambert, C ML 4793 (*Elgar: Wand of Youth).*

The charm of Sitwell's reading is lost on me, wherefore I can only regard the text as an intrusion on the lively music by Walton. By its absence, the Columbia competition for itself is automatically enhanced, especially as Lambert's master hand has rarely been better employed, and the recording, if not razor-edge fi, is high enough in all other qualities for enjoyment. ("Fanfare," "Polka," "Swiss Yodeling Song," "Valse," "Tango-Pasodoblé," "Country Dance," "Popular Song," "Scotch Rhapsody," *"Tarantella Sevillana," "Noche Espagnole,"* and "Old Sir Faulk.)"

Works for Orchestra and Voices

Belshazzar's Feast. SYM, Boult, soloist, chorus, W WL 5248.

One of the most powerful of contemporary reproductions, with Boult a highly suitable interpreter and Noble, as before, a fine voice for the solo part.

WARLOCK, PETER (1894-1930)

*Capriol Suite. BNO, Neel, L LL 801 (*Britten: Variations on a Theme by Bridge).*

Sensitive, well-controlled direction by Neel. Very good sound.

WEBER, BEN (1916-)

*Symphony on Poems of William Blake. HIS, Stokowski, V LM 1785 (*Harrison: Suite).*

Rather pretentious, overwritten treatment of four songs. Warren Galjour is the able singer, and the sound is very distinct.

WEBER, CARL MARIA VON (1786-1826)

Concertos

For Clarinet and Orchestra, Nos. 1 in F minor and 2 in E. Heine, SAL, P. Walter, Per SPLP 529.

Messrs. Heine and Walter awaken these works, so to speak, but hardly bring them to life. As may be suspected from Weber's writing for wind instruments in various operas, his clarinet writing is fluent and idiomatic. The recording is clear, not marked by many subtleties.

For Piano and Orchestra, Nos. 1 in C and 2 in E flat. Wührer, PRO, Swarowsky, Vox PL 8140.

Soloist and conductor share an ingratiating estimate of these works, which should be better known. Wührer has an excellent sound for the filigree of the music, and the reproduction is uncommonly good.

Concertino

*For Clarinet and Orchestra, in C minor. Bürkner, BPH, Schrader, U URLP 7012 (*Symphony No. 2; Oberon, Euryanthe overtures).*

The tonal qualities of Kell's earlier version are lacking here, as is the artistic leadership of Goehr. This is straightforward, rather dry performance, clearly reproduced without much resonance.

Konzertstück

*In F minor. Casadesus, CO, Szell, C ML 4588 (*Liszt: Concerto No. 2).*

Dashing performance by Casadesus, well supported by Szell and brightly reproduced.

Opera Excerpts (Orchestral)

*Abu Hassan: Overture. BAM, Leitner, 10" D DL 4057 (*Euryanthe, Preciosa overtures).*

Leitner makes this lively work sparkle, and the recording is better than fair.

*Euryanthe: Overture. VPH, Böhm, L LP 354 (*Oberon, Preciosa, Peter Schmoll). BAM, Leitner, 10" D DL 4057 (*Preciosa, Abu Hassan).*

Neither of these conforms to classical standards in this exacting music, but the Böhm shows the culture of the Viennese strings to advantage, and the sound is excellent. Leitner's is energetic, rather wiry in sound.

*Der Freischütz: Overture. NBC, Toscanini, 10" V LRM 7028 (*Oberon; Donizetti: Don Pasquale overture). PHO, Ormandy, 10" C ML 2043*

(*Invitation to the Dance; Weinberger: Schwanda excerpts; Glinka: Russlan and Ludmilla overture*).

Ormandy's performance seems more than creditable until compared with the dazzling Toscanini version transferred by RCA from its former V 11-9172. Not only is it powered by a different order of dramatic impulse, it also comes off better as a recording.

*Oberon: Overture. NBC, Toscanini, 10" V LRM 7028 (*Freischütz overture; Donizetti: Don Pasquale). VPH, Böhm, L LP 354 (*Euryanthe, Preciosa, Peter Schmoll). BPH, Jochum, 10" D DL 4006 (*Mendelssohn: Midsummer Night's Dream overture).*

The virtues of the Vienna and Berlin Philharmonics, both well conducted, are substantial, but the NBC on the date of this recording was a greater orchestra than either in precision, responsiveness, and superbly animal animation. The sound is big, if slightly coarse. The Jochum is the best recording of the three.

*Peter Schmoll und Seine Nachbarn: Overture. VPH, Böhm, L LP 354 (*See Euryanthe).*

An appropriate introduction for a comic opera, one of Weber's earliest, and neatly carried off by Böhm. Fine sound.

*Preciosa: Overture. VPH, Böhm, L LP 354 (*See Euryanthe). BAM, Leitner, 10" D DL 4057 (*Euryanthe, Abu Hassan).*

Tone quality here favors Böhm. Leitner's performance is quite satisfactory if one prefers his miscellany to Böhm's.

Overture

*Jubilee. MIN, Mitropoulos, C RL 3038 (*Beethoven: Coriolan, Leonore No. 3 overtures; Brahms: Variations on a Theme by Haydn).*

At the price, this sequence is certainly generous, provided that one is steeled to resist its shrill, penetrating tone characteristic and Mitropoulos's preference for vigor above all.

Symphony

*No. 2 in C. AUS, Rabhuber, Rem 199-112 (*Mozart: Symphony No. 29). ORB, Heger, U URLP 7012 (*Concertino for Clarinet; Euryanthe, Oberon overtures).*

Neither of these is ear-assuaging, but the direction of Rabhuber is more to the point of this "Schubertian" (Franz Peter was barely five when it was written) work than Heger's. A highly absorbing link in the musical chain, and one that bears on the harmonic features of the romanticism to come.

Arrangement

*Invitation to the Dance. PHI, Markevitch, V LBC 1028 (*Sibelius: Finlandia; Elgar: Pomp and Circumstance No. 1; Wolf-Ferrari: Intermezzi from Jewels of the Madonna; etc.). PHO, Ormandy, 10" C ML 2043 (*Der Freischütz overture, etc.). NEW, Fistoulari, 10" L LD 9108 (*Minkus: Pas de deux from Don Quichotte).*

None of these is anything memorable, wherefore a priority to Markevitch on behalf of low price, assorted goodies of all sorts, and generally good reproduction of all. At least he keeps the tempo steady, which is more than can be said for Ormandy (this is a pre-LP reproduction). Fistoulari does better than on his previous opportunity, and has much the best sound. However, the overside Minkus work is, to recall a popular item of the Lunceford repertory, for dancers only.

WEINBERGER, JAROMIR (1896-)

*Schwanda: Polka and Fugue. PHO, Ormandy, 10" C ML 2043 (*Weber: Invitation to the Dance, Freischütz overture; Glinka: Russlan and Ludmilla overture).*

Excellent performance of this opera excerpt and clear but not too resonant reproduction in the early LP manner. Note that this disc contains more music than AL 12, and is worth the extra cost.

WIENIAWSKI, HENRI (1835-1880)

Concerto for Violin and Orchestra, No. 2 in D minor. Elman, ROB, Hilsberg, 10" V LM 53. Stern, NYPH, Kurtz, 10" C ML 2012.

Although Stern's performance has been available longer than the Elman, it is decidedly a better-sounding treatment of this music. As between violinists, the values are substantially even, hence the alphabetical presentation. Stern has what advantage there is.

WOLF, HUGO (1860-1903)

*Italian Serenade. GPH, Keilberth, 10" Cap H 8131 (*Mozart: Symphony No. 32*).

The predecessor-group of the one now based in Bamberg is the orchestra involved here, and the playing is thoroughly good, as is Keilberth's estimate of the situation. However, the recording is a little washed-out by contemporary standards.

WOLF-FERRARI, ERMANNO (1876-1948)

*The Jewels of the Madonna: Intermezzos. LSO, Bellezza, V LBC 1028 (*Sibelius: Finlandia; Elgar: Pomp and Circumstance; etc.). ROB, Mitropoulos, 10" C ML 2053 (*Menotti: Sebastian; etc.).*

The margin between these is narrow, to be determined largely on the basis of associated materials. Bellezza's version of No. 2 is especially good, the recording excellent. On the Mitropoulos disc (also well recorded), the Wolf-Ferrari material is preceded by the intermezzos from *Manon Lescaut* and *Cavalleria.*

*The Secret of Suzanne: Overture. ASO, Gui, Rem 199-142 (*Cherubini: Water Carrier; Rossini: Siege of Corinth, Italiana in Algeri overture, etc.).*

Reasonably deft direction by Gui, marred by shallow sound, lacking bass.

INDEX

The text of this book was set on the Vari-Typer, in the Bodoni Book Style (by Coxhead). Composition by *The Science Press*, Lancaster, Pennsylvania. Printed by *The Murray Printing Company*, Wakefield, Massachusetts. Paper manufactured by *S. D. Warren Company*, Boston, Massachusetts. Bound by *H. Wolff*, New York. Designed by *Harry Ford.*